Critical Dialogic TESOL Teacher Education

Critical Approaches and Innovations in Language Teacher Education

SERIES EDITOR: Bedrettin Yazan (University of Texas at San Antonio, USA)

The series is dedicated to advancing critical language teacher education research that can transform the dominant practices of language teaching in educational contexts around the world. Language education has become more important than ever, to facilitate the crossing of physical and ideological borders of nation-states, and to meet the needs of increasingly ethnically and linguistically diverse student populations. This series helps inform the preparation of resilient and agentive language teachers with critical social justice orientations. It presents state-of-the-art research to support the formation of teachers who identify as democratic, social agents of formal schooling, and devoted to improving learning experiences of marginalized students. The titles in this series appeal to language teachers, teacher educators, and researchers and can be used as educational materials in graduate and undergraduate studies.

ADVISORY BOARD

Darío Banegas (University of Edinburgh, UK)
Osman Barnawi (Royal Commission Colleges & Institutes, Saudi Arabia)
Yasemin Bayyurt (Boğaziçi University, Turkey)
Ester de Jong (University of Florida, USA)
Andy Xuesong Gao (University of New South Wales, Australia)
Icy Lee (Chinese University of Hong Kong, Hong Kong)
Gloria Park (Indiana University of Pennsylvania, USA)
Ingrid Piller (Macquarie University, New South Wales, Australia)
Richard Smith (University of Warwick, UK)
Zia Tajeddin (Tarbiat Modares University, Iran)

Forthcoming in the series:
Critical Autoethnography in Language Teacher Education, Bedrettin Yazan
International Perspectives on Critical English Language Teacher Education: Theory and Practice, edited by Ali Fuad Selvi and Ceren Kocaman
Language Teacher Education Beyond Borders: Multilingualism, Transculturalism, and Critical Approaches, edited by Fernando Zolin-Vesz, Dario Luis Banegas and Luciana C. de Oliveira
Language Teacher Education, edited by Fernando Zolin-Vesz, Dario Luis Banegas and Luciana C. de Oliveira
Teacher Education for Global Englishes Language Teaching, Denchai Prabjandee
Social-Emotional Learning in Language Teacher Education: A Guidebook for Language Teacher Educators, Administrators and Leaders, Gilda Martínez-Alba and Luis Javier Pentón Herrera
Activism in Language Teaching and Language Teacher Education, edited by Amber N. Warren and Natalia A. Ward

Critical Dialogic TESOL Teacher Education

Preparing Future Advocates and Supporters of Multilingual Learners

Edited by Fares J. Karam and Amanda K. Kibler

BLOOMSBURY ACADEMIC
LONDON • NEW YORK • OXFORD • NEW DELHI • SYDNEY

BLOOMSBURY ACADEMIC
Bloomsbury Publishing Plc, 50 Bedford Square, London, WC1B 3DP, UK
Bloomsbury Publishing Inc, 1359 Broadway, New York, NY 10018, USA
Bloomsbury Publishing Ireland, 29 Earlsfort Terrace, Dublin 2, D02 AY28, Ireland

BLOOMSBURY, BLOOMSBURY ACADEMIC and the Diana logo are
trademarks of Bloomsbury Publishing Plc

First published in Great Britain 2024
Paperback edition published 2026

Copyright © Fares J. Karam, Amanda K. Kibler and Contributors, 2024, 2026

Fares J. Karam, Amanda K. Kibler and Contributors have asserted their right under the
Copyright, Designs and Patents Act, 1988, to be identified as Authors of this work.

For legal purposes the Acknowledgments on p. xvi constitute an
extension of this copyright page.

Cover design: Grace Ridge
Cover image © rudchenko and Anastasia Shemetova/iStock

All rights reserved. No part of this publication may be: i) reproduced or transmitted in any form, electronic or mechanical, including photocopying, recording or by means of any information storage or retrieval system without prior permission in writing from the publishers; or ii) used or reproduced in any way for the training, development or operation of artificial intelligence (AI) technologies, including generative AI technologies. The rights holders expressly reserve this publication from the text and data mining exception as per Article 4(3) of the Digital Single Market Directive (EU) 2019/790.

Bloomsbury Publishing Plc does not have any control over, or responsibility for, any third-party websites referred to or in this book. All internet addresses given in this book were correct at the time of going to press. The author and publisher regret any inconvenience caused if addresses have changed or sites have ceased to exist, but can accept no responsibility for any such changes.

A catalogue record for this book is available from the British Library.

Library of Congress Cataloging-in-Publication Data

Names: Karam, Fares J., editor. | Kibler, Amanda, editor.
Title: Critical dialogic TESOL teacher education : preparing future advocates and supporters of multilingual learners / edited by Fares J. Karam and Amanda K. Kibler.
Description: London ; New York : Bloomsbury Academic, 2024. | Series: Critical approaches and innovations in language teacher education | Includes bibliographical references and index. |
Summary: "This edited volume showcases how teacher educators around the world engage with critical and dialogic approaches to prepare TESOL professionals. Chapters include duoethnographic accounts, critical discourse analytic approaches, and case studies from various EFL and ESL contexts such as the United States, Morocco, New Zealand, Italy, Thailand, and Turkey"– Provided by publisher.
Identifiers: LCCN 2023048382 (print) | LCCN 2023048383 (ebook) |
ISBN 9781350342071 (hardback) | ISBN 9781350342118 (paperback) |
ISBN 9781350342095 (epub) | ISBN 9781350342088 (ebook)
Subjects: LCSH: English language–Study and teaching–Foreign speakers. |
English teachers–Training of. | Critical pedagogy. | LCGFT: Essays.
Classification: LCC PE1128.A2 C6978 2024 (print) | LCC PE1128.A2 (ebook) |
DDC 428.0071–dc23/eng/20240215
LC record available at https://lccn.loc.gov/2023048382
LC ebook record available at https://lccn.loc.gov/2023048383

ISBN: HB: 978-1-3503-4207-1
PB: 978-1-3503-4211-8
ePDF: 978-1-3503-4208-8
eBook: 978-1-3503-4209-5

Series: Critical Approaches and Innovations in Language Teacher Education

Typeset by Integra Software Services Pvt. Ltd.

For product safety related questions contact productsafety@bloomsbury.com.

To find out more about our authors and books visit www.bloomsbury.com
and sign up for our newsletters.

Contents

List of Figures	ix
List of Tables	x
Series Foreword	xi
Acknowledgments	xvi

Introduction: A Vision for Critical Dialogic Education within the Context of TESOL Teacher Education *Fares J. Karam and Amanda K. Kibler* 1

Part One: Reimagining Curricula and Pedagogies to Prepare Dialogic and Critical TESOL Professionals

1 The Role of Curriculum in the Development of Teacher Expertise to Enact Critical Dialogic Education *Aída Walqui* 23

2 Sustaining a Holistic Stance or Not?: Language and Language Pedagogies in Teacher Education *Laura D. Turner and María E. Fránquiz* 45

3 Cultivating Pre-Service Language Teachers' Critical Multilingual Language Awareness: A Macau Perspective *Rui Eric Yuan, Kailun Wang, and Jiahui Li* 65

Part I Commentary: How Critical Dialogic Education Can Contribute to Equity-Oriented Pedagogy and Curriculum *Megan Madigan Peercy* 89

Part Two: Reimagining the Roles of Teacher Candidates and Teacher Educators

4 "I Just Really Want to Focus on Expressing How Valuable Each Student Is": Impact of Collaborative Exploration of Problems of Practice on Teachers' Visions of Critical Dialogic Education *Heather M. Meston and Emily Phillips Galloway* 107

5 Critical Reflections on Dialogic Education and Practice: A Duoethnographic Approach by Teacher Educators *Naashia Mohamed, Christine Biebricher, and Rosemary Erlam* 127

6   Toward More Inclusive Classroom Practices in the Turkish EFL
    Contexts: A Case Study on the Integration of Critical and Dialogic
    Approaches to Field Placement   *Ayşe Kızıldağ and Işıl Günseli Kaçar*   147

Part II Commentary: Reimagining the Roles of Teacher Candidates and
Teacher Educators: How Identities, Voices, and Power Are Taught and
Learned   *Camille Ungco and Manka Varghese*   167

Part Three: Reimagining Online TESOL Teacher Education: Creating
Dialogic and Critical Online Spaces

7   Creating a Dialogic Online Space for Preparing Critically Reflective
    TESOL Educators   *Guofang Li and Yue Bian*   183
8   Interrogating Raciolinguistic Ideologies through Role-Play: A
    Critical Dialogic Approach   *Fares J. Karam, Amanda K. Kibler, and
    Patricia J. Arnold*   205

Part III Commentary: Reimagining Online TESOL Teacher Education:
Creating Dialogic and Critical Online Spaces   *Yasemin Tezgiden-Cakcak*   225

Conclusion: Toward a Future CDE Research Agenda   *Fares J. Karam
and Amanda K. Kibler*   239

List of Contributors   248
Index   254

Figures

0.1	Ideologies in language teacher education	xiii
1.1	Spiraling organization of Unit 3	32
1.2	Notice and describe: from individual to joint activity	34
1.3	Students present their collaboratively written dialogues, NYC, July 2022	39
4.1	CDE and visioning professional development protocol	113
5.1	Population breakdown of Auckland from 2018 census data	131

Tables

I.1	Critical dialogic transformations	10
2.1	CDE and the take-up of a translanguaging stance	48
2.2	Participants	51
2.3	Participant moves over time and across contexts	53
3.1	Shared tenets of CDE and CMLA	70
3.2	Main topics of the course	71
3.3	Forum discussion tasks	72
3.4	Suggested topics for the final reflection essay	73
4.1	Participating educators	114
4.2	Mattie's visions	118
7.1	TESOL module summary	189

Series Foreword

Critical Approaches and Innovations in Language Teacher Education

When I was preparing the initial proposal for this book series with Bloomsbury Academic, I was asked to justify why there should be a whole separate book series on critical and innovative language teacher education (LTE). The scholarly conversation on LTE has taken place in venues that have a broader scope and occurs in fields of applied linguistics, TESOL (Teaching English to Speakers of Other Languages), modern/world language education, or general teacher education. While this interdisciplinarity gives the field of LTE both scope and depth, at times it feels scattered across these various venues of scholarship. Thus, the first aim of this series was to curate and compile volumes centered around the common topic of LTE. The second aim in the series is to highlight the need in our field to focus on critical approaches to innovating LTE due to the ways that language (and therefore, language teaching) is intertwined with cycles of privilege and marginalization and power dynamics among speakers. I feel that this need to bring together scholarship that is critical and simultaneously innovative in nature has been clear to us as members of the research communities who are interested in studying policies, pedagogies, and practices of teacher education. Therefore, the inception of this series was timely.

With the generous support of the contributing authors, editors, editorial board members, and external peer reviewers, what I seek to accomplish with this series is to bring together colleagues from around the world to share their efforts in pedagogy-oriented research in LTE and extend the existing scholarly work further toward the direction of continued criticality and innovation in the interest of social justice. At the same time, practitioners and researchers of LTE can use the publications in this series, partly or fully, as resources in advancing their work.

The two significant constructs undergirding this book series are *criticality* and *innovation*, and their relationship therein. Ideally, *innovation*, or the process of engaging in continuous efforts to create new ways of supporting teachers and teacher educators at all phases of their careers in response to changing dynamics at their institutions and society in general, in LTE should contribute to teachers', teacher educators', researchers', and administrators' increasingly critical approaches to language teaching and learning. What I mean by *criticality* here are the combined efforts to address oppressive language ideologies that inform institutions' and people's stances, decisions, and actions, thus shaping their professional practices as educators writ large. Those language ideologies are never about "language" per se; they are always intertwined with ideologies of culture, nationality, race, ethnicity, gender, sexuality, and ableism, amongst others (see Kubota, 2020; Lin et al., 2004; Motha, 2014; Park, 2017).

Very much contextually bound and situated, language ideologies operate invisibly and impact the activities within the scope of LTE at three interlocking layers: language learning, language teaching, and language teacher education (See Figure, 0.1 below). To parse them out, at one layer, language ideologies influence how we understand the nature, acquisition, and use of language, which subsequently impacts our understanding of the identity positions hierarchically available for language users and learners (Pavlenko & Blackledge, 2004). At another layer, we have ideologies that pertain to teaching languages and being language teachers, and the most salient of such ideologies being the monolingual fallacy, the "native" speaker fallacy, and the subtractive fallacy as discussed by Phillipson (2013). As examples, these three fallacies provide dichotomous identity positions for language teachers, reducing the nuance and complexity of teacher identity and essentializing what "good" teachers and teaching practices should be. At a third layer, we encounter ideologies about the formal preparation of language teachers, as well as what it means to become and grow as a language teacher within local educational contexts where economic and cultural globalization are variably accepted or opposed as national educational goals (Hawkins, 2011). Those ideologies include the hierarchical positioning of certain academic content as superior to or more important than others based on or aligned with the standards or directives coming from governing bodies that manage the activities of teacher education (e.g., Higher Education Council in Türkiye, State legislative mandates on K-12 curriculum content in the United States). Such hierarchies are typically perpetuated through external high-stakes assessments which operate as gate-keeping mechanisms. Additionally, to reiterate their interconnected nature, ideologies of LTE also encompass the ideologies in circulation around language teaching which therefore also involve the ideologies around language learning and language use. Ideologically laden hierarchies, variably based on the socio-political context, define and confine

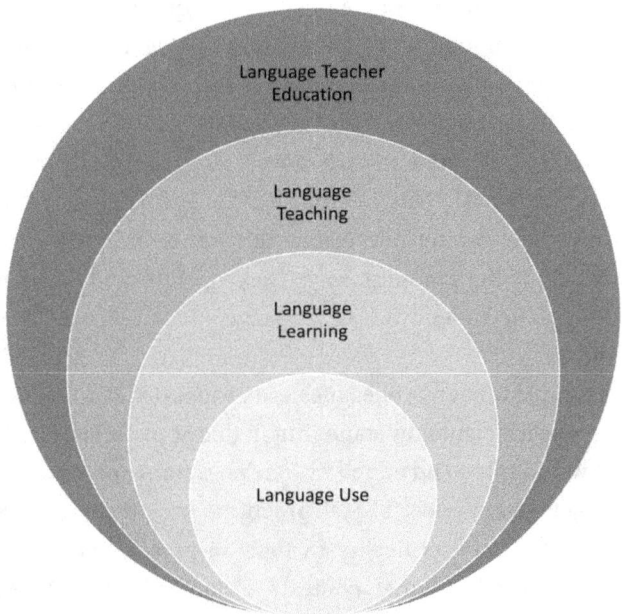

Figure 0.1 Ideologies in language teacher education.

what a language teacher educator is allowed and supposed to be, do, and feel when preparing teachers to work with language learners.

In the last three decades, critical scholarship in our field (e.g., Canagarajah, 2020; Norton & Toohey, 2004; Pennycook, 1999; Varghese et al., 2016) has called for persistent pushback against dominant language ideologies and the corresponding ways in which institutions and the people ultimately maintain the asymmetrical power relations in society. As the "mission" of LTE is to prepare language teachers (who experience varying degrees of privilege and marginalization) who are going to work with language learners (who also experience varying degrees of privilege and marginalization), LTE practices have strong potential to effect change in society. It is my hope that the scholarly work published in this series will contribute to that change in various educational contexts around the world. I suggest that we, as practitioners and researchers of LTE, keep in mind these two aspects of being critical: first, there are many ways of being critical and acting critically in our contexts and our practices, and identities that inform our criticality are situated at the intersection of personal, professional, and political dimensions of language learning, teaching, and teacher education (Rudolph, 2022). Second, being critical requires us to keep critiquing our own criticality by self-reflexively questioning, reconsidering, and innovating our practices to address oppressive forces, uneven power relations, and systemic inequities that impact our efforts as teacher educators (Yazan, 2023). Such reflexivity in which we engage and model for our students could also involve endeavors toward developing "political and ideological clarity" (Bartolomé, 2004). This clarity includes identifying, problematizing, examining, and reflecting on our orientation vis-à-vis dominant ideologies to better understand the complex ways they operate and we construct our sociopolitically situated identities as language users, learners, teachers, and teacher educators.

Reviewed multiple times by colleagues as a proposal and full manuscript, this volume you are reading right now stands out in this book series as another strong collection that was curated and edited by Fares J. Karam and Amanda K. Kibler. The editors bring together select TESOL practitioners and researchers of teacher education who foreground criticality in their in-person and online practices across varying socio-educational contexts around the world (e.g., Macau, Türkiye, New Zealand, the United States). Those practitioners and researchers share their critical dialogic ways of addressing language ideologies explicitly in TESOL teacher education. The editors note in the introduction chapter that their goal is to "showcase how dialogic and critical approaches can be infused into TESOL teacher education programs through reimagining curricula, pedagogies, the roles of pre—and in-service teachers and teacher educators, and online language education spaces" (p. 3). That conceptual and practical impetus toward reimagination of TESOL teacher education is reflected in the organization of the chapters around three parts (e.g., Reimagining Curricula and Pedagogies to Prepare Dialogic and Critical TESOL Professionals). In addition to individual chapters, Karam and Kibler invited colleagues (Peercy, Ungco & Varghese, and Tezgiden-Cakcak) to comment on the chapters in each part. These insightful commentaries are helpful in incorporating a dialogic dimension to the composition of this volume.

This outstanding volume presents distinct research-based illustrative examples for the intentional incorporation of what Kibler et al. (2021) conceptualized as "critical dialogic education" in TESOL teacher education. It makes a resounding contribution to critical language teacher education to have students, teachers, and teacher educators dialogically attend to ideologies that influence English language learning, use, teaching, and teacher education. I believe its high-quality content with compelling writing will captivate the reader from cover to cover.

References

Bartolomé, L. I. (2004). Critical pedagogy and teacher education: Racializing prospective teachers. *Teacher Education Quarterly, 31*(1), 97–122.

Canagarajah, A. S. (2020). *Transnational literacy autobiographies as translingual writing.* Routledge.

Hawkins, M. R. (Ed.). (2011). *Social justice language teacher education* (Vol. 84). Multilingual Matters.

Kibler, A. K., Valdés, G., & Walqui, A. (Eds.). (2021). *Reconceptualizing the role of critical dialogue in American classrooms: Promoting equity through dialogic education.* Routledge.

Kubota, R. (2020). Confronting epistemological racism, decolonizing scholarly knowledge: Race and gender in applied linguistics. *Applied Linguistics, 41*(5), 712–32.

Lin, A., Grant, R., Kubota, R., Motha, S., Sachs, G. T., Vandrick, S., & Wong, S. (2004). Women faculty of color in TESOL: Theorizing our lived experiences. *TESOL Quarterly, 38*(3), 487–504.

Motha, S. (2014). *Race, empire, and English language teaching: Creating responsible and ethical anti-racist practice.* Teachers College Press.

Norton, B., & Toohey, K. (Eds.). (2004). *Critical pedagogies and language learning.* Cambridge University Press.

Park, G. (2017). *Narratives of East Asian women teachers of English: Where privilege meets marginalization.* Multilingual Matters.

Pavlenko, A., & Blackledge, A. (Eds.). (2004). *Negotiation of identities in multilingual contexts.* Multilingual Matters.

Pennycook, A. (1999). Introduction: Critical approaches to TESOL. *TESOL Quarterly, 33*(3), 329–48.

Phillipson, R. (2013). TESOL expertise in the empire of English. *TESOL in Context, 22*(2), 5–16.

Rudolph, N. (2022). Narratives and negotiations of identity in Japan and criticality in (English) language education: (Dis)Connections and implications. *TESOL Quarterly.* Advance online. https://doi.org/10.1002/tesq.3150

Varghese, M., Motha, S., Trent, J., Park, G., & Reeves, J. (Eds.). (2016). Language teacher identity in multilingual settings. *TESOL Quarterly, 50*(3), 545–71.

Yazan, B. (2023). Being a transnational language teacher educator and researcher: Borderlands, ideologies, and liminal identities. In M. Gemignani, Y. Hernández-Albújar, & J. Sládková (Eds.), *Migrant scholars researching migration: Reflexivity, subjectivity, and biography in research* (pp. 121–132). Routledge.

Acknowledgments

We would like to thank Dr. Guadalupe Valdés and Dr. Aída Walqui for their generosity in allowing us to draw upon their initial conceptualization of critical dialogic education (CDE) with Dr. Amanda K. Kibler. We are thankful for the opportunity to continue to explore CDE and share their passion for educating young minds and preparing equity-oriented TESOL professionals.

We also extend our gratitude to the chapter contributors in this volume and their commitment to preparing dialogic, critical, and inclusive TESOL professionals.

Introduction: A Vision for Critical Dialogic Education within the Context of TESOL Teacher Education

Fares J. Karam and Amanda K. Kibler

This edited volume builds upon Kibler, Valdés, and Walqui's (2021) conceptualization of critical dialogic education (CDE). CDE envisions classrooms as spaces that have the potential to support the education of all students through "equity-focused classroom pedagogies that are dialogic, critical, and inclusive" (p. 1). While Kibler and colleagues' previous efforts centered the classroom as the core space where radical and transformative change can occur, this edited volume's focus is Teaching English to Speakers of Other Languages (TESOL) teacher education. More specifically, we argue that in order for teachers to be able to create equitable classroom environments that support the academic and intellectual development of linguistically minoritized students, teacher educators need to infuse dialogic, critical, and inclusive approaches into their teacher education programs in the first place. In relation to the field of TESOL, we note that such actions have specific urgency given the hierarchies in which the teaching and learning of English are placed worldwide and the necessity of bringing critical perspectives to that phenomenon, but we acknowledge the utility of CDE in teacher preparation for language education more generally.

Although more experienced TESOL teachers may be able to agentively implement critical and dialogic approaches to instruction (e.g., Karam, 2021; Karam, Barone, & Kibler, 2021), we know little about what TESOL teacher educators do to help train and prepare language teachers who can do exactly that. To address this gap in our knowledge, we bring together a group of scholars who share their visions of how to use CDE to prepare critical, dialogic, and inclusive TESOL professionals who in turn can advocate for and support their multilingual learners through the adoption and implementation of CDE principles themselves. Since language teachers are at the forefront of supporting the academic and social needs of increasingly ethnically and linguistically diverse student populations (Duran, 2019; Hawkins & Norton, 2009; Karam, Oikonomidoy, & Kibler, 2021), preparing critical and dialogic TESOL teachers with social justice orientations becomes increasingly essential to helping multilingual learners (MLs) of English fulfill their academic and linguistic potential. Such an orientation is also in line with recent calls for a decolonial pedagogy that acknowledges teachers' role as "nothing short of world-makers and heart-changers" (Canagarajah, 2023, p. 10) in their transformational role of helping students develop critical dispositions.

We start this introductory section by providing an overview of the status of the field with respect to preparing TESOL professionals, with a focus on dialogic and critical efforts. We then transition to elaborating on the principles underlying CDE and how these apply to and intersect with TESOL teacher education. Finally, we share an overview of chapters included in this edited volume and conclude with our CDE vision for preparing critical, dialogic, and inclusive TESOL professionals.

TESOL Teacher Education: Current Status of the Field

What qualities make a great TESOL teacher?

To answer this important question, Coombe (2020) conducted a review of the literature and identified ten characteristics of excellence with respect to TESOL teachers. Such characteristics included professional knowledge, instructional effectiveness, good communication skills, and willingness to go the extra mile—among others. Although this list is by no means comprehensive, we emphasize good communication skills as an essential quality that contributes to the profile of an excellent TESOL teacher. Building on this key quality is going the extra mile and engaging in dialogic teaching based on the essential belief that knowledge is constructed jointly through quality classroom interactions (e.g., Haneda, 2017).

While there is ample empirical evidence that highlights the effectiveness of dialogic approaches in supporting the language development (e.g., Philp et al., 2013; Sato & Ballinger, 2016) as well as the academic achievement of students (e.g., Resnick et al., 2015), dialogic classrooms remain rare (Cui & Teo, 2021; Kibler et al., 2021). Moreover, teachers may not be well equipped to plan for and facilitate classroom dialogue (Lyle, 2008): such a situation can inadvertently lead to furthering inequities in the classroom rather than ameliorating them. For those reasons, while Kibler et al. (2021) acknowledge the importance of dialogic teaching, they call for adding a critical dimension to dialogic pedagogies through questioning power structures of classroom talk and placing equity at the center of any pedagogies that aim at providing quality education for students, especially those from linguistically minoritized backgrounds.

In TESOL teacher education, dialogic and critical approaches to prepare and train current and future language educators are often treated separately. A unique contribution of this edited volume is to showcase how dialogic and critical approaches can be infused into TESOL teacher education programs through reimagining curricula, pedagogies, the roles of pre- and in-service teachers and teacher educators, and online language education spaces. Before we present our vision for CDE in teacher education contexts, we survey the literature on dialogic and critical language teacher education. We cover such approaches and contexts as dialogic gatherings, dialogic learning communities, dialogic online interactions, and dialogic collaborations and advocacy. We also outline some of the major and more recent attempts at implementations of critical approaches such as translanguaging, self-reflexivity, critical multilingual language awareness, and narrative and identity approaches—among others.

Dialogic Language Teacher Education

Grounded in Bakhtin's (1935/1981) notion of dialogism and Vygotsky's (1978) sociocultural theory of learning, dialogic teaching encourages students to negotiate and co-construct knowledge through questioning, challenging, and engaging in dialogue with peers and other sources of knowledge (e.g., teachers and textbooks) (Alexander, 2017; Mercer et al., 2020; see Kibler et al., 2021). Such a pedagogy becomes increasingly important for students from linguistically minoritized backgrounds as language is the medium through which students learn and demonstrate their learning to teachers (Cazden, 2001). Teo (2019) even argued that dialogic pedagogy is a key twenty-first-century skill for teachers to be able to encourage students to think critically and develop their own opinions. Indeed, in an age where misinformation abounds, there is an increasing "need for learners to sift through layers of (mis/dis)information in order to uncover what is of value and relevance" (p. 175).

Despite this urgent need for preparing teachers for dialogic pedagogies, inconvenient truths regarding second-language teacher education persist. The relative scarcity of dialogic pedagogies means that in many cases neither pre-/in-service teachers nor teacher educators have participated in dialogic classrooms settings as learners, making it difficult to implement what they have not experienced themselves. Further, Farrell (2019) reminds us of the theory/practice gap and the sense of inadequacy that many newly qualified teachers experience. Novice teachers often embark on teaching multilingual learners in classrooms that rarely resemble what they have learned about during their teacher education programs. To address such serious issues and reclaim the relevance of L2 teacher education, Johnson (2015) underscores the importance of

> the dialogic interactions between teacher educators and teachers, where teacher educators can see, support, and enhance the professional development of L2 teachers. Exploring these dialogic interactions, as they unfold and within the sociocultural contexts in which they occur, not only opens up the practices of L2 teacher education for closer scrutiny, but it also holds teacher educators accountable to the L2 teachers with whom they work and, of course, the L2 students their teachers teach.
>
> (p. 515)

Despite the importance of such dialogic interactions, Cui and Teo (2021) emphasize the ambiguity resulting from the different *models* of dialogic teaching. To bring more clarity to dialogic pedagogies, they reviewed, compared, and critiqued several dialogic education models and proposed a new framework of dialogic education with four components: dialogic environment, teaching goal, classroom talk, and dialogic moves. An important conclusion that Cui and Teo arrive at is that "dialogic education is not a one-size-fits-all" and is largely dependent on local school and classroom contexts (Lefstein & Snell, 2014) where teachers play a vital role in navigating the complexities of classroom talk.

To showcase such diversity in implementing dialogic approaches in language teacher education, we provide a brief overview of different attempts utilizing different dialogic approaches in various contexts to help prepare language educators to facilitate dialogic pedagogies in their own classrooms. Barros-del Rio et al. (2021) documented the implementation of dialogic gatherings (DGs) in TESOL teacher education in Spain. DGs involve previously selected works of literature that are read and then discussed by participants. DGs are often facilitated by a moderator who ensures equitable turn-taking and participation. What Barros-del Rio et al. found was that the careful inclusion of critical readings as part of the course in addition to the joint reflections as part of the DGs helped their seven participants develop a critical understanding of teaching English as a foreign language, promote critically responsive practices, and construct professional identities as language teachers. Similar to Barros-del Rio et al.'s efforts in Spain, McClure and Vasconcelos (2011) explored creating dialogic learning communities within the context of an English for Speakers of Other Languages (ESOL) teacher education course in the United States. Their findings suggested that adopting dialogic and humanizing approaches (e.g., inviting students to take part in the course design and weekly agendas) in the first author's course helped challenge the traditional teacher–student hierarchical structure and create an environment where students developed a "sense of collective responsibility for each other's learning throughout the course, positioning their peers as important knowledge-producers that contributed to their learning" (p. 118).

Efforts to create dialogic spaces were not restricted to in-person contexts. Suh and Michener (2019) examined how dialogic online discussion prompts (weekly questions based on course readings in addition to a minimum of three responses to classmates) contributed to the preparation of linguistically responsive teachers. Analyzing over fifty online discussion prompts, the authors found that while teacher candidates engaged critically with hegemonic language ideologies and English-only policies, it was more challenging to engage with each other as interlocutors in a critical manner (e.g., most responses to classmates were positive and encouraging but did not critically challenge or provide alternate perspectives to the original posts). Another important finding emphasized the importance of perspective taking. When teacher candidates put themselves in the shoes of linguistically diverse students and families, this helped them better understand their students' linguistic diversity and consequently be better prepared to advocate for them and support their instruction. The same authors, in another study (Michener & Suh, 2023), explore the dialogic dimension in advocacy work to support historically marginalized students labeled as English learners. More specifically, they tracked a group of teachers' advocacy work (e.g., advocating for ensuring access to equitable instruction and language learning programs) throughout their ESL certification into their teaching work in a school district in New Jersey. The researchers analyzed various forms of dialogic discussions that took place both during and after the participants' completion of their teacher certification (e.g., weekly online discussions prior to course work completion and focus groups and email discussion after completion of course work). Their findings emphasized the importance of dialogic discourse in mediating teachers' advocacy work.

In summary, the work reviewed in this section (albeit not comprehensive) suggests that dialogic pedagogies are essential in TESOL teacher education programs as they hold the promise of preparing TESOL professionals who are well equipped to value the perspectives and diversity of multilingual learners and their families, advocate on their behalf, and effectively scaffold their instruction. Such promise of dialogic pedagogies can be enacted within online spaces of teacher education and can be more powerful if combined with a critical perspective.

Critical Language Teacher Education

Critical approaches to education and applied linguistics abound. Within the context of language teacher education, Hawkins and Norton (2009) described this critical dimension as "a focus on how dominant ideologies in society drive the construction of understandings and meanings in ways that privilege certain groups of people, while marginalizing others" (p. 31). In building the case for critical language teacher education, they explained how ideologies and assumptions are transmitted and expressed through language. As such, language is by no means neutral and is

> shot through with meanings, inflections, intentions and assumptions. Rather than have learners internalize such meanings as normal and right, critical language teachers work with their students to deconstruct language, texts, and discourses, in order to investigate whose interests they serve and what messages are both explicitly and implicitly conveyed.
>
> (p. 32)

The onus then is on teacher educators to help language teachers develop critical practices (e.g., critical awareness, critical self-reflection, and critical pedagogical relations) that can facilitate their work with students to challenge dominant narratives and inequitable language ideologies and policies (Hawkins & Norton, 2009). But what does this look like within the context of TESOL teacher education? While it is beyond the scope of this introductory chapter to present a complete review of the literature, we highlight some recent studies—drawing upon various critical paradigms and practices—that showcase efforts to prepare critical language teachers.

Cultivating critical awareness (e.g., Alim, 2005; Fairclough, 2014; Janks, 1999) is a key focus in TESOL teacher education where teacher educators endeavor to raise awareness about power relations and inequities that limit the possibilities for the student populations that TESOL professionals serve (Cinaglia & De Costa, 2022). Drawing upon critical multilingual language awareness (CMLA;

García, 2015), Deroo and Ponzio (2023) analyzed pre-service teachers' multimodal representations of the relationship between language, identity, and power. Findings from their study suggest that creating such digital representations and engaging in reflective journal entries and drawing connections to course readings helped the pre-service teachers develop their CMLA and critically challenge monoglossic ideologies. Another critical orientation in TESOL teacher education programs is promoting an understanding of translanguaging (Andrei et al., 2020; Deroo et al., 2019; Tian et al., 2020) and translingual awareness (Flores & Aneja, 2017). For example, adopting a case study design, Deroo et al. (2019) documented how a pre-service and an in-service teacher navigated adopting a translanguaging stance. Findings revealed that integrating course work and field work was essential to connect translanguaging theory with practice and in order to efficiently develop a translanguaging stance. The authors emphasized the importance of supporting teachers throughout their field work through adequate course content that bridges theory into practice and through appropriate placements and mentor teachers whenever possible. From a different perspective, Andrei et al. (2020) found that translanguaging theory was a contentious topic in the teacher education classroom they studied, which required thoughtful facilitation of discussions to elicit and honor students' multiple perspectives and critiques. Examining a TESOL course that they taught, Flores and Aneja (2017) also found that engaging "non-native" speaking students with translingual projects and content can support their development of more positive and asset-based identities as multilingual teachers.

An additional focus is promoting critical reflection (e.g., Farrell, 2015; Peercy & Sharkey, 2022). Farrell (2015) presented a framework for TESOL teachers to be able to reflect on various aspects of their practice, including not only (meta)cognitive and intellectual, but also emotional and moral dimensions encompassing their teaching. Farrell's (2016) literature review regarding this topic suggests that overall, "the research indicates that both preservice and inservice teachers are interested in, and feel they benefit from, reflecting on various aspects of their practice" (p. 241).

An identity-oriented approach to TESOL teacher education has also been gaining popularity and increased interest (e.g., Barkhuizen, 2017; De Costa & Norton, 2017; Varghese et al., 2016). Again, this is a broad field with various theoretical and methodological orientations; however, several employ explicitly critical approaches. By means of example, we share Yazan's (2019) case study of a teacher candidate's authoring of her critical autoethnographic narrative (CAN). Yazan analyzed various types of data (e.g., discussion board posts, CAN presentation, and feedback sessions) documenting how the teacher candidate used narrative to construct her teacher identity and challenge ideological binaries such as native/nonnative and correct/incorrect forms of language. More importantly, Yazan presented CAN as a powerful tool to support teacher candidates' learning and help them "analyze their lived experiences to make sense of the intricate interplay between the personal and the cultural in their identity construction with specific focus on the role of language ideologies in shaping the identity options available" (p. 6).

In summary, while there is considerable research on dialogic and critical approaches to TESOL teacher education, it is rare to find studies combining both lenses. While we recognize the immense responsibility of teacher educators to prepare TESOL professionals who are ready to address the specific needs of multilingual learners, we also acknowledge the need to avoid characterizing teacher educators as "supermen/superwomen" and emphasize "the need to humanize them as whole people by recognizing their unique strengths and struggles as well as diverse learning needs" (Yuan et al., 2022, p. X). Just like TESOL teachers, teacher educators also are under constant pressure to do more with increasingly limited resources. This volume is an attempt at sharing examples of how some teacher educators adopted CDE to help prepare dialogic, critical, and inclusive TESOL professionals. We hope these examples inspire similar efforts in various contexts. In the next section, we present our vision of how CDE can be infused into teacher education contexts and how teacher educators can utilize CDE to help language teachers be agents of change and proponents of equity and social justice in support of their multilingual learners.

CDE as a Framework for Preparing Language Teachers

In order to envision CDE as a framework for preparing TESOL teachers, it is important to clarify what is unique about this educational approach and how it synthesizes both dialogic and critical perspectives. Kibler et al. (2021) argue for the importance of dialogic classroom discourse practices, and in TESOL contexts, such practices must respond to and develop the multilingual resources learners bring to the classroom. They also emphasize that discourse practices must be embedded in critical perspectives that help both teachers and students challenge the linguistic and racialized norms and expectations that often limit multilingual youth's opportunities.

One way to differentiate CDE from dialogic approaches more generally is to consider the key goals and the role of equity in each. For many scholars working in dialogic traditions, main goals or outcomes achieved by dialogic teaching are students' academic, linguistic, and intellectual development. Typically, equity has been considered a secondary or "embedded" goal (Resnick et al., 2015, p. 3). Kibler et al. (2021) differentiate critical and dialogic teaching and learning (CDE) by proposing equity for marginalized populations as the primary goal, which is achieved *through* academic, linguistic, and intellectual development. They argue that if equity is only a secondary or embedded goal, and not a primary one, it is unlikely that such efforts will achieve either the academic, linguistic, and intellectual development, or the equity itself. Further, the term "dialogic" is purposefully used in CDE in multiple and overlapping senses: it includes the practical notion of dialogue or classroom talk, the Bakhtinian concept of multivoicedness (1935/1981), and the Freirean notion of problem-posing pedagogies (1973; 2005).

But what specifically is necessary to move classrooms from being dialogic to being critical and dialogic? Table I.1 provides an overview of some commonly agreed-upon features of dialogic talk that Kibler et al. (2021) identified: that it is co-constructed, intellectually purposeful, respectful, adaptive, contextually responsive, and learnable. These are all important and valuable elements of dialogic teaching and learning, but they require certain transformations to be both critical and dialogic. We describe each briefly below before turning to implications for their integration into TESOL teacher education contexts to support language teachers' enactment of CDE in and beyond their classrooms.

First, dialogic teaching in CDE is not only co-constructed among teachers and learners: students have active and agentive roles in building learning around questions that are authentic and relevant to them. In TESOL teacher education contexts, this means that teacher educators must create learning spaces centered on key topics related to language, learners, and pedagogy that are compelling and relevant to pre-/in-service teachers' classroom practice. Likewise, discussions should be structured to give pre-/in-service teachers the agency (and responsibility) to build this knowledge alongside each other and their instructors, rather than waiting for the "right" answers to be given to them.

Second, in CDE dialogue is not only intellectually purposeful: it also elicits multiple voices and perspectives, many of which might be overlooked in traditional classroom spaces. This is accomplished by taking a critical stance on knowledge, whether that be the perspectives presented in curriculum or textbooks, or the knowledge shared by others in the classroom about their real-

Table I.1 Critical dialogic transformations*

Common dialogic talk features	Critical dialogic transformations
Co-constructed	Offers active, agentive roles for students in talking about authentic and relevant questions
Intellectually purposeful	Elicits multiple voices and perspectives through critical stances toward knowledge
Respectful	Utilizes equitable and reciprocal community norms
Adaptive	Grounds teachers' adaptation in their knowledge of power dynamics and a firm belief that all students can participate
Contextually responsive	Responds in ways that recognize no contexts are neutral
Learnable	Acknowledges that students can learn to engage dialogically with greater expertise, but that does not automatically lead to empowerment

* Adapted from Kibler et al. (2021).

life experiences. In this sense, critical awareness is developed through dialogic interactions with others, with attention to experiences of bias and discrimination as well as awareness of the structures and assumptions that normalize powerful and dominant ways of understanding, speaking, and engaging with the world. Such an approach may lead to difficult and uncomfortable conversations for pre-/in-service teachers, but teacher educators must go beyond a skill-centered or technical approach to teaching multilingual learners in developing pre-/in-service teachers' pedagogical knowledge. TESOL teacher educators are therefore called upon to develop critical but culturally responsive means to encourage critical stances in their pre-/in-service teachers, and to encourage them to do the same with their own students.

A third shift relates to the respectful norms that are highlighted in dialogic teaching and learning: in CDE, these norms must go beyond respect to be reciprocal and equitable, in which everyone is understood as a "talk-worthy partner" (Alvarez et al., 2021) whose contributions are valued and necessary to develop new understandings in a community of learners. In TESOL teacher education, this means that teacher educators must support pre-/in-service teachers—who may represent widely varied social, geographic, and political contexts—in exploring and valuing each other's diverse experiences, goals, and perspectives. Both explicit norm-setting and relationship-building collaborative activities can help foster these agreed-upon ways for pre-/in-service teachers (and their instructor) to engage with each other, which can serve as a model for pre-/in-service teachers' own classroom practice.

A fourth element of CDE is that dialogue is not only adaptive, responding to the flow of conversation as students and teachers engaging in learning together: teachers should adapt talk in the moment based on their knowledge of power dynamics inside and outside the classroom and students' positioning in these hierarchies, and on a firm belief that all students can participate in dialogic teaching. For TESOL teacher educators, this requires them to reflect—in the moment and retrospectively—on classroom dialogue by considering not only what is said and who says it, but what is *not* said, and who does *not* speak. Seeking input from pre-/in-service teachers themselves can also deepen their perspectives about ways they may need to adapt talk to support all students' learning. Making these reflective processes visible to pre-/in-service teachers is important in helping them embody an approach to adaptation that is reflective and equity-oriented.

Fifth is a shift from simply seeing talk as responsive to context—looking and sounding different depending on the setting and the people in the classroom—to understanding that no contexts are neutral, and that taken-for-granted ways of engaging in talk may disadvantage multilingual learners for a variety of reasons. Similar to the fourth principle, this requires self-reflection from TESOL teacher educators on their own classroom discourse patterns, as well as helping pre-/in-service teachers understand common barriers to equity in classroom discourse and practical ways to apply that knowledge to the structure and content of classroom conversations.

And finally, although over time teachers and students can learn to participate in dialogic talk in increasingly sophisticated ways, doing so with more success in classrooms does not automatically resolve the many inequities and discrimination facing linguistically and racially marginalized multilingual learners inside or outside of schools. TESOL teacher educators are therefore called to build pre-/in-service teachers' commitment to not only building equitable classroom spaces but also seeking opportunities to advocate for systemic changes in their schools, communities, and other institutions. Such advocacy-oriented professional dispositions are critical for classroom teachers as they move through their careers.

These transformations have multiple important implications for TESOL teacher education. In terms of curriculum, teacher education content and standards must develop pre-/in-service teachers' critical awareness and dialogic teaching expertise by engaging pre-/in-service teachers in CDE practices as learners and then later as the designers and facilitators of these spaces. In both teacher education and school contexts, curricula should connect learners to key global issues that reflect and impact their daily lives and provide space for students to use their personal and lived experiences, as well as their existing linguistic and cultural assets, as a means of entering new and complex topics. Teacher educators also need guidance in how to re-envision the classroom curriculum they receive and how to self-reflect on their own teaching so that they can apprentice pre-/in-service teachers to do this in their own classrooms.

The transformations that CDE entails also require new approaches to the language pedagogies that are taught to pre-/in-service teachers. Similar to other approaches, it is clear that planned scaffolding and in-the-moment contingent scaffolding are necessary to guide students through a lesson, and such guidance is familiar to many TESOL teacher educators. However, the goal of that scaffolding in CDE is not to achieve linguistic accuracy or correctness through practice on simplified tasks. Rather, scaffolds should facilitate students' fluency and language exploration through engaging with complex ideas. As a result, pre-/in-service teachers must learn to develop such scaffolds around rich and relevant topics rather than around language forms or functions. Further, CDE is predicated upon a usage-based approach to language development, in which language development emerges from use rather than being a prerequisite for use. Pedagogical reliance on the pre-teaching of vocabulary or sequenced grammatical forms is therefore misplaced: engagement with meaningful ideas and concepts gives rise to opportunities to learn and develop language. With time and opportunities to learn alongside each other, students' language and concepts will develop in tandem: pre-/in-service teachers must therefore learn to understand, trace, and document students' development through careful observation and formative assessment. And finally, teacher educators must take great care to avoid uncritical approaches to language teaching that hold simplistic views of "correctness" and ignore the ways that power, prestige, identity, and audience have shaped the development of language varieties and the ways they are used inside and outside the classroom. Helping pre-/in-service teachers take such critical and descriptive views of language is a complex task and requires explicit reflections on pre-/in-service teachers' own ideologies about language and language users.

A last set of considerations that CDE transformations require of TESOL teacher education is to carefully rethink the roles of both students and teachers in the classroom. Students—regardless of their language proficiencies or pedagogical training—are capable knowers and thinkers who bring expertise and have much to teach each other and their instructors. Teachers, in turn, are knowledgeable guides but lead as facilitators and fellow learners, rather than experts; they also bring a critical stance and asset-oriented mindset to their work with multilingual learners. Such roles may be deeply unfamiliar and uncomfortable to some teacher educators, and such perspectives undoubtedly need to be taken up and transformed to fit the ways of being and cultural practices in each setting. However, modeling such roles is important if pre-/in-service teachers are expected to draw upon them in their classroom settings.

Overview of Chapters

In Part I, authors present different ways to enact critical and dialogic approaches in teacher education through reimaging curricula and language pedagogies. In the first chapter, *The role of curriculum in the development of teacher expertise to enact critical dialogic education*, Aída Walqui explores how teacher practices can shift from prescriptive and form-oriented approaches of teaching language to more creative, critical, and dialogic approaches of engaging students labeled as long term-English learners. In that chapter, we see how innovative curriculum design can positively influence teacher expertise and help teachers prepare students for civic lives.

The second chapter, *Sustaining a holistic stance or not?: Language and language pedagogies in teacher education* by Laura D. Turner and María E. Fránquiz, combines a CDE lens with translanguaging to examine how four pre-service teachers position themselves in a course that adopted multilingual pedagogies. Their findings emphasize the importance of context in whether pre-service teachers sustain their belief in a more holistic and inclusive stance on language and language ideologies. As such, CDE pedagogy can benefit from a future focus on the diverse contexts where CDE is enacted.

The final chapter in this section, *Cultivating pre-service language teachers' critical multilingual language awareness: A Macau perspective* by Rui Eric Yuan, Kailun Wang, and Jiahui Li, examines how pre-service teachers enrolled in the authors' introductory course in Applied Linguistics develop their critical multilingual language awareness. Through integrating critical dialogic learning activities, pre-service teachers are able to develop a multilingual mindset and a more critical stance pertaining to how they will teach English. The chapter emphasizes the importance of intentional curricular design and planning in effecting change in teacher education courses.

Part I concludes with a commentary by Megan Madigan Peercy that summarizes the first three chapters and discusses the possibilities of employing CDE to help frame equity-oriented pedagogy and curriculum in TESOL teacher education.

The chapters in Part II illuminate and critically examine how CDE can contribute to reimagining the roles of pre-/in-service teachers and teacher educators. In *"I just really want to focus on expressing how valuable each student is": Impact of collaborative exploration of problems of practice on teachers' visions of critical dialogic education*, Heather M. Meston and Emily Phillips Galloway describe their collaborative efforts with four in-service teachers of multilingual students with interrupted formal education (SIFE) and how the authors work with these teachers to help them enact their visions of CDE. The chapter describes how the authors adopt a collaborative, dialogic, and critical approach to help the teachers address their problems of practice and realize their classroom visions through multivocal discussions. The authors reimagine the role of teacher educators as facilitators and supporters of teachers' visioning rather than sources of knowledge that prescribe solutions to teachers' problems.

Critical reflections on dialogic education and practice: A duoethnographic approach by teacher educators is by Naashia Mohamed, Christine Biebricher, and Rosemary Erlam. The authors adopt a duoethnographic design to critically reflect on their own practices as teacher educators in New Zealand. More specifically, they use narratives to examine how their lived experiences shape their practice and how CDE is embodied in their teaching. The authors contribute to reimagining the role of teacher educators in how they learn from each other and respect their different ways of incorporating and struggling with CDE in their own practice.

The next chapter in Part II, by Ayşe Kızıldağ and Işıl Günseli Kaçar, is entitled *Toward more inclusive classroom practices in the Turkish EFL contexts: A case study on the integration of critical and dialogic approaches to field placement*. This chapter examines how the authors adopt a Notice-Problematize-Implement (NPI) approach to incorporate CDE into a Teaching English as a Foreign Language (TEFL) field placement experience within the context of Turkiye. The chapter's unique contribution is presenting how CDE is enacted within a context beyond the United States and how teacher educators can help support pre-service teachers through re-envisioning classroom talk and decentering the teacher educator as the authority figure.

The commentary by Camille Ungco and Manka Varghese concludes Part II, providing a synthesis of the chapters in this section and discussing the important role that identities, voices, and power structures play in preparing future TESOL professionals.

Part III focuses on online TESOL teacher education and how teacher educators can create dialogic and critical online spaces. The first chapter in Part III is titled *Creating a dialogic online space for preparing critically reflective TESOL educators* by Guofang Li and Yue Bian. The chapter documents the authors' efforts in designing and piloting online modules with the aim of promoting teacher candidates' dialogic and critical learning. The chapter presents valuable insights into the lessons learned in developing safe online spaces for dialogic and reflective learning that can help teacher candidates become more aware of the struggles that multilingual learners face. Li and Bian underscore the potential of action research as a tool for teacher educators' professional learning.

The final chapter in Part III, by Fares J. Karam, Amanda K. Kibler, and Patricia J. Arnold, is entitled *Interrogating raciolinguistic ideologies through role-play: A critical dialogic approach*. This chapter investigates how a group of graduate students in a TESOL course grapple with raciolingusitic ideologies. More specifically, the chapter examines how students worked in small groups to write and enact fictional scenarios at the intersection of language, race, and identity. Findings suggest that role-playing can be one effective tool in providing students a space, albeit online, to interrogate raciolinguistic ideologies and draw upon their own and peers' experiences to develop a deeper understanding of the inequities surrounding race and language.

Part III concludes with a commentary by Yasemin Tezgiden-Cakcak in which she discusses how the chapters in this section address employing CDE in online contexts. She also reflects on her personal journey of reconsidering the possibilities of applying critical and dialogic pedagogies through online modes of delivery.

In the conclusion, we as editors return to reflect upon how chapters in this volume align with the CDE transformations described earlier in this introduction and suggest implications for integrating CDE in TESOL teacher education that can help us prepare dialogic, critical, and inclusive advocates and supporters of multilingual learners.

References

Alexander, R. J. (2017). *Towards dialogic teaching: Rethinking classroom talk* (5th Ed.). Dialogos.

Alim, H. S. (2005). Critical language awareness in the United States: Revisiting issues and revising pedagogies in a resegregated society. *Educational Researcher, 34*(7), 24–31.

Alvarez, L., Capitelli, S., De Loney, M., & Valdés, G. (2021). English learners as agents: Collaborative sense-making in an NGSS-aligned science classroom. In A. Kibler, G. Valdés, & A. Walqui (Eds.), *Reconceptualizing the role of critical dialogue in American classrooms: Promoting equity through dialogic education* (pp. 78–104). Routledge.

Andrei, E., Kibler, A. K., & Salerno, A. S. (2020). "No, professor, that is not true": First attempts at introducing translanguaging to pre-service teachers. In Z. Tian, L. Aghai, P. Sayer, & J. L. Schissel (Eds.), *Envisioning TESOL through a translanguaging lens: Global perspectives* (pp. 329–44). Springer. https://doi.org/10.1007/978-3-030-47031-9_5

Bakhtin, M. (1935/1981). *The dialogic imagination* (V. Liapunov & K. Brostrom, Trans.). University of Texas Press.

Barkhuizen, G. (Ed.). (2017). *Reflections on language teacher identity research*. Routledge.

Barros-del Rio, M. A., Álvarez, P., & Molina Roldán, S. (2021). Implementing Dialogic Gatherings in TESOL teacher education. *Innovation in Language Learning and Teaching, 15*(2), 169–80.

Canagarajah, S. (2023). Decolonization as pedagogy: A praxis of "becoming" in ELT. *ELT Journal, 77*(3), 283–93. https://doi.org/10.1093/elt/ccad017

Cazden, C. (2001). *Classroom discourse: The language of teaching and learning* (2nd Ed.). Heinneman.

Cinaglia, C., & De Costa, P. I. (2022). Cultivating critical translingual awareness: Challenges and possibilities for teachers and teacher educators. *RELC Journal, 53*(2), 452–59.

Coombe, C. (2020). Quality education begins with teachers what are the qualities that make a TESOL teacher great? In J. D. M. Agudo (Ed.), *Quality in TESOL and teacher education from a results culture towards a quality culture* (pp. 171–84). Routledge.

Cui, R., & Teo, P. (2021). Dialogic education for classroom teaching: A critical review. *Language and education, 35*(3), 187–203.

De Costa, P. I., & Norton, B. (Eds.). (2017). Transdisciplinarity and language teacher identity. *Modern Language Journal, 101*, S1. https://doi.org/10.1111/modl.12368

Deroo, M. R., & Ponzio, C. M. (2023). Fostering pre-service teachers' critical multilingual language awareness: Use of multimodal compositions to confront hegemonic language ideologies. *Journal of Language, Identity & Education*, 22(2), 181–97.

Deroo, M. R., Ponzio, C. M., & De Costa, P. I. (2019). Reenvisioning second language teacher education through translanguaging praxis. In Z. Tian, L. Aghai, P. Sayer, & J. L. Schissel (Eds.), *Envisioning TESOL through a translanguaging lens: Global perspectives* (Vol. 42, pp. 214–31). Springer.

Duran, C. S. (2019). On issues of discrimination and xenophobia: What can TESOL practitioners do to support and advocate for refugee students? *TESOL Quarterly*, 53(3), 818–27.

Fairclough, N. (2014). *Critical language awareness*. Routledge.

Farrell, T. S. C. (2015). *Promoting reflection in second language education: A framework for TESOL professionals*. Routledge.

Farrell, T. S. C. (2016). Anniversary article: The practices of encouraging TESOL teachers to engage in reflective practice: An appraisal of recent research contributions. *Language Teaching Research*, 20(2), 223–47.

Farrell, T. S. C. (2019). "My training has failed me": Inconvenient truths about second language teacher education (SLTE). *TESL-EJ: The Electronic Journal for English as a Second Language*, 22(4), 1–16. http://www.tesl-ej.org/wordpress/issues/volume22/ej88/ej88a1/

Flores, N., & Aneja, G. (2017). "Why needs hiding?" Translingual (re) orientations in TESOL teacher education. *Research in the Teaching of English*, 51, 441–63.

Freire, P. (1973). *Pedagogy of the oppressed* (M. Berman Ramos, Trans.). Seabury Press.

Freire, P. (2005). *Teachers as cultural workers: Letters to those who dare to teach*. Westview.

García, O. (2015). Critical multilingual language awareness and teacher education. In J. Cenoz, D. Gorter, & S. May (Eds.), *Language awareness and multilingualism* (pp. 1–17). Springer. https://doi.org/10.1007/978-3-319-02325-0_30-1

Haneda, M. (2017). Dialogic learning and teaching across diverse contexts: Promises and challenges. *Language and Education*, 31(1), 1–5. https://doi.org/10.1080/09500782.2016.1230128

Hawkins, M., & Norton, B. (2009). Critical language teacher education. In A. Burns & J. Richards (Eds.), *Cambridge guide to second language teacher education* (pp. 30–9). Cambridge University Press.

Janks, H. (1999). Critical language awareness journals and student identities. *Language Awareness*, 8(2), 111–22.

Johnson, K. E. (2015). Reclaiming the relevance of L2 teacher education. *The Modern Language Journal*, 99(3), 515–28.

Karam, F. J. (2021). Re-envisioning the ESOL classroom through a virtues-based curriculum: Contributions to critical dialogic education. *TESOL Journal*, 12(3), e582.

Karam, F. J., Barone, D., & Kibler, A. K. (2021). Resisting and negotiating literacy tasks: Agentive practices of two adolescent refugee-background multilingual students. *Research in the Teaching of English*, 55(4), 369–92.

Karam, F. J., Oikonomidoy, E., & Kibler, A. K. (2021). Artifactual literacies and TESOL: Narratives of a Syrian refugee-background family. *TESOL Quarterly, 55*(2), 510–35. https://doi.org/10.1002/tesq.3001

Kibler, A. K., Valdés, G., & Walqui A. (Eds.). (2021). *Reconceptualizing the role of critical dialogue in American classrooms: Promoting equity through dialogic education.* Routledge.

Lefstein, A., & Snell, J. (2014). *Better than best practice: Developing teaching and learning through dialogue.* Routledge. https://doi.org/10.4324/9781315884516

Lyle, S. (2008). Dialogic teaching: Discussing theoretical contexts and reviewing evidence from classroom practice. *Language and Education, 22*(3), 222–40.

Manan, S. A., & David, M. K. (2021). Deprescriptivising folk theories: Critical multilingual language awareness for educators in Pakistan. *The Language Learning Journal, 49*(6), 668–85.

McClure, G., & Vasconcelos, E. F. D. S. (2011). From "I am" to "we could be": Creating dialogic learning communities in ESOL teacher education. *Pedagogies: An International Journal, 6*(2), 104–22.

Mercer, N., Wegerif, R., & Major, L. (Eds.). (2020). *The Routledge international handbook of research on dialogic education.* Routledge.

Michener, C. J., & Suh, S. (2023). The development of collaborative advocacy: Dialogic engagements over time and texts. *Journal of Teacher Education, 74*(4), 398–412.

Peercy, M. M., & Sharkey, J. (2022). Who gets to ask "Does race belong in every course?": Staying in the anguish as White teacher educators. In A. Martin (Ed.), *Self-studies in urban teacher education: Preparing U.S. teachers to advance equity and social justice* (pp. 95–112). Springer.

Philp, J., Adams, T., & Iwashita, N. (2013). *Peer interaction and second language learning.* Routledge. https://doi.org/10.4324/9780203551349

Resnick, L. B., Asterhan, C. S. C., & Clarke, S. N. (2015). Introduction: Talk, learning, and teaching. In L. B. Resnick, C. S. C. Asterhan, & S. N. Clarke (Eds.), *Socializing intelligence through academic talk and dialogue* (pp. 1–12). American Educational Research Association.

Sato, M., & Ballinger, S. (Eds.). (2016). *Peer interaction and second language learning: Pedagogical potential and research agenda.* John Benjamins.

Sharkey, J., Peercy, M. M., Solano-Campos, A., & Schall-Leckrone, L. (2022). Being a reflexive practitioner and scholar in TESOL: Methodological considerations. In E. R. Yuan & I. Lee (Eds.), *Becoming and being a TESOL teacher educator: Research and practice* (pp. 127–46). Routledge. https://doi.org/10.4324/9781003004677-9

Suh, S., & Michener, C. J. (2019). The preparation of linguistically responsive teachers through dialogic online discussion prompts. *Teaching and Teacher Education, 84*, 1–16.

Teo, P. (2019). Teaching for the 21st century: A case for dialogic pedagogy. *Learning, Culture and Social Interaction, 21*, 170–8.

Tian, Z., Aghai, L., Sayer, P., & Schissel, J. L. (2020). *Envisioning TESOL through a translanguaging lens: Global perspectives.* Springer.

Varghese, M. M., Motha, S., Trent, J., Park, G., & Reeves, J. (Eds.). (2016). Language teacher identity in multilingual settings. *TESOL Quarterly, 50,* 545–71. https://doi.org/10.1002/tesq.333

Vygotsky, L. (1978). *Mind in society: The development of higher psychological processes.* Harvard University Press.

Yazan, B. (2019). Toward identity-oriented teacher education: Critical autoethnographic narrative. *TESOL Journal, 10*(1), e00388.

Yuan, R., Lee, I., De Costa, P. I., Yang, M., & Liu, S. (2022). TESOL teacher educators in higher education: A review of studies from 2010 to 2020. *Language Teaching, 55*(4), 434–69.

Part One

Reimagining Curricula and Pedagogies to Prepare Dialogic and Critical TESOL Professionals

1

The Role of Curriculum in the Development of Teacher Expertise to Enact Critical Dialogic Education

Aída Walqui

Opportunities offered students to interact in sustained exchanges about a text or topic, hypothesizing, combining facts, critiquing, applying, are at the heart of learning (Alexander, 2020; Glick & Walqui, 2021). When the work helps students scrutinize their realities, assuming a critical and constructive lens, it becomes more powerful. How then, do practicing teachers develop a dialogic stance in their pedagogical practice and learn to invite and support students' engagement in critical talk? What role do—and can—published educational materials play in the growth of teacher expertise to offer multilingual learners of English critical and dialogic learning opportunities across a variety of settings? To explore these questions, and to explore the possibilities of dialogic exchanges that are critical, I draw on data from an ongoing study.[1] The data used include 1) review of materials currently used in English language arts (ELA) secondary classes; 2) notes on design and redesign considerations of the materials to incorporate critical and dialogic perspectives; 3) a one-semester pilot implementation of the materials by four middle school ELA teachers; 4) a three-week intensive summer implementation by the authors of the curriculum[2]; and 5) reflections and suggestions made by participating teachers, students, and the authors on the implementations of the curriculum. The chapter will provide an overview of relevant literature on the development of teacher expertise and the role of instructional materials in supporting teachers' instruction. It will also describe the development of an innovative curriculum based on CDE principles and discuss lessons learned from how that curriculum influenced the teaching practices of four in-service eighth-grade ELA teachers participating in this study.

The curriculum proposal builds on experiences of several decades of work carried out by the author, and jointly with colleagues for two decades, using sociocultural approaches in classrooms with teachers to promote quality and equitable opportunities to learn for adolescent English Learners[3] (Walqui, 2000; Walqui & van Lier, 2010). Within the United States, bi/multilingual students who are in the process of learning English as an additional language are often classified by their schools as English Learners. To this perspective, a Critical Dialogic Education (CDE) approach has been added in the last three years (Kibler et al., 2021). Central to the curriculum proposal is the belief that critical dialogic pedagogy is not only desirable in the schooling experiences of all students, but essential in the education of English Learners. These students contend daily with societal inequities and need to develop an analytical and reasoned voice to redress them. CDE proposes that dialogic participation is pivotal in the joint development of knowledge: apprenticeship and individual appropriation of practices, all features of sociocultural theory. Moreover, CDE affirms that in this apprenticeship curricular materials should function not as factory machines automatically triggering worker responses, but as tools that invite the exploration of personal and societal relationships, structures, and practices, contesting them all for the common good (Kibler et al., 2021). This approach is especially needed by long-term English Learners—students who have been in the English Learner denomination for more than six years, received repetitive, impoverished educational opportunities, and as a consequence, have been denied opportunities to advance academically (Brooks, 2019; 2022).

The Development of Teacher Expertise

The development of teacher knowledge and the ability to implement it in practice, expertise, should be a life endeavor given the constant changing nature of society, advances in learning, and the increasing need for a critically educated citizenry (Noguera, 2021). However, in US educational contexts, once teachers receive a teaching degree, the opportunities available to them to keep re-examining and growing their expertise are few, not necessarily coherent, and oftentimes driven by publishers with profit goals. Thus, teacher ability to offer students, especially English Learners, quality opportunities to learn and develop their social and academic potential, voice, and autonomy is limited (Villegas & Lucas, 2016). Economic, time, and vision constraints preclude school leaders from creating spaces and processes for teachers to collaboratively reflect on their practice and its impact, to redirect it for the benefit of schools and communities.

Reorienting teachers' vision of learning, of their students and what they can do, and of their practice is imperative. The world of today is no longer factory-based. The "information" age requires judicious citizens who can probe messages, compare them to other positions, and make up their own minds, justifying the reasons for their decisions. To be able to do that, English Learners require classes where they are offered interactive, well-supported, enticing, opportunities to learn which they perceive as relevant and worthwhile, and which will prepare them for reasoned participation in society.

The Impact of Instructional Materials

After observing multiple classes,[4] interacting with teachers, and interviewing them, it became clear that because of the limited opportunities and time teachers have available to keep developing their expertise while at work, pedagogical materials have ended up playing a significant role in defining what is valuable in learning, how students learn, the right progressions for developing students' knowledge and skills, and how to provide learners with practice to attain valued goals. This situation has worsened as a result of the pandemic since due to shortages (Leider et al., 2021) teachers lack "prep periods" as they have to teach classes where colleagues are absent. Adding to that problem, nationally teacher supply has decreased significantly in the last four years.

My colleagues and I carried out an examination of currently used ELA materials in middle and high school. We were interested in the "mainstream curriculum" and what it offered English Learners because many students classified as Long-term English Learners take regular English classes and repeatedly fail them. We were interested in understanding the quality of materials and the guidance they offered teachers to challenge and support students in critical and dialogic ways.

Key findings from this review revealed that, in general, current ELA curricular materials lack the qualities to be good guiding companions for the development of teachers' or students' practices. Specifically, we identified seven features that gravitate against CDE:

1. *Monolingual and essentialized student audience:* Because commercial curricula are published for a national audience, they assume non-descript

generalized students as users of this curriculum. English Learners specifically do not find themselves in these materials.

2. *Linear progressions*: Units present individual "teaching points" aligned to ELA standards, with lessons traveling from one idea to another, or from skill to skill. Teaching points tend to function as checklists, once "taught" there is no need to "cover" them again, with the assumption being that students learn once, and after that, the understandings and skills are owned and can be used.

3. *Coverage is extensive and superficial*: Textbooks present "a mile wide and an inch deep" sequence of texts. In one, for example, the first unit of study has seven stories. The concern is not about the quality of the texts, in fact, each constitutes an excellent example of literature originally written in English by writers that include Ray Bradbury, Roald Dahl, and Margaret Atwood. There is, however, no attempt to critically explore themes and relate them to students' realities, actions, and knowledge in consequential ways.

4. *Lack of academic rigor*: Our definition of rigor states that it exists when classroom activities invite students to explore key ideas presented in a text (oral, visual, written, or multimodal) and offers them the opportunity to weave these with other supporting and related ideas, while using analytic thinking (Valdés, et al., 2014; Walqui & van Lier, 2010). Rigorous schoolwork—which should always be beyond students' individual ability to engage in on their own—provides collective opportunities for teams of students in a class to critically apprentice into the practices that define discipline-specific communities. For example, in a widely used curriculum, after reading a powerful story, "Bread," by Margaret Atwood, students (those whose parents only speak English as well as English Learners) are asked to name the amount of bread present in each of the five contexts presented in the text using a two-entry note taker. In the story the amount of bread is almost irrelevant. The significant and humanly relevant question is: what role does bread play in the lives of five different characters? The exercise is trivial, irrelevant, and busy work, above all, it is not consequential, thus not respectful, inviting, nor productive.

5. *Activities promote transmission-oriented approaches to teaching*: Most materials currently provide scripts for teachers to read, suggesting there is one right way to teach (not to learn) and recommending that teachers avoid "deviations." In teaching, however, all classes are different, and even

when tooled with the best of plans, teachers have to adjust contingently to meet the ongoing needs of each class. Relatedly, students regularly express how boring it is to hear the teacher talking all the time—except when they are supposed to engage in reading silently. There is growing agreement that learning occurs when students are provided with opportunities to purposefully talk about the subject at hand (Haneda, 2017; Mercer, 2019, among others). As they listen to each other, consider what has been said, and engage in responses, interlocutors grow. Talk also provides students with opportunities to develop their voice and autonomy. In CDE, autonomy does not entail individualism but a keen sense of responsibility to others (Kibler et al., 2021), and the awareness that one's individual voice contributes to the common good (van Lier, 2004).

Talk provides English Learners with opportunities not only to share ideas, but to practice new language uses, to gain comfort, and to hear how others, and they themselves talk. Disregarding this important idea, course book recommendations suggest that students "turn to your partner and tell them ..." Telling is not engaging in dialogic interaction. Another common suggestion is "Have students answer each essential question and discuss them *briefly* with a partner." There is no description, or modeling, of the expected quality the engagement should promote nor of how to structure opportunities for all students to talk in sustained engagements.

6. *Absence of high intellectual challenge matched by high levels of pedagogical support:* A good pedagogical proposal has two components: students are invited to work with consequential texts beyond their understanding, and they are supported as they jointly—and then individually—appropriate practices, deal with ambiguity, grapple with uncertainty, and develop their competence (Hammond, 2022). Both components are accomplished through deliberate and contingent scaffolding that offers learners temporary targeted support until their autonomy in the specific practice is developed. In this way they "help students participate with peers and teachers to explore complex topics" (Kibler et al., 2021, p. 14). For English Learners, scaffolding amplifies (Walqui & Bunch, 2019), not simplifies intellectual access and engagement. However, most activities contained in published curriculum are simplistic, unenticing, do not invite any type any student to work at the edge of their competence, and do not create classrooms with civic and intellectual vitality.

7. *Focus on language:* ELA textbooks address language as form: grammar, lexis, in a vacuum of meaning. This approach often leads to misinterpretations of the text and actions being referred to. Instead of asking students to be critical about situations presented, suggestions are to focus on grammar, usually misinterpreted. Another example comes from the same ninth-grade ELA textbook that uses Atwood's *Bread*. In the book the author presents the different meanings bread has for people across highly diverse circumstances: in a comfortable home, in prison, where bread is used as a tool of torture, during a famine, between siblings in strained family relations. To invite the reader's emotional engagement, Atwood uses the second-person narration, enticing readers to imagine and situate themselves in the concrete situations she presents. However, the textbook highlights the opening sentence used in Atwood's book, written in the imperative, as a command given to the reader to think of a piece of bread. Furthermore, it guides students to understand that with commands, it is implied that the subject is the reader (you). If the subject were to be explicitly stated, Atwood's command would read, "*You* [the reader] imagine a piece of bread." In other words, as CDE proposes, "it is learners' exposure to and use of language in real-life settings that is the key mechanism for development (Ellis & Wulff, 2015), not the careful sequencing of language forms or the breaking down of language into smaller bits and pieces" (Kibler et al., 2021, p. 15).

I have selected a few items to critique in ELA instructional materials to demonstrate the dangers of teachers following uncritically the guidance offered by books. The recommendations lead to students who are increasingly alienated from classroom work and school, and the potential to develop articulate, socially minded, critical, and contributing citizens is lost.

As we have seen, suggestions for work with English Learners can further isolate them from their peers, from relevant content, and in general preclude them from access and valuable engagement. For teachers, the curriculum functions almost as the lesson plan, and the discrete linear progression of teaching points leads their students astray. Even if they "mastered" the teaching points, the result would be inert, not generative knowledge. While most of the texts contained in published ELA curriculum are good, the pedagogical treatment proposed reduces them to a focus on isolated, almost irrelevant knowledge. As Allwright (2005) commented once referring to the prevalence of teaching points in curriculum directed at English Learners, "We cannot sensibly measure the overall success of a lesson simply in terms of the percentage of teaching points successfully learned. Focusing on these points may imperil the potential richness of the overall experience, from which so much more might be learned" (Allwright, 2005, p. 14). The shift, as Allwright suggests, is to encourage teachers of English as a second language to move from teaching points to learning opportunities revolving around the question of student uptake, what students can do with that knowledge in and beyond the classroom. We add to his words, students need critical dialogic engagement.

Development of Replacement Educative Materials

Heeding Allwright's advice, and our own discontent with published materials, one of the Studies in the Center's portfolio of work[5] was to develop replacement educative curriculum for teachers who had classes where students bureaucratically classified as long-term English Learners studied alongside a diversity of peers. The curriculum is intended to replace published materials during a quarter of the academic year, and to deepen teacher expertise through the experience.

The materials are educative (Davis et al., 2017) because beyond containing proposals for teaching students, they also aim to contribute to the growth of teacher expertise. They do not only advice teachers on what they may do with students, they contain annotations explaining why these suggestions are offered, providing a theoretical rationale for them. They also assume that students will respond differentially to invitations to learn, thus, annotations present options and offer teachers choices for reacting to students' engagement in supportive and formative ways. The materials were designed in highly interactive sessions by the Walqui, Hartman, Schmida, and Feldman team.

We had originally intended to develop units iteratively, adjusting the practices as a result of deliberate observations of ongoing implementation. However, as we were going to start the process in 2020, schools closed because of the pandemic, so we decided to develop that first year, and to refine materials during the next year with teachers who piloted them. The observations and interactions we had with teachers, and amongst the team around design and implementation were immensely valuable. For example, during a focus group, teachers commented that they found the annotations useful because they pointed to key ideas in the text, highlighting how they interconnected. In this way we could see the growth of an important aspect of teacher expertise, subject matter knowledge (Ball & Cohen, 1996; Hill & Charalambous, 2012).

During the second year, four eighth-grade Los Angeles Unified School District (LAUSD) ELA teachers received professional development, used the materials, and were coached during implementation. We also run focus groups with them and their students. To compensate for having missed a second year of iterative design, and to test issues that emerged from teacher implementation, three of the authors taught a summer academy each in NYCPS in 2022, four hours a day for three weeks. The data used for this article come from these implementations. In all cases the classes had between 30 and 40 percent of students who had been bureaucratically designated as Long-term English Learners, about 30 percent of English-only students, and the rest fluctuated at all levels of English proficiency.

The Replacement Curriculum: Assumptions and Components

The curriculum design team has collectively worked with teachers of English Learners in secondary schools for fifty-eight years at WestEd. Lee Hartman, Mary Schmida, and Shirley Feldman are specialists in the Quality Teaching for English Learners initiative which I direct. We share a sociocultural perspective to development and have recently adopted critical dialogic education as a result of collaboration with one teacher in NYC in particular, Yael Glick; and Amanda Kibler and Guadalupe Valdés, long-time colleagues. Based on these experiences, and our continued critical reading of the literature, we decided to have the following assumptions guide our work, with the first one being the overarching one from which the others follow:

- School is the place where students develop the ability to both understand themselves and the world in which they live, consider alternatives, critique the status quo, envision, tool themselves, and act on the possibilities of change for the common good.
- The way in which students apprentice into critical academic practices in school is by being invited to participate with others in critical dialogic activity. Talk is rigorous, it focuses on central ideas related to a text and offers students opportunities to reflect on how these ideas connect to build larger ELA-specific, individual, and social understandings. As one student talks, the other one(s) listen attentively so that responses build on, or

critique the reasoning of the first interlocutor gauging its social. As students "interthink" (Mercer, 2019), they grow.

- The development of academic, discipline-specific practices entails the simultaneous growth of conceptual, analytic, and language practices (Valdés et al., 2014). As students experience the power of talk that engages their interest, they advance understanding, expand ideas, and build and evaluate arguments, empowering them for lifetime learning and democratic engagement (Alexander, 2020). More importantly, as they engage in critical activity, students understand and challenge "inequitable power dynamics, issues that are intricately interconnected to the social, cultural, linguistic, racial, and historical con-texts in which students live and attend school" (Kibler et al., 2021, p. 185).

- Ecologically speaking, the process of development is complex, nonlinear, and adaptive (van Lier, 2004). In school, students should be offered affordances; be surrounded by enticing meaning-making potential, so that as they perceive their surroundings, each one picks up what critically resonates with them (van Lier, 2004, p. 93). Affordances make both multisensory environments essential and dialogic exchanges indispensable for the appropriation of new repertoires of practice (Gutiérrez & Rogoff, 2003) and for the development of a "proactive vision that gives voice to students and disrupts inequitable power dynamics inside and beyond classrooms" (Kibler et al., 2021, p. 5).

- Because students are in the process of developing the academic discipline, thinking habits, and their language is growing, they are bound to produce "imperfect" English. Thus, intersubjectivity is necessary, that is, a tacit understanding that everybody in the class will do their best to understand and support each other during communication.

- The ways of reading, speaking, writing, valued by the academic community the classroom represents are visible to everybody, they are discussed explicitly, and dialogic practice is offered all students to appropriate them.

Six main components characterize the design of the materials. These guidelines have been developed for the last three decades through individual and collective reflection with many scholars, mainly among them, Leo van Lier. For the last twenty-three years I have also had wonderful colleagues at WestEd, and added to that my intellectually rich collaboration with Guadalupe Valdés and Amanda Kibler. Critical interactions with all of them have infused my perspectives with clarity, depth, and strength:

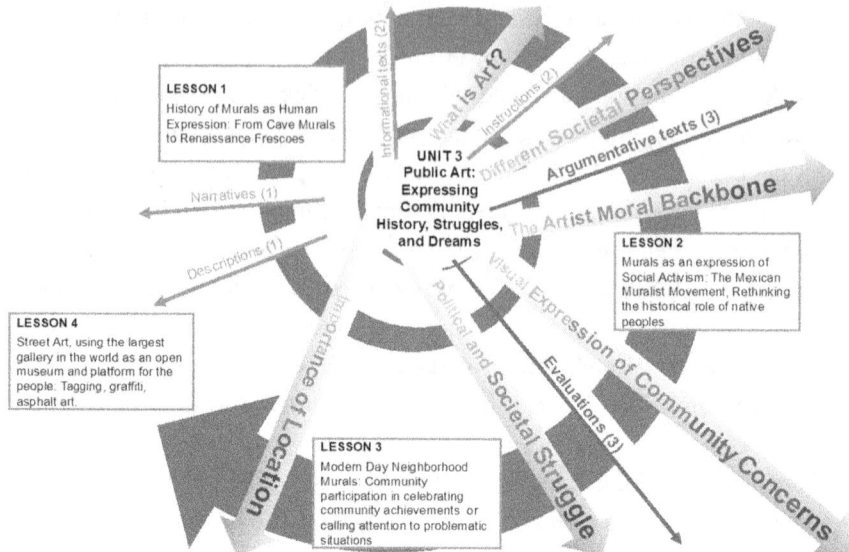

Figure 1.1 Spiraling organization of Unit 3.

1. *Thematically organized learning tools*: Rather than offering students a parade of isolated texts and topics, we designed three thematic units which together explore the overarching question: *How have human beings across time and space interpreted their environment and tried to control it?*. The units focus on mythology (three lessons), pandemics (three lessons), and murals and public art (four lessons). Each lesson is intended to take about five class periods, adding to a total of 10–12 weeks.

    Ideas and practices are explored in a spiraling way, making it possible for students to develop increasingly more complex ideas, critical skills, and language over time. Figure 1.1 represents this conceptually linked organization intended to build students' deep and generative expertise. Shadowed analytic practices are new in the lesson, while as they bolden, they signal that the practices introduced in a prior lesson (lighter), are now gaining strength and deepening knowledge to support continuous further development. The variety of texts used, with a number in parenthesis, indicate when those types were first introduced, and are spiraled later on in other lessons and units.

2. *Lesson architecture*: All lessons follow a three-structure design, each fulfilling a specific purpose. During *Preparing Learners* teachers invite students to engage in interaction as they activate relevant experiences, and pertinent funds of knowledge. Students' attention is focused through interactions on a main broad concept, and, if needed, students are

introduced in contextualized dialogic tasks to a few key constructs and the language that names them, what our Australian colleagues (Derewianka & Jones, 2016) call *Building the Field*.

During *Interacting with the Text*, students explore and unpack texts and ideas in the text. Finally, during *Extending Understanding*, the explored text is connected to other texts, and to the personal and societal lives of students. Well-structured and supported invitations are given students to amplify understanding by engaging in collaborative and individual activity.

3. Tasks used within moments constitute concrete invitations given students to engage in an activity. Tasks follow a routine structure to facilitate learner participation. The structure of the task, which scaffolds development, is flexible and generative. Once it is appropriated, students and teachers vary them and/or phase them out.

4. *Engineered texts*: We want English Learners, and especially students bureaucratically classified as long-term English Learners to read, discuss, and understand complex, long texts. Thus, texts are engineered, broken into their main meaningful components, adding subheadings to each section that do not reveal the content of the fragment, but add critical questions to guide students' attention to key aspects of the text without "directing" them to answers. Engineered texts make complex texts accessible by highlighting key elements, presenting students with manageable reading tasks, and offering questions that help them focus on essential aspects of the text.

5. Simultaneous development of oracy (Alexander, 2020; Mercer, 2019; Walqui, 2019; Wilkinson, 1965), reading of multimodal texts, and writing. Diverse ways of reading, mostly interactive, but sometimes individual; writing (taking notes, providing alternative versions of texts, composing essays); and talking (in small groups, in larger groups, presentations to the class, etc.) are interwoven to support the overall academic growth of students.

6. *Affordances*: Learning disciplinary practices in an additional language does not result from input–output sequences, where the teacher teaches something and the student learns it. Development rather occurs from a complex ecological process in which the same meaning-making element in the pedagogical environment affords different perceptions and uses for different students (van Lier, 2000). An affordance does not unequivocally cause specific learning but is the source of that learning. In our curriculum, we offer students semiotic budgets so that they each can use them differently and as they interact with each other, are able to appreciate varied perspectives and grow their understanding.

> You will be given the picture of an old painting by the Dutch master Peter Paul Rubens, painted at the beginning of the 17th Century. The painting, called *The Fall of Phaeton* is now at the National Gallery of Art in Washington, DC. Because of its name, you now know, the central character in the painting is Phaeton. In this lesson you will be learning much more about him. Because the painting is very busy, we are also giving you a draft Rubens made before he worked in the full painting which enables us to see the main details in the pictorial composition.
>
> First take a couple of minutes to observe both pieces and see what you notice. Jot down a few ideas. Then, working with the classmate next to you, spend three minutes collaboratively describing what you see in the sketch and in the painting. Who seems to be the main character? How does the title of the painting help you determine that? What appears to be happening? What may be going on? Do not worry about speculating as long as your speculation has a point of support in the painting or the sketch.
>
> *The sketch* 
>
> *The painting*

Figure 1.2 Notice and describe: from individual to joint activity.

For example, in the task above, which prepares students to read the myth of Phaeton students are given the sketch Rubens first prepared, and then, the resulting painting to observe. They prepare some notes that they will soon share. Both sketch and painting constitute affordances: they offer students the same contextual element, but what students notice tends to vary. Then, as they discuss their individual observations and interpretations, teammates appreciate their alternative perceptions.

Lessons Learned from the Implementation of the Replacement Units

Four Los Angeles Unified School District eighth-grade ELA teachers, varying in experience from 2 to 10 years implemented the three units with their students. These teachers taught the same class four or five times a day, so they had the opportunity to try the materials several times. Prior to implementation they received two days of professional development and during the quarter they were coached four times each. Based on conversations with teachers, their notes, and critical focus groups, these were some of the most important lessons learned during this first experience. They reflect key assumptions in CDE that require teachers to rethink both their pedagogies and their beliefs about students, as well as their assumptions about what "good" classroom talk entails (Kibler et al., 2021).

Teachers' Vision of Their Students Is Malleable

Teachers' awareness and recognition of their own implicit bias for what multilingual students classified as long-term English Learners can do and accomplish can be facilitated by educative pedagogical materials accompanied by professional development and coaching. Research literature on the adoption of innovative curriculum confirms our experience. For example, it has been documented that teachers accommodate new pedagogical ideas into their existing incompatible understandings and practices (Coburn & Woulfin, 2012) or they adopt ideas in isolation, selectively inserting them into current practices. In general, teachers fail to reflect proposers' intent after all, they are not explicitly addressed—and implementation frequently takes different interpretations from one classroom to the next, even within the same school and district (Coburn, 2004; Spillane & Zeuli, 1999). Sometimes enactment does not at all capture the essence of the innovation, thus leading to "lethal mutations" (Brown, 1992). All of this makes sense since changing old habits and the vision of learners requires major support.

Sustained, Critical Student Talk Is Possible

During the first days of professional learning, which took place the first days of January 2022, during their vacation, teachers expressed that they liked the materials but they thought both texts and notes were demanding. Nevertheless, they thought their students would enjoy the readings if they could work through them. They commented that their students could not talk as much, nor in the sustained ways the curriculum promoted.

As the quarter began, and teachers started to use the materials, they were surprised about the level of engagement generated, and how students seemed to handle texts that were quite demanding. They also noticed a positive impact on student attendance in class. During the first week a student said to another who wondered why he was not as usual absent from school, "I did not want to miss what happened to the dude who killed his father and married his mother," referring to the myth of Oedipus that starts the lesson. When we talked to students later on, they said they did not mind reading long texts because as they read, they had conversations with their peers as they enjoyed working together through their reading. One student commented, "I never thought I would enjoy reading about mythology, I did not even know that word before, but now I see how important it was for people's lives a long time ago. These stories help me understand myself and others better."

It became clear to their teachers that talk was both the means of communicating with others, and an apprenticeship tool. Pedagogically they saw how important it was to structure and support the invitation to students to engage in interactive practice to appropriate new conceptual, analytic, and language practices. This talk, an essential part of our curriculum, they commented, is typically neglected in learning and teaching, an observation shared by multiple educators (Mercer, 2019). One teacher's comment echoed those of her colleagues: "I really did not think our students could talk about stubbornness, greed, and other problems in Greek mythology and then refer to them in contemporary life. I was amazed about their thinking power" (interview notes, 12/19/22).

The Value of Task Structure to Foment a Rich Process

For teachers the novelty was that if they understood the structure of each task, and its value, they could engage all students in productive activity at the same time. They did not need to control students from the front of the classroom, nor be concerned about possible distractions, thus allocating to all the opportunity to consider, share, and respond to each other's comments. Teachers also observed that this organization benefitted all students, whether they were English Learners or not. They realized that if they provided learners with norms for talk which may have seemed constraining at first, they actually brought comfort to their students and they could gradually increase their competence.

Additionally, the sustained exploration of key ideas and their ramifications led to appropriation over time by students, who now, in other contexts, could use ideas, thinking practices, and language. When interviewed, students manifested their excitement at being able to read long, demanding texts, and their enjoyment interacting with their peers over well-structured opportunities. These comments proved that curriculum materials can be a lever for effecting change in classrooms (Ball & Cohen, 1996), impacting teachers and students alike, resulting in all students' critical and democratic engagement in substantive discussions.

Old Habits Die Hard

However, to our concern, teachers took longer than expected in working through the materials. In fact, during the first trial, the three units took them almost two quarters as opposed to the expected one quarter. We had two explanations for this phenomenon. The first was the fear of abdicating control until students got things right. This led teachers to overextend or repeat activities—something we observed during coaching—until learners "got them." In fact, the notion of fossilization of errors was mentioned. We tried to tell teachers that English Learners needed to build their competence not at once, but over time. The second explanation was that teachers wanted students to understand every single detail in the readings. We had emphasized during the professional learning days that if students understood what was essential for purposes of the course, they should learn to tolerate ambiguity, that over time, because of the spiraling nature of the curriculum, they would be able to gain deeper and fuller understanding of the practices explored. Teachers seemed to be reluctant to accept this was the case.

Teachers Need Support to Grow

While teachers initially thought their students could not do what was proposed in the materials, after they tried it with support, they were very excited to see that their own students could be focused, productive, and actually enjoy the interaction. They feared that inviting their students to work on interactive tasks meant they would be abdicating their control of the class. This concern turned into a recognition that students could talk to each other on topic, within time limits, and be motivated by the exchange. In fact, these teachers were so enthusiastic about their experience that they volunteered to try a redesigned version of the materials starting January 2023.

Regardless of their experience, though, we realized teachers say they do not have the time to plan. This is indeed the case, especially after the pandemic. For example, when we visited, we could see that teachers had not read the curriculum to be taught in advance. First period was tentative, teachers asked students to read the instructions aloud. As they became familiar with the moves after a couple of periods, classes began to flow more efficiently. While we know that typically teachers need at least three iterations with materials before they begin to use them purposefully (Loucks-Horsley et al., 2003) and ideally to adapt them in principled ways, it is important also that during professional development, teachers be given the opportunity to read the curriculum they will implement.

Use of Rich, Demanding, and Longer Texts Is Possible

The requirement is that the pedagogy amplifies for students the opportunity to interactively engage with them. Teachers can learn to use complex texts and both engineer them as well as scaffold their approach in classes with multilingual learners of English. For example, in Unit 2, lesson 2, one of the texts used in the educative materials is Poe's Masque of the Red Death (Poe, 2010). Instead of simply asking students to read the text silently and annotate it, we engineered (chunked out) the story into five component episodes, each subtitled, added questions to guide students' attention to key aspects of the episode and their relationship to the whole (without "pre-teaching"). Multiple interactive tasks are proposed to teachers so they unpack the text supported by deliberate scaffolds that enable students to jointly perform beyond their individual ability and apprentice in the process. Proposing meaningful episodes with headings is productive during *Interacting with Text*, as tasks are formulated to work through it. Then, during *Extending Understanding*, tasks like the Collaborative Dialog Writing (Figure 1.3 depicts students presenting their work) can benefit from the same chunking of text. In this activity, groups of students are assigned a segment to write the dialogues that characters in the section may have enacted with each other. Students need to use their knowledge of the text and the world to construct these interactions. All students in a team are asked to keep a full script, and then, in sequence, all dialogues are performed in class. Students in one of the summer groups performed the following dialogue. As the transcript makes clear, students are concerned about the hierarchical and callous response of Prince Prospero to the fate of his subjects, a theme that was later discussed by students critically. In fact, they compared it to incidents in which high political figures in the United States and Great Britain had had parties while other people were suffering from Covid-19.

Group 1, Prince Prospero invites his friends to move to his castle with him to escape the pandemic

>S1: Come to the palace and hide with me, I have plenty of food for all of us. We will live well here and have fun.
>S2: Prince Prospero, thank you for inviting us to this ball.
>S3: But Prince Prospero, how can we have fun inside when there is a lot of people dying outside? Shouldn't we be concerned about them?
>S1: I don't care about them, that is not my problem.
>S2: Prince Prospero, but what would happen here if someone is affected here? We all can die from the red death. I am not sure this is a good idea.

Figure 1.3 Students present their collaboratively written dialogues, NYC, July 2022.

S1: Don't worry, we are all safe here. The red death will not reach us.
S3: Ok, if you say so, I guess we are all safe and can have fun, but I am still worried about those who do not have our protection. What will become to them?

Changes to the Curriculum

Through critical dialogic encounters with teachers first, during the academic year, and then through critical conversations the designers had about our teaching experience summer 2022, we decided on three types of changes to the first version of the curriculum:

1. Streamline activities. We had designed many activities that could be easily skipped if prior ones were carried out in depth and accomplished their purpose. We certainly experienced that as we taught, we deleted tasks as we went along. It was fascinating for us to find out during debriefs at the end of the day, that separately, we had skipped many of the same tasks. Extra activities will now go into a section of the teacher (educative) materials as alternatives to be used when needed. More importantly, we realized that graphic organizers that require students to write down answers should be used at a minimum. Although the questions, for

example in a Compare/Contrast Matrix, asked students to think critically, students had the tendency to copy text verbatim, and teachers thought that was fine. When asked why they did so, students explained that copying information, a practice familiar to them, was all they did during the pandemic. While sometimes very useful, we will now emphasize that organizers require students to infer, compare, justify, etc.

2. In our minds, the conceptual connections between lessons and across units were very clear. Observing our four teachers as we coached, talking with students, and experiencing teaching ourselves we realized that for them, this was not the case. We will now emphasize these connections and link them to activities throughout the materials to promote deeper thinking.

3. Educative notes will be made more varied to entice teachers to read them. We are now writing brief vignettes of implementation and will use 2–3-minute video clips—to be filmed during the third year of implementation—to accompany explanations of purpose and structure of activities. In our own work, we have found videos to be powerful for conveying visions of what is possible and for illustrating pedagogical practices and moves. Our colleagues in LAUSD will be filmed during their teaching for some of these videos during the second semester of 2023.

Conclusion

There is immense power for all students in critical dialogic engagement, and this is especially the case for students bureaucratically classified as Long-term English Learners. They have been minoritized, instruction for them has been simplified, and then they have been made responsible for their educational failure. We need to assume the responsibility of teachers, and especially of materials writers, in this failure. We must remind ourselves that schools are places destined not just to prepare students for jobs. Most importantly, we are preparing students for civic lives. And while dialogue is not a panacea, …, curricular materials are essential to engage teachers and students in purposive social action. Teachers in this second-year implementation have realized that students are critical thinkers; that they have dreams of a more equitable society; that after all, they came to this country following an American Dream of fairness and justice, an idea they can help realize. In the United States, and elsewhere in the world today, "dialogue is essential to how we respond to the cultural, [social] and existential crises that confront us, but only if we are to defend those of its ingredients that are currently under attack: voice, argument, and truth" (Alexander, 2020, p. 198). Critical Educational Curriculum plays a pivotal role in that change.

Notes

1. The iterative design and testing of the replacement curriculum for eighth-grade English Language Arts is part of the portfolio of work funded by the Institute of Education Sciences for a National Research and Development Center to Improve the Education of English Learners in Secondary Schools, grant # R305C00008. While the funding supports this work, the opinions expressed in this paper are solely the author's.
2. Designers of the ELA curriculum were Leland Hartman, Mary Schmida, Shirley Feldman, and Aída Walqui.
3. I have opted to use the full "English Learners" denomination throughout the article instead of the acronym because I believe that the use of acronyms tends to be interpreted as if the individuals captured by the abbreviation were a fixed and monolithic reality rather than a collective of diverse individuals in flow. I realize the repetition can be tedious, but I think it is far worse to signify the category is absolute.
4. For this study, forty teachers were observed systematically. However, given that my work and that of my colleagues involve teacher professional learning, we have observed hundreds of classes and interacted with a great amount of teachers.
5. The portfolio of work includes two development and research studies, one focused on eighth-grade English Language Arts, which this article addresses, and the other one in mathematics.

References

Alexander, R. (2020). *A dialogic teaching companion*. Routledge.

Allwright, D. (2005). From teaching points to learning opportunities and beyond. *TESOL Quarterly, 39*(1), 9–33.

Ball, D., & Cohen, D. K. (1996). Reform by the book: What is—or might be—the role of curriculum materials in teacher learning and instructional reform? *Educational Researcher, 25*(9), 6–8, 14.

Brooks, M. (2019). Pushing past myths: Designing instruction for long-term English learners. *TESOL Quarterly, 52*(1), 221–33.

Brooks, M. D. (2022). What does it mean? EL-identified adolescents' interpretations of testing and course placement. *TESOL Quarterly, 56*(4), 1218–41.

Brown, A. (1992). Design experiments. Theoretical and methodological challenges in creating complex interventions. *Journal of the Learning Sciences, 2*(2), 141–78.

Coburn, C. (2004). Beyond decoupling: Rethinking the relationship between the institutional environment and the classroom. *Sociology of Education, 77*(3), 211–44.

Coburn, C., & Woulfin, S. (2012). Reading coaches and the relationship between policy and practice. *Reading Research Quarterly, 47*, 5–30.

Davis, E. A., & Krajcik, J. (2005). Designing educative curriculum materials to promote teacher learning. *Educational Researcher, 34*(3), 3–14.

Davis, E. A., Palincsar, A., Smith, S., Arias, A., & Kademiam, S. (2017). Educative curriculum materials: Uptake, impact, and implications for research and design. *Educational Researcher, 46*(6), 293–304.

Derewianka, B., & Jones, P. (2016). *Teaching language in context*. Oxford University Press.

Ellis, N., & Wulff, S. (2015). Usage-based approaches in second language acquisition. In B. van Patten & J. Williams (Eds.), *Theories in second language development. An introduction* (pp. 75–93). Routledge.

Glick, Y., & Walqui, A. (2021). Affordances in the development of student voice and agency: The case of bureaucratically labeled long-term English learners. In A. Kibler, G. Valdés, & A. Walqui (Eds.), *Reconceptualizing the role of critical dialogue in American classrooms: Promoting equity through dialogic education* (pp. 23–51). Routledge.

Gutiérrez, K. D., & Rogoff, B. (2003). Cultural ways of learning: Individual traits and repertoires of practice. *Educational Researcher, 32*, 5.

Hammond, J. (2022). Scaffolding: Implications and equity for diverse learners in mainstream classes. In L. De Oliveira & R. Westerlund (Eds.), *Scaffolding for multilingual learners in K-12 schools* (pp. 3–28). Routledge.

Haneda, M. (2017). Dialogic learning and teaching across diverse contexts: Promises and challenges. *Language and Education, 31*(1), 1–5.

Hill, H., & Charalambous, C. (2012). Teaching (un) connected mathematics: Two teachers' enactment of the pizza problem. *Journal of Curriculum Studies, 44*(4), 467–87.

Kibler, A. K., & Valdés, G. (2016). Conceptualizing language learners: Socioinstitutional mechanisms and their consequences. *The Modern Language Journal, 100*(S1), 96–116.

Kibler, A. K., Valdés, G., & Walqui, A. (2021). *Reconceptualizing the role of critical dialogue in American classrooms: Promoting equity through dialogic education.* Routledge.

Lefstein, L. B., & Snell, J. (2014). *Better than best practice: Developing teaching and learning through dialogue.* Routledge.

Leider, C. M., Colombo, M., & Nerlino, E. (2021). Decentralization, teacher quality, and the education of English learners: Do state education agencies effectively prepare teachers of Els?. *Education Policy Analysis Archives, 29*(January–July), 100. https://doi.org/10.14507/epaa.29.5279

Loucks-Hosley, S., Love, N., Stiles, K., Mundry, S., & Hewson, P. (2003). *Designing professional development for teachers of science and mathematics* (2nd Ed.). Corwin Press.

Mercer, N. (2019). *Language and the joint construction of knowledge: The selected works of Neil Mercer*. Routledge.

Noguera, P. (November, 2021). *Address given to the National Association of Independent Schools*. https://www.youtube.com/watch?v=D-S8zSkAMIU

Paris, D. (2012). Culturally sustaining pedagogy: A needed change in stance, terminology, and practice. *Educational Researcher, 41*(3), 93–7.

Poe, E. A. (2010). *The masque of the red death*. Guttenberg Project. https://www.gutenberg.org/ebooks/1064

Spillane, J., & Zeuli, J. (1999). Reform and teaching: Exploring patterns of practice in the context of national and state Mathematics reform. *Education, Evaluation & Policy Analysis, 21*(1), 1–27.

Umansky, I. M., & Dumont, H. (2021). English learner labeling: How English learner classification in kindergarten shapes teacher perceptions of student skills and the moderating role of bilingual instructional settings. *American Educational Research Journal, 58*(5), 993–1031. https://doi.org/10.3102/0002831221997571

Valdés, G., Kibler, A., & Walqui, A. (2014). *Changes in the expertise of ESL professionals: Knowledge and action in an era of new standards*. TESOL International Association.

van Lier, L. (2000). From input to affordance: Social interactive learning from an ecological perspective. In J. Lantolf, (Ed.), *Sociocultural theory and second language learning: Recent advances* (pp. 245–25). Oxford University Press.

van Lier, L. (2004). *The ecology and semiotics of language learning: A sociocultural perspective*. Kluwer Academics.

Villegas, A., & Lucas, T. (2016). Preparing culturally responsive teachers: Rethinking the curriculum. *Journal of Teacher Education, 53*(1), 20–32.

Walqui, A. (2019). Shifting from the teaching of oral skills to the development of oracy. In L. De Oliveira (Ed.), *The handbook of TESOL in K-12* (pp. 181–97). John Wiley and Sons Ltd.

Walqui, A. (2000). *Access and engagement: Program design and instructional approaches for immigrant students in secondary schools*. Center for Applied Linguistics.

Walqui, A., & Bunch, G. (2019). *Amplifying the curriculum: Designing quality learning opportunities for English learners*. Teachers College Press.

Walqui, A., & van Lier, L. (2010). *Scaffolding the academic success of adolescent English learners. A pedagogy of promise*. WestEd.

Walqui, A., Koelsch, N., Hamburger, L. et al. (2010). *What are we doing to middle school English learners? Findings and recommendations for change from a study of California EL programs* (Research Report). WestEd.

Wilkinson, A. (1965). *Spoken English*. University of Birmingham Press.

2

Sustaining a Holistic Stance or Not?: Language and Language Pedagogies in Teacher Education

Laura D. Turner and María E. Fránquiz

Introduction

Traditionally, methods or approaches of teaching English to linguistically minoritized children and youth have been situated within a monolingual frame of reference (Martínez, 2018; Ortega, 2013). Researchers have argued that this traditional frame is problematic as it does not provide space for students to utilize their full repertoire for meaning-making, in addition to linguistic resources already acquired across and beyond named languages (Cenoz & Gorter, 2011; Cummins & Early, 2011; García & Wei, 2014). By focusing solely on standardized constructions of English, monolingual approaches to language and language pedagogies lose sight of the whole child, positioning linguistically minoritized children and youth in relation to an imagined norm and to the construct of the ideal native speaker (Cook, 1999). However, in recent years, research across fields has increasingly called for the dismantling of monolingual assumptions and discriminatory language practices, arguing instead to focus on the everyday languaging practices of multilinguals (García, 2009; Ortega, 2013). This call positions the act of languaging as a dynamic process and posits that language-minoritized students leverage their communicative resources for a variety of purposes both within and outside of the classroom (García & Wei, 2014). In this sense, language becomes something that we *do*, rather than something that we *have*. We *language* (García, 2009).

Holistic languaging pedagogies have been described through various conceptualizations of translanguaging theory (García & Wei, 2014; Otheguy et al., 2015, 2019) and theories supporting the utilization of the full repertoire for meaning-making (Cenoz & Gorter, 2011; García & Otheguy, 2020; Hall, 2019).

Otheguy, García, & Reid (2015) define translanguaging as "the deployment of a speaker's full linguistic repertoire without regard for the watchful adherence to the socially and politically defined boundaries of named (and usually national and state) languages" (p. 283). Although translanguaging as a theoretical concept is not new, in recent years, it has gained increased attention in teacher education. Its pedagogical potential has been highlighted by scholars across the literature (Conteh, 2018; García & Kleyn, 2016; García et al., 2017), and it has been underlined as a framework with potential to prepare preservice teachers to challenge monolingual ways of approaching multilingualism (Barros et al., 2021; Deroo & Ponzio, 2019). Although translanguaging has also been debated in linguistics as a potential challenge to dual correspondence theory (see MacSwan, 2017; Otheguy et al., 2015, 2019), its impact as a theoretical framework, or conceptual lens, has predominately taken shape as a critical praxis within classrooms (García & Wei, 2014; García et al., 2017; García & Kleyn, 2016). A great deal of this work has taken place in the US context, with translanguaging theory serving as the take-up and enactment of a pedagogical stance, or disposition, in the education of multilingual children and language-minoritized students.

Enacting a Translanguaging Stance and Critical and Dialogic Approaches in TESOL Teacher Education

In teacher education, Kleyn (2016) encourages preservice teachers to consider whether or not multilingual students are *viewed* through a holistic lens in their field placements. Menken and Sánchez (2019) also point to the importance of *seeing* multilingual students holistically. Translanguaging—conceptualized as a pedagogical stance and critical praxis—has been highlighted in teacher education as a framework that places power dynamics at the center, and positions language equity as a right. As a pedagogical tool, translanguaging grants permission for students to utilize their full repertoire of communicative resources in the classroom, and pushes educators to challenge the existence of language hierarchies and normative languaging practices in schools (García et al., 2017). This positioning has been theorized as the educator's take-up and enactment of the translanguaging *stance*—a transformative disposition that maintains "using the child's full repertoire will transform language hierarchies in school" (García & Kleyn, 2016, p. 21). In this line, enacting a translanguaging stance serves as a means to disrupt and reposition (Deroo et al., 2020), thus restoring language to the students and communities we serve. However, as translanguaging's potential to challenge discriminatory language practices takes shape across the literature, teacher educators continue to explore how to foster the take-up of this critical stance, and nourish its sustained enactment over time.

In recent years, research in teacher education has consistently pointed to a need to prepare all teachers to teach multilingual and language-minoritized students (de Jong, 2013; Lucas & Grinberg, 2008; Lucas & Villegas, 2013). Teacher educators have called for this preparation in a variety of ways, but the majority of frameworks have underlined the importance of viewing language, culture, and identity as interconnected (de Jong & Harper, 2005; Lucas & Villegas, 2013; Palmer & Martínez, 2013), and of placing equity and inclusivity at the center (García et al., 2017; Kibler et al., 2021). Recent studies have also moved to examine preservice teachers' take-up and embodiment of a translanguaging theory (Barros et al., 2021; Deroo & Ponzio, 2019; Deroo et al., 2020; Ponzio, 2020). Although this uptake has been documented in university courses, little is known as to how this disposition, or holistic stance, potentially sustains throughout teacher preparation and beyond. This also holds true when considering the enactment of dialogic approaches and the shaping of preservice teachers' adoption of a critical dialogic stance, or mindset (Kibler et al., 2021). Both pedagogical approaches—translanguaging and dialogic education—require a focused level of support within and beyond the university classroom. For teacher preparation, this means thinking of new ways to not only capture their uptake, but to also explore their sustained enactment over time. In response to this need, in this chapter we position critical dialogic education (Kibler et al., 2021) as a framework with potential to work in tandem with translanguaging theories challenging linguistic norms. In Table 2.1, we highlight aspects of both frameworks that can work in communion in the preparation of preservice teachers, particularly as they navigate spaces to push back upon, challenge, and transcend discriminatory languaging practices and normative language pedagogies.

In order to support preservice teachers toward the enactment of equitable classroom pedagogies, teacher educators must instill a clear vision of what an equitable language classroom entails. By utilizing a dual translanguaging and CDE framework, teacher educators can begin to guide preservice teachers toward this collective vision across local contexts and over time. Within both frameworks, centering multiple voices or perspectives ensures that all students have permission to not only utilize their full repertoire for meaning-making, but most importantly, that this repertoire is positioned as a strength in language

Table 2.1 CDE and the take-up of a translanguaging stance

Critical dialogic education	The educator's take-up of a translanguaging stance
1. **Equity** for marginalized populations is centered as the primary goal and classroom settings are truly **inclusive**.	Teachers "must first develop a stance that **bilingualism is a *resource* at all times** to learn, think, imagine, and develop commanding performances in two or more languages" (García and Kleyn 2016, p. 21).
	The teacher recognizes that students' **language and cultural practices "work *juntos* and enrich each other**" (García et al. 2017, p. 28).
2. Teachers have deep knowledge of **power dynamics** in (and beyond) the classroom and their students' positioning in these hierarchies.	The teacher's *stance* "must position **language in the lips and minds of the children**, and not in external standards or regulations" (García and Kleyn 2016, p. 21).
	Families and communities are positioned **as *resources*** to be leveraged for learning (García & Kleyn, 2016).
3. **Democratic vision** that prioritizes marginalized voices and participation.	**Classrooms are seen as "a democratic space** where teachers and students *juntos* co-create knowledge, challenge traditional hierarchies, and work toward a more just society" (García et al. 2017, p. 28).

classrooms. In this sense, student voice is leveraged to disrupt power dynamics both *within* and *beyond* the classroom context, and language pedagogies and curricula are designed to dismantle traditional practices. Pushing back upon monolingual assumptions, across both frameworks, teacher educators, in turn, facilitate a deep understanding of power dynamics and student agency, and underline how these dynamics play out in and beyond the classroom (i.e., ideologies surrounding language and race, the role of external standards in language classrooms, etc.).

With an aim to address how current understandings of language and language pedagogies need to be collectively reenvisioned, in this chapter, we discuss how a critical and dialogic approach to preparing preservice teachers can influence their roles and identities as they come into contact with institutional structures and entrenched linguistic norms. We then consider the implications for TESOL teacher education, and position CDE as a pedagogical tool to better foster and sustain commitment to additive language pedagogies and practices challenging linguistic norms in the preparation of language educators.

Methods

Context

In fall 2019, the first author taught a course with undergraduate students before they entered the professional development sequence for elementary education certification as ESL generalists in a teacher preparation program in the Southwestern United States. After completing university core curriculum and major coursework, the professional development sequence takes place across three semesters, and consists of thirty-nine hours of additional coursework and placement in the field as an Intern 1, Intern 2, and Student Teacher. The initial timepoint outlined in this study took place directly before entry into this sequence during the eighteen-hour requirement of major coursework. Organized around the pedagogical knowledge and skills teachers need to know about language (Wong-Fillmore & Snow, 2018), the course sought to provide undergraduate students with the sociocultural and sociopolitical knowledge (De Jong, 2013; García & Kleyn, 2016) necessary to take up and enact more holistic and inclusive approaches to language and language pedagogies. To reach this aim, the course addressed topics ranging from the historical trajectory of language policy in the US context, to topics in educational linguistics, and explored language loss, immigration, and migration, and translanguaging. As a key component, undergraduate students engaged in a ten-hour service-learning experience, which consisted of a tutoring assignment with an emergent bi/multilingual student in a local elementary school. As an ongoing part of the field experience, the enrolled undergraduate students completed an intensive final project exploring the full communicative repertoire of their tutoring student from a holistic and additive lens. Using audio recordings, writing samples, student drawings, and observational fieldnotes, undergraduates explored a variety of linguistic components in context (i.e., phonology, semantics, pragmatics, morphology, and syntax), and enacted a descriptive lens by highlighting their tutoring students' hybrid languaging practices and use of semiotic resources beyond the linguistic.

Through the course content and the tutoring experience, the first author's intention as the instructor was to provide a space for the students to begin to challenge monolingual assumptions and ideologies. She also aimed to provide an entry point toward the understanding of a more holistic and dynamic view of language and bilingual/multilingual children. Undergraduate students were encouraged to view their tutoring students' languaging practices as both a resource and right (García & Kleyn, 2016; Ruiz, 1984), and to support and leverage their student's full use of the communicative repertoire, an underlying tenet in the take-up of a translanguaging stance (García et al., 2017). In their final projects, the undergraduates were invited to enact this developing stance and describe the dynamic languaging practices of their students across linguistic components. This included entering into a critical and dialogic space to reflect upon their perceptions and biases surrounding language use, in addition to their own languaging practices in the negotiation of meaning. Due to the undergraduate students' engagement with the course material, as the course progressed, the first author became increasingly interested in whether or not, or *how*, the emerging development of this stance would sustain over time. To further explore these curiosities, she developed a qualitative study to (1) examine the undergraduate students' take-up of the course content and (2) understand more about the ways in which a critical and dialogic approach to teacher preparation can influence preservice teachers' roles, identities, and positionalities over time—particularly as they grapple with structural inequities, entrenched linguistic norms, and perceptions of language and bilingualism/multilingualism in situated contexts. To avoid potential bias, the second author served as a thought partner and mentor as the participants were followed over time across the course of the study.

Participants

The participants represented a diverse sample of cultural and linguistic backgrounds and lived experiences in relation to language and multilingualism. Although all participants self-identified as cisgender female, their experiences in relation to languages beyond English also varied. In Table 2.2, we provide a brief snapshot of the research participants' self-reported identity information.

It is key to note that like many preservice teachers during this unprecedented time, the Covid-19 pandemic impacted all four participants' lives and experiences while moving across teacher preparation and the professional development sequence. Other than their face-to-face tutoring experience in the first author's course, the majority of their training in the field took place online or in hybrid settings.

Data Collection Methods and Procedures

We utilized case study design (Cresswell, 2007) and approached our objectives from a qualitative perspective. Favoring "intensity and depth" (Blanco, 2015), we anchored our research process in the voices, experiences, and positionalities

Table 2.2 Participants

Participant	Certification	Racial and/or ethnic identity	Language identity
Ilyana	Early Childhood to Sixth Grade ESL Generalist	South Asian	Bilingual [Urdu, English]
Adriana	Early Childhood to Sixth Grade ESL Generalist	Hispanic and White	Monolingual [English]
Anna	Early Childhood to Sixth Grade ESL Generalist	White	Monolingual [English]
Haley	Early Childhood to Sixth Grade ESL Generalist	White	Monolingual [English]

of the four preservice teacher participants over time. Through this process, we also sought to understand more about the complexities and nuances involved in the uptake of new learning across contextually situated timepoints. Data were collected over the course of a two-year period and included preservice teacher coursework, fieldnotes and researcher reflections, language learning histories, and a series of interviews with participants over time. Informal check-ins were also completed with participants in fall 2021 and spring 2022 after induction into the teaching profession.

In tandem with preservice teacher coursework, the first author conducted initial interviews with each participant after the completion of the course, in addition to follow up interviews over time. The interviews were semi-structured and open-ended, and lasted approximately one hour. Through dialogue and reflection, participants explored their own perceptions and positionings in relation to multilingualism and bilingual/multilingual students. They also engaged in guided reflection with the first author to explore their thoughts on student languaging practices. Participants interrogated their perceptions of these topics as children and young adults, and pulled from their lived experiences in school and beyond. This dialogue provided a space for each participant to begin to interrogate the potential implications for their future teaching and move toward action—building on each other's ideas, posing questions, and connecting the past to the present.

The first author also explored participants' language learning histories (LLHs) (Barkhuizen et al., 2013) to gain insight into their experiences with language, and to learn more about participants' linguistic and cultural backgrounds. She then completed a series of follow-up interviews with each preservice teacher, circling back to the topics addressed in the course at specific timepoints in their teacher training. In spring 2021, participants engaged in their final in-depth follow-up conversation, approximately one year after the transition to online and hybrid instruction as a result of the Covid-19 global pandemic. During this timepoint, participants were graduating from the teacher preparation program and moving into teacher induction. In fall 2021 and spring 2022, informal check-ins were also completed with participants after induction. Our focus across the timepoints was to facilitate an inclusive, collaborative, and critical reflection process, moving with the preservice teachers in tandem across space and time. To ensure trustworthiness (Miles et al., 2020), we placed participant voice at the center of the research design and supplemented participant voice with prolonged engagement with participants over time.

During the data analysis process, we used thematic content analysis to identify themes, or *participant moves*, that emerged from the participant data over time and across contexts. As the data set was intensive, we developed an organizational structure, or matrix, to facilitate this process, highlighting key aspects of CDE and the take-up of a translanguaging stance. While participants moved across the timepoints, the matrix captured participants' thinking, reflections, and experiences surrounding these key aspects. For example: centering equity for marginalized populations, positioning bilingualism/multilingualism as a resource at all times, envisioning classrooms as democratic spaces where teachers and students co-create knowledge, and challenging traditional language hierarchies and discriminatory languaging practices in their placements over time, etc. (see Table 2.1). All data across the timepoints was organized by participant in chronological order, and the analysis process was ongoing and reflective (Cresswell, 2007; Marshall et al., 2022). During this reflective process, we took note of aspects of CDE and the take-up and embodiment of a translanguaging stance, and paid close attention to nuances, complexities, and contradictions across the arc of the data. As a final step, we identified the themes, or *participant moves*, that emerged across the arc of the data as participants experienced different settings over time. Using the matrix as a guide, across all participants, we identified a sequence that contradicted a linear progression in the uptake of new learning. When it came to taking up, engaging with, and enacting more holistic views of language and language pedagogies, the participant process was complex. All four participants moved across, through and back the progression fluidly—engaging with the content, grappling with contradictions, re(imagining) possibilities, and questioning their role. We highlight these moves in Table 2.3.

Table 2.3 Participant moves over time and across contexts

Centering critical dialogic education & the educator's take-up of a translanguaging stance			
Participant moves over time and across contexts			
Engaging with content and initial uptake	**Grappling with contradictions**	**Re(imagining) possibilities**	**Questioning their role**
Embracing theory while moving toward practice	*Interrogating practice through a theoretical lens*	*Engaging in critical dialogue to (re)imagine translingual and dialogic spaces*	*Reflecting upon a lack of agency when confronting entrenched linguistic norms*
Trying on aspects of a dual CDE and Translanguaging Stance framework	Identifying contradictions between course content and learning in context	Addressing setbacks and roadblocks through the creation of dialogic spaces over time between preservice teachers and mentors/teacher educator guides	Reflecting on the feasibility of enacting aspects of a dual CDE and Translanguaging framework in educational spaces

Findings

Across the data arc, all four participants' inclination to challenge linguistic norms in their placements was context-driven. Institutional structures, entrenched linguistic norms, limited on-site mentoring opportunities, and power dynamics all contributed to the ways in which the participants approached language and language pedagogies in their placements over time. With this in mind, engaging in critical dialogue with participants at specific timepoints generated an ongoing reflective space to identify and address potential roadblocks or setbacks—creating and nourishing spaces for participants to continue to reflect upon their evolving roles and identities as language educators. Using aspects of a combined CDE and translanguaging stance framework as a guide: (1) *Equity*: Centering bilingualism as a resource at all times; (2) *Power dynamics*: Language in the lips and minds of children; and (3) *Democratic vision*: Teachers and students co-create knowledge, challenge traditional hierarchies, and work toward a more just society (García et al., 2017; Kibler et al., 2021), in the following section, we explore a series of contextual factors that emerged as participants navigated teacher preparation over time, and how these factors interacted within the framework. These factors, in turn, contributed to the nonlinear participant moves highlighted in Table 2.3, and demonstrate the complexity involved in the uptake of new learning and its potential sustained enactment over time.

Equity: Centering Bilingualism as a Resource at All Times

For a classroom to be truly equitable, positioning bilingualism as both a resource and right should always be centered. In this sense, in an inclusive classroom, the classroom teacher recognizes and upholds that "students' language and cultural practices work *juntos* and enrich each other" (García et al., 2017, 28). With this in mind, Ilyana's transition from pre-professional development sequence to the Intern 1 setting underlined the importance of considering context when taking-up and engaging with more holistic and equitable language pedagogies in the classroom. Throughout the initial course, Ilyana's emerging holistic lens, or approach to language and language pedagogies was equity-based and child-focused. However, as she transitioned into her field experiences, she did not have an opportunity to expand upon this developing lens hand-in-hand with a mentor teacher. As Ilyana moved into the professional development sequence and into her Intern 1 placement, she was placed in an English-only ESL classroom, and although 90 percent of the student population spoke Spanish at home, she described the school environment as "very strict about everything." She reported that as a rule, students in her placement classroom were discouraged by their teacher to speak or write in Spanish. In one of our follow-up interviews, Ilyana reflected upon a moment that "she didn't feel okay with," and that contradicted what she was learning in her university coursework. In the following anecdote, we place this classroom moment into perspective:

> So I was circulating with my co-intern and supporting the students as they wrote. One student was writing and he used the phrase *mi amigo* [my friend] and everything else was in English. The teacher made him erase the whole thing. I was excited that he was using both languages, and so when he showed it to me, I was like "Yeah, that's great," but when he showed it to his teacher he had to change it. And the teacher was also Spanish-speaking and fluent in Spanish. So seeing that, it was just a little—I wouldn't work like that I guess. It just went against everything that we'd learned in your class and in our other classes as well.

Although Ilyana quickly identified a situation in her placement that did not center equitable language pedagogies, she was surprised to see the disconnect between what she was learning in her university courses and what she was experiencing in practice. In contradiction to her university preparation, in her placement, the ESL classroom was positioned as a monolingual space. Within this space, Spanish and hybrid languaging practices fell outside of what was considered acceptable within the classroom context. In this sense, by interrogating this classroom practice through her emerging theoretical lens, Ilyana highlighted an approach to language instruction that did not align with a dual framework placing multivocality and student agency at the center. By pointing out and confronting this contradiction, Ilyana recentered the student's voice by lifting up her student's use of his full repertoire of meaning-making.

Like Ilyana, when Adriana moved into her Intern 1 placement, she also began to point to contradictions in our reflections. Although she expressed that she "felt sad" about some of the things she experienced, instead of presenting a pedagogical alternative, she decided to just "do what she could" while she was on site. Discussing two emergent bilingual children in her placement classroom, Adriana described how she felt:

> The teacher had said that there wasn't space for them in the bilingual classrooms, so they were placed in ESL. It just made me sad when they weren't getting the support they needed. The teacher sat them at different tables, and so I was like, they can only talk to each other, and yet, they're not sitting together. They really didn't talk to anyone. And so I would try to talk to them as much as I could because I felt like they weren't talking to anyone. They just kind of sat back there.

Like Ilyana, Adriana contrasted this experience with what she had learned in the course. In both classroom moments, Ilyana and Adriana argued that bi/multilingualism was not centered in their placement classrooms, and English-only was the primary focus and goal. The ESL classroom continued to be a monolingual space, with the use of languages beyond English accepted in bilingual classrooms. In their first field experiences in ESL contexts, Spanish and languages beyond English were not positioned as a resource, and were instead aspects of the classroom to be erased or silenced in subordination to English. As outlined in her anecdote, in Adriana's experience, utilizing a language beyond English was also positioned as a problem, and led to the silencing of bilingual children, in addition to their physical location in the classroom. As Adriana grappled with this contradiction, her emerging theoretical lens conflicted with her collaborating teacher's way of positioning both students. When taking up a more holistic view of language and language pedagogies, from a critical and dialogic perspective, teachers should have "deep and evolving knowledge of students, their resources, and their accomplishments" (Kibler et al., 2021).

However, in Adriana's placement classroom, the students' meaning-making repertoires remained invisible. In both Ilyana and Adriana's cases, although their placements stood in contrast to their university preparation, by engaging in critical dialogue at these specific timepoints, we generated a collective space to reflect upon these scenarios together, moving from theory toward an imagined alternative practice. Through questioning and guided reflection, the first author sought to move both participants toward action, discussing the ways in which they would have done things differently and pointing to power dynamics as a potential barrier preventing them to enact change.

Power Dynamics: Language in the Lips and Minds of Children

As highlighted in the previous two examples, as participants transitioned into their placements in ESL classrooms, power dynamics also came into play. Using a dual framework centering CDE and translanguaging pedagogies, preservice teachers must have deep knowledge of power dynamics in and beyond the classroom when it comes to language and language pedagogies. They should also be deeply aware of their students' positioning within these hierarchies, particularly when it comes to policy measures. As participants moved across contextually situated time points toward the upper elementary grades and responsibilities shifted, acting upon these power dynamics became increasingly complex. As mandated English language testing became a reality, centering language in the lips and minds of children began to serve as a challenge. Pointing to the pressures involved with standardized testing, for Haley, as a monolingual identifying teacher, when her placement students used languages beyond English in the classroom, not being able to understand students in particular situations, at times, made her worry that they were not receiving what they needed from her. Anna also placed this into perspective in one of our follow-up conversations before graduation. After substituting in a bilingual classroom after her student teaching experience, for Anna, it became clear that when students are provided space to utilize all of their linguistic resources in the classroom, they are able to have more in-depth academic conversations. However, she expressed that as a monolingual identifying teacher, sometimes she felt like this was perhaps not as helpful for the teacher. In many ways, this also had to do with her perception of her own language use, and her ability to communicate with her students in languages beyond English.

> I mean, I think it's great. They're definitely able to have more elaborate academic conversations because they have the vocabulary in Spanish. So I have no problem

with it at all. Um, but then obviously, it's not helpful as a teacher. Like, I feel like I can't help them and I feel like I don't understand their thinking. Just because I cannot speak the same language.

When I asked Anna to elaborate a bit more as to how she felt during these interactions, she expressed the following:

> Just kind of like helpless. It can feel like I'm not being helpful, and I'm not doing my job. And I feel like I'm doing them a disservice because I can't be like their teacher.

In this sense, for both Haley and Anna, as the teacher, it is important to be able to understand students through a shared language due to the institutional pressures associated with being an ESL teacher. In addition, as Haley highlighted, the role of the ESL teacher within the situated context of a public-school classroom is also a role that is responsible for guiding students toward an English test—essentially, to "test out" of services. This role in many ways contradicts the take-up of a more holistic stance that positions language first and foremost "in the lips and minds of the children, and not in external standards or regulations" (García & Kleyn, 2016, 21). Over time, these conversations generated spaces across the participants to discuss the external pressures that come into play when teaching emergent bilingual/multilingual children in the ESL classroom (e.g., testing, external regulations, standards, etc.). At the end of the professional development sequence, when asked to identify something she was surprised about when it came to becoming certified in ESL, Anna pointed to testing without hesitation.

> The amount of testing that's required was a surprise. I did not realize that you have to qualify for ESL. I thought it would just kind of be like these are additional supports that you, as a teacher, should know and should use, if you happen to have students whose first language isn't English. I didn't realize that it was much more structured, like the different exit periods and all that kind of stuff, and that they have to test out. I didn't realize the structure of it.

For all four participants, the structure of ESL in practice created a variety of stressors for teachers and students that challenge bi/multilingual perspectives. Haley underlined these challenges in a conversation at the end of her student teaching.

> A challenging part has not been able to understand exactly what my students are going through. I didn't have that experience. I don't know what it's like to speak to your parents in one way, but then be expected to take the same test. You

know, everyone just took the STAAR [State of Texas Assessments of Academic Readiness] test and it's like a huge disadvantage for students learning English. You're getting tested and maybe you didn't understand the math question, but you know how to do the math. I don't know, it just gets to me. I didn't think about it before.

When it came to sustaining a more holistic approach to language and language pedagogies, testing in English served as a challenge participants faced as they moved across contexts during their field experiences. Although all four participants had knowledge of power dynamics in (and beyond) the classroom, in addition to their students' positioning in these hierarchies, navigating how to push back upon external standards and regulations felt beyond their control. As they moved further across the sequence, this also led participants to question the feasibility of enacting aspects of a dual CDE and translanguaging framework due to institutional constraints. As highlighted in Table 2.3, this setback, or roadblock, goes against a linear sequence in the uptake of new learning. As they progressed through the professional development sequence, all four participants increasingly found themselves navigating a complex system that in many ways contradicted what they had learned in their courses.

Democratic Vision: Teachers and Students *Juntos*

Within a combined framework, both CDE and the educator's take-up of a translanguaging stance also call for a focused democratic vision. This vision "prioritizes marginalized voices and participation" (Kibler et al., 2021), and sees classrooms as "democratic spaces where teachers and students *juntos* co-create knowledge, challenge traditional hierarchies, and work toward a more just society" (García et al., 2017, 28). In a language classroom, the importance of teachers and students working together to challenge traditional hierarchies cannot be understated. Ilyana embodied this approach to viewing language and language pedagogies while working with her tutoring student during the initial course.

My student was from Afghanistan and recently moved to the United States with his parents.

> His first language was Pashto but he knew a lot of Afghani-Persian or Dari vocabulary, both Dari and Pashto being the official languages of Afghanistan. I realized that I was working with an emergent trilingual which also explained

this student's rapid acquisition of the English language and his great confidence in communicating with me in English. He would then teach me a word in Pashto and would ask me the word in Urdu (my first language). He would get very excited when the words turned out to be quite similar or the exact same. He realized during our language exchange how skilled he was in the Dari language as a lot of Urdu words are borrowed from Farsi. I believe that this realization encouraged him to learn English, as it made him realize how capable he was in learning languages.

Although Ilyana was quick to position her tutoring students' diverse cultural and linguistic repertoire as a critical asset, during her field experience, she expressed concern that her student appeared to be isolated in his second-grade classroom. She was surprised to discover that his classroom teacher did not know where he was from, in addition to the languages he spoke at home with his family. Although she engaged her student by tapping into his wealth of resources for meaning-making, his dynamic linguistic repertoire was invisible in a second-grade classroom shaped by a normative monolingual approach toward language and language pedagogies.

Spaces were also generated with participants that highlighted moments of agency and resistance for both students and teacher. For Ilyana, although students in her Intern 1 placement were discouraged to speak and write in Spanish, she described instances across her experience where the students and teacher contradicted this norm. In one such circumstance, she described the use of Spanish.

> So everything was taught in English, but the other Spanish English class [bilingual] was filled up, and they didn't have any space, and they would send over some students who were learning English. So they sent them to the class, and the teacher had to translate sometimes for them. And there was one girl, no one told her to do anything, but she just took the responsibility of translating all the time and talking to the kids and supporting them. I mean, we're talking kindergarten. It was just awesome to see.

In this sense, Ilyana describes a young child who took on the role of using her linguistic resources to support her classmates as they continued to add English to their repertoire. Due to space constraints, although the use of Spanish in this moment was denoted as a special circumstance, both teacher and students worked *juntos* to ensure the new students received the content they needed, pushing back upon classroom language policy and making space for languages beyond English.

Implications

In recent years, translanguaging has crossed over as a transdisciplinary framework in the fields of Second Language Acquisition (SLA) and language teaching (see Leung & Valdés, 2019). Increasingly, it is also being employed as a theoretical framework and pedagogical tool in ESL contexts internationally. Provided the interest in translanguaging theory as a theoretical framework, or conceptual lens, there remains a need in TESOL teacher education to examine how preservice teachers are taking up, engaging with, and enacting more holistic views and practices surrounding language and language pedagogies. There also remains a need to learn more about how teacher education programs are preparing preservice teachers to develop more comprehensive and nuanced understandings of language and multilingualism.

The importance of moving over time with participants as they navigate new classroom contexts during teacher preparation is a key implication of this study. This need has also been highlighted throughout the literature on preparing teachers to teach emergent bilingual/multilingual children (Mills et al., 2020; Solano-Campos et al., 2020). Moving across situated contexts, preservice teachers can come into contact with language pedagogies that contradict new learning as they shift into new field experiences in schools and classrooms. Although eager to place new learning into practice, power dynamics can shape interactions with cooperating teachers and administrators, and place preservice teachers in a complex space where they are required to mediate what they are learning in their courses, and at times, what they are experiencing in the field. This is particularly challenging as preservice teachers grapple with the uptake of new learning in practical settings across contexts over time. As demonstrated in the previous section, taking up, engaging with, and enacting new learning is not a linear process. All four participants moved both within and across the progression detailed in Table 2.3 fluidly as they engaged with new content, grappled with contradictions in their placements, re(imagined) possibilities with the first author, and questioned their roles in enacting change. As TESOL and bi/multilingual teacher educators, it is our responsibility to ensure that preservice teachers' expanding perceptions of language and language pedagogies *sustain* as they transition from the university classroom and into the field. We must also find creative ways to support preservice teachers as they move toward action and enacting change. To do so, there must be a thread connecting theory to practice, and focused dialogic spaces where potential contradictions can be reimagined.

Critical and dialogic conversations over time encourage preservice teachers' agency in the classroom and guide them toward action. In this sense, creating these spaces over time has potential to provide the tools, support, and mentorship over time to actively—and confidently—push back upon monolingual assumptions and discriminatory languaging practices within teaching placements when necessary, and to present pedagogical alternatives. As the experiences and positionalities in this study highlight, following preservice teachers across contextually situated timepoints as they progress across field experiences can also lead to individualized mentorship over time. Moving across contexts to carve out critical dialogic spaces that facilitate decision making aligned to theory is key to this process, particularly as preservice teachers move toward induction. As a first step, by generating spaces that are critical, inclusive, and dialogic, teacher educators and preservice teachers can work in communion over time, as they *together* identify and reimagine setbacks and roadblocks, both within and outside of ourselves.

References

Barkhuizen, G. P., Benson, P., & Chik, A. (2013). *Narrative inquiry in language teaching and learning research.* Routledge. https://doi.org/10.4324/9780203124994

Barros, S., Domke, L. M., Symons, C., & Ponzio, C. (2021). Challenging monolingual ways of looking at multilingualism: Insights for curriculum development in teacher preparation. *Journal of Language, Identity & Education, 20*(4), 239-54. https://doi.org/10.1080/15348458.2020.1753196

Blanco, G. L. (2015). Qualitative research genres. In C. Marshall & G. B. Rossman (Eds.), *Designing qualitative research* (pp. 13-42). Sage.

Cenoz, J., & Gorter, D. (2011). Towards a holistic approach in the study of multilingual education. In J. Cenoz & D. Gorter (Eds.), *Multilingual education: Between language learning and translanguaging* (pp. 1-15). Cambridge. https://doi.org/10.1017/9781009024655.002

Conteh, J. (2018). Translanguaging as pedagogy—a critical review. In A. Creese & A. Blackledge (Eds.), *The routledge handbook of language and superdiversity: An interdisciplinary perspective* (pp. 473-87). Routledge. https://doi.org/10.4324/9781315696010-33

Cook, V. (1999). Going beyond the native speaker in language teaching. *TESOL Quarterly, 33*, 185-209. https://doi.org/10.2307/3587717

Cresswell, J. W. (2007). *Qualitative inquiry and research design: Choosing among five approaches* (2nd Ed.). Sage.

Cummins, J., & Early, M. (2011). *Identity texts: The collaborative creation of power in multilingual schools.* Trenthan Books.

de Jong, E. J. (2013). Preparing mainstream teachers for multilingual classrooms. *Journal of the Association of Mexican-American Educators, 7*(2), 40–9.

de Jong, E. J., & Harper, C. A. (2005). Preparing mainstream teachers for English—language learners: Is being a good teacher good enough? *Teacher Education Quarterly, 32*(2), 101–24.

Deroo, M. R., & Ponzio, C. M. (2019). Confronting ideologies: A discourse analysis of In-Service teachers' translanguaging stance through an ecological lens. *Bilingual Research Journal, 42*(2), 214–31. https://doi.org/10.1080/15235882.2019.1589604

Deroo, M. R., Ponzio, C., & De Costa, P. I. (2020). Reenvisioning second language teacher education through translanguaging praxis. In Z. Tian, L. Aghai, P. Sayer, & J. L. Schissel (Eds.), *Envisioning TESOL through a translanguaging lens: Global perspectives* (Vol. 42, pp. 214–31). Springer International Publishing. https://doi.org/10.1007/978-3-030-47031-9_6

García, O. (2009, 2011). *Bilingual education in the 21st century: A global perspective*. Wiley-Blackwell Publishers.

García, O., & Kleyn, T. (Eds.). (2016). *Translanguaging with multilingual students: Learning from classroom moments*. Routledge.

García, O., & Otheguy, R. (2020). Plurilingualism and translanguaging: Commonalities and divergences. *International Journal of Bilingual Education and Bilingualism, 23*(1), 17–35. https://doi.org/10.1080/13670050.2019.1598932

García, O., & Wei, L. (2014). *Translanguaging: Language, bilingualism and education*. Palgrave Macmillan. https://doi.org/10.1057/9781137385765_4

García, O., Johnson, S. I., Seltzer, K., & Valdés, G. (2017). *The translanguaging classroom: Leveraging student bilingualism for learning*. Caslon.

Gort, M., & Sembiante, S. F. (2015). Navigating hybridized language learning spaces through translanguaging pedagogy: Dual language preschool teachers' languaging practices in support of emergent bilingual children's performance of academic discourse. *International Multilingual Research Journal, 9*, 7–25. https://doi.org/10.1080/19313152.2014.981775

Grosjean, F. (1989). Neurolinguists beware! The bilingual is not two monolinguals in one person. *Brain and language, 36*, 323–54. https://doi.org/10.1016/0093-934X(89)90048-5

Gutiérrez, K. D., Baquedano-López, P., & Tejeda, C. (1999). Rethinking diversity: Hybridity and hybrid language practices in the third space. *Mind, Culture, and Activity, 6*, 286–303. https://doi.org/10.1080/10749039909524733

Hall, J. K. (2019). The contributions of conversation analysis and interactional linguistics to a Usage-Based understanding of language: Expanding the transdisciplinary framework. *Modern Language Journal, 103*, 80–94. https://doi.org/10.1111/modl.12535

Kibler, A. K., Valdés, G., & Walqui, A. (Eds.). (2021). *Reconceptualizing the role of critical dialogue in American classrooms: Promoting equity through dialogic education*. Routledge. https://doi.org/10.4324/9780429330667

Kleyn, T. (2016). Setting the path: Implications for teachers and teacher educators. In O. García & T. Klein (Eds.), *Translanguaging with multilingual students: Learning from classroom moments* (pp. 202–20). Routledge.

Leung, C., & Valdés, G. (2019). Translanguaging and the transdisciplinary framework for language teaching and learning in a multilingual world. *The Modern Language Journal, 103*(2), 348–70.

Lucas, T., & Grinberg, J. (2008). Responding to the linguistic reality of mainstream classrooms: Preparing all teachers to teach English language learners. In M. Cochran-Smith, S. Feiman-Nemser, & J. McIntyre (Eds.), *Handbook of research on teacher education: Enduring issues in changing contexts* (pp. 606–36). Erlbaum.

Lucas, T., & Villegas, A. M. (2013). Preparing linguistically responsive teachers: Laying the foundation in preservice teacher education. *Theory into Practice, 52*(2), 98–109. https://doi.org/10.1080/00405841.2013.770327

MacSwan, J. (2017). A multilingual perspective on translanguaging. *American Educational Research Journal, 54*(1), 167–201. https://doi.org/10.3102/0002831216683935

Marshall, C., Rossman, G. B., & Blanco, G. L. (2022). *Designing qualitative research*. Sage.

Martínez, R. A. (2018). Beyond the English learner label: Recognizing the richness of bi/multilingual students' linguistic repertoires. *The Reading Teacher, 71*(5), 515–22. https://doi.org/10.1002/trtr.1679

Menken, K., & Sánchez, M. T. (2019). Translanguaging in English-only schools: From pedagogy to stance in the disruption of monolingual policies and practices. *TESOL Quarterly, 53*(3), 741–67. https://doi.org/10.1002/tesq.513

Miles, M. B., Huberman, A. M., & Saldaña, J. (2020). *Qualitative data analysis: A methods sourcebook* (4th Ed.). Sage.

Mills, T., Villegas, A. M., & Cochran-Smith, M. (2020). Research on preparing preservice mainstream teachers for linguistically diverse classrooms. *Teacher Education Quarterly, 47*(4), 33–55.

Ortega, L. (2013). SLA for the 21st century: Disciplinary progress, transdisciplinary relevance, and the bi/multilingual turn. *Language Learning, 63*, 1–24. https://doi.org/10.1111/j.1467-9922.2012.00735.x

Ortega, L. (2019). SLA and the study of equitable multilingualism. *The Modern Language Journal, 103*, 23–38. https://doi.org/10.1111/modl.12525

Otheguy, R., García, O., & Reid, W. (2015). Clarifying translanguaging and deconstructing named languages: A perspective from linguistics. *Applied Linguistics Review, 6*(3), 281–307. https://doi.org/10.1515/applirev-2015-0014

Otheguy, R., García, O., & Reid, W. (2019). A translanguaging view of the linguistic system of bilinguals. *Applied Linguistics Review, 10*(4), 625–51. https://doi.org/10.1515/applirev-2018-0020

Palmer, D., & Martínez, R. A. (2013). Teacher agency in bilingual spaces: A fresh look at preparing teachers to educator latina/o bilingual children. *Review of Research in Education, 37*(1), 269–97. https://doi.org/10.3102/0091732X12463556

Ponzio, C. (2020). (Re)Imagining a translingual self: Shifting one monolingual teacher candidate's language lens. *Linguistics and Education, 60*, 1–11. https://doi.org/10.1016/j.linged.2020.100866

Ruiz, R. (1984). Orientations in language planning. *NABE Journal, 8*(2), 15–34. https://doi.org/10.1080/08855072.1984.10668464

Seltzer, K. (2019). Reconceptualizing "Home" and "School" language: Taking a critical translingual approach in the English classroom. *TESOL Quarterly, 53*(4), 986–1007. https://doi.org/10.1002/tesq.530

Solano-Campos, A., Hopkins, M., & Quaynor, L. (2020). Linguistically responsive teaching in preservice teacher education: A review of the literature through the lens of cultural-historical activity theory. *Journal of Teacher Education, 7*(2), 203–17.

Tian, Z., Aghai, P., Sayer, P., & Shissel, J. L. (Eds.). (2020). *Reenvisioning TESOL through translanguaging lens: Global perspectives* (pp. 111–34). Springer.

Wong-Fillmore, L., & Snow, C. E. (2018). What teachers need to know about language. In C. T Adger, C. E. Snow, & D. Charistian (Eds.), *What teachers need to know about language* (pp. 8–35). Multilingual Matters. https://doi.org/10.21832/9781788920193-003

3

Cultivating Pre-Service Language Teachers' Critical Multilingual Language Awareness: A Macau Perspective

Rui Eric Yuan, Kailun Wang, and Jiahui Li

Introduction

The spread of English across the globe, while being celebrated as a crucial part of the process of globalization accompanied by talent mobility, technology advancement, and economic gains, has its dark side owing to the colonial history of English and its related issues such as social discrimination and linguistics bias. With such complexities in mind, many scholars (Dwomoh et al., 2023; Hawkins & Norton, 2009; Karam, 2021; Kibler et al., 2021) in second language teacher education (SLTE) have been advocating the need to embrace a critical and dialogic stance in preparing and developing future language teachers. In particular, increased attention has been paid to language teachers' language awareness (Lourenço et al., 2018; Otwinowska, 2017), which entails their knowledge and ability "to both examine their own biases and to unpack linguistic parochialism and prejudice within policy, curriculum, and student interaction" (Gage, 2020, p. 227). García (2017) proposed "Critical Multilingual Language Awareness" (CMLA) as a more specific term to denote teachers' understanding of language as socially created and changeable, and thus entangled with linguistic hierarchies and power struggles experienced by individuals (especially linguistic minority students). Equipped with CMLA, language teachers are encouraged to adopt a socially just perspective of language teaching and learning to give voice to all students and educate them equitably (Deroo & Ponzio, 2023).

However, cultivating language teachers' CMLA is often fraught with challenges especially at the pre-service stage of SLTE, where the traditional mode of knowledge transmission prevails and student teachers may lack linguistic competence and relevant contextual knowledge (Dwomoh et al., 2023; Lourenço et al., 2018). Particularly in many English-as-a-foreign-language (EFL) contexts, student teachers are often unaware of the social, cultural, and political nature of language with its embedded ideologies, values, and practices owing to their past language-learning experiences dominated by mechanical drills and memorization. Meanwhile, traditional curricula tend to treat student teachers as followers of curricula and consumers of knowledge, offering limited opportunities for dialogic reasoning and critical thinking (Kibler et al., 2021). Resultatively, they are bound by a technical view of language and a monolingual mindset with little regard for the linguistic diversity and complexities embedded in the multilingual and multicultural reality (Iversen, 2022).

The present study was conducted against such a backdrop to investigate how a group of student teachers fostered their CMLA in a pre-service language teacher education course informed by the principles of critical dialogic education (CDE) at a Macau university. CDE, which emphasizes the role of dialogue as a means of promoting critical thinking, creativity, and social change (Karam, 2021; Kibler et al., 2021), is pivotal to individuals' personal growth and well-being as they try to understand complex social issues and navigate power dynamics in their daily lives. In the course taught by the first author, the student teachers were exposed to a range of critical topics (e.g., gender, race, and native-speakerism) relating to the English language and its use in schools and the wide society. Also, different tasks (e.g., online forum discussion, group presentations, and reflective writing) were organized to facilitate the student teachers' collaborative meaning-making and negotiation in a critical and dialogic manner.

As opposed to previous studies which focused on the language awareness of in-service teachers (e.g., Dwomoh et al., 2023) or pre-service teachers at a more mature stage in their situated programs (e.g., Dubiner, 2018; Godley et al., 2015), the course reported in the study was provided for student teachers who just entered the university as freshmen after high school graduation. Such an arrangement was intentionally made to confront them with the dynamic, multi-layered, power-laden, and potentially contested nature of English, challenge and transform their existing language ideologies, and cultivate their CMLA for their continuous professional learning in the four-year program. By tracking and analyzing the student teachers' experiences in the course and the possible development of their CMLA, it is hoped that the study can generate insights for current SLTE regarding how to instill CMLA in language teachers to support their development of equitable and inclusive pedagogy in language classrooms.

Literature Review

Understanding CMLA

Teacher language awareness (TLA), generally perceived as "a teacher's ability to use, analyze, and teach language" (Lindahl, 2019, p. 85), is a widely explored concept with rich connotations owing to over three decades' research in applied linguistics. The word "awareness" inherently denotes a cognitive orientation, referring to teachers' explicit knowledge about language and their ability to recognize and understand specific processes, structures, and patterns in a linguistic system for instructional purposes (Thornbury, 1997; Wright & Bolitho, 1993). In language classrooms, teachers are often encouraged to play the role of a language analyst (Svalberg, 2007)—not only should they engage in an ongoing investigation of language as a dynamic phenomenon, but they also need to involve learners in analysis, exploration, and discovery of the meaning and use of language (Borg, 1994; Otwinowska, 2017).

TLA also entails a critical dimension implicated in the intertwined relationship between language, society, and power (Fairclough, 1990). Transcending the cognitive, instrumental orientation of language awareness as a "linguistic radar" (Wright, 2002), this view places a premium on teachers' critical understanding of the complex ideologies and systems that dictate what languages are privileged or oppressed in classrooms and society. Consequently, as Godley et al. (2015, p. 43) claimed, teachers should "teach students to question existing language ideologies and become aware of the ways in which language upholds systems of privilege and discrimination." More recently, García (2017) developed the framework of CMLA, dedicated to the promotion of social and language activism in the multilingual and multicultural world. She differentiated CMLA from a traditional notion of language awareness by asserting that CMLA entails a humanized, dynamic, and socio-constructed view of bilingualism and plurilingualism. As she elaborated below:

> Teachers are expected to have not only knowledge of the speakers of the languages and their bilingualism (their knowledge of, and about, their languages and practices), but also of three additional factors: (1) the plurilingualism in their mindset, (2) the histories of the speakers and their struggles, and (3) the social construction of the language of school in order to keep privilege in the hands of few.
>
> (García, 2017, p. 269–70)

The aspects mentioned above thus lie at the core of CMLA, which confronts monoglossic and raciolinguistic ideologies prevalent in language education. Meanwhile, García (2017) also emphasized that the notion of CMLA was not made merely for minoritized populations but for *all*. Therefore, by fostering CMLA, language teachers can build up a linguistically responsive pedagogy, encompassing their sociolinguistic consciousness, value for linguistic diversity, and an inclination to advocate for English language learners, with a view to promoting equitable learning and social justice in language classrooms (Dwomoh et al., 2023; Lucas et al., 2014).

Following the socio-cultural turn and emergence of critical pedagogy in SLTE, cultivating student teachers' CMLA has become a consensus among language teacher educators. Dubiner (2018), for instance, tracked a group of student teachers' reflective learning facilitated by vocabulary notebooks. The research findings spoke to the power of reflections in fostering the participants' meta-cognitive awareness about vocabulary acquisition and deepening their self-understanding as agentive, autonomous language learners. In Deroo and Ponzio's (2023) study, the student teachers were invited to create their own visual representations that showed the relationship between language, identity, and power, and then engage in journal writing to explain the images based on course readings. Such a multimodal reflective task, connecting their personal experiences and the theoretical input from the course, allowed the student teachers to critically examine and interrogate implicit language ideologies across social settings and develop their CMLA. Student teachers' pedagogical exploration based on their emergent CMLA was further probed in Ponzio and Deroo (2023), where they were guided to engage with the notion of translanguaging through a cycle of multimodal learning tasks (e.g., creating visual metaphors and writing reflective responses). Salient in the findings was the student teachers' enhanced awareness of the potential of translanguaging enacted through the use of multilingual, multimodal, and multisensory resources brought by language learners (Yuan & Yang, 2023). Thus, the participants questioned the monoglossic, restrictive language norm and emphasized the need to adopt translanguaging in their future classroom teaching.

Despite these positive, promising findings, there is research evidence pointing to the challenges faced by language teachers in their CMLA development. For instance, as reported by Lourenço et al. (2018), school teachers might feel unprepared to incorporate a critical perspective in their teaching, due to their past language-learning experiences dominated by a monolingual approach as well as fear of risk-taking in pedagogical innovations. For pre-service teachers reported in Godley et al.'s (2015) study, they tended to avoid acknowledging their own white privilege and showed a lack of willingness and skills in teaching about power structures and struggles associated with language learning and use. Such issues, on the one hand, suggest the sensitivity and vulnerability that CMLA can induce for language teachers as they engage in self-examination and self-interrogation about their linguistic ideologies and practices; on the other hand, they highlight the need for SLTE programs to create positive learning environments that are "personally comfortable, racially and ethnically inclusive, and intellectually stimulating" (Gay, 2006, p. 343). As such, language teachers at all levels can feel secure and supported in fostering and refining their CMLA to inform their classroom practice.

Linking CMLA with CDE

CDE encourages "equity-focused classroom pedagogies that are dialogic, critical, and inclusive" (Kibler et al., 2021, p. 1). One of the important elements of CDE is dialogic teaching and learning, which views education as a process of collaborative meaning construction and negotiation between teachers and students in the classroom community (Haneda, 2017; Kibler et al., 2021; Suh & Michener, 2019). Building on such premises, Kibler et al. (2021) further highlighted two important components of CDE pedagogies, that is, "a critical dialogic perspective that is firmly grounded in classroom talk, and a proactive vision that seeks to give voice to students and disrupt inequitable power dynamics inside and beyond classrooms" (p. 5).

Our literature review shows many empirical attempts made to examine how CDE could be enacted in classroom settings. In their edited book, Kibler et al. (2021) invited researchers in the United States to demonstrate instructional efforts with a specific CDE design. The six studies, conducted with participants in a wide range of educational settings (e.g., immigrants and African-American students), generally attested to the pivotal role of CDE in promoting equity and inclusion in education. Karam (2021) focused on the design and implementation of a virtue-based curriculum in an ESOL classroom and identified that putting sociopolitical issues (e.g., inequity and justice) at the center of instruction and facilitating active participation in authentic classroom talk can enhance students' academic and social adjustment.

The empirical evidence, albeit limited, has revealed the power of CDE principles in creating a dialogic space for students to critically examine sociopolitical issues and develop their critical awareness (Karam, 2021; Kibler et al., 2021). However, research on CDE is still limited in the field of SLTE. In the present study, we intentionally draw a link between CDE and CMLA by proposing that CDE can serve as a useful pedagogical framework to help pre-service language teachers foster and strengthen their CMLA. Firstly, the relationship between CDE and CMLA can be seen in their shared emphasis on the heterogeneous nature of an increased population of language learners from various ethnic, linguistic, and social backgrounds; it is thus crucial to create dialogic spaces to promote students' active participation and language learning on an equal and collaborative basis. Secondly, the issue of power negotiation and struggle should be made explicit for language learners and teachers, through which they can foster their critical awareness about language use and become active participants in the negotiation of power dynamics in multilingual contexts. Thirdly, both theories pay heightened attention to students from linguistic minority groups by legitimizing a variety of semiotic resources and strategies (e.g., via translanguaging) in classroom instruction. Table 3.1 presents a summary of the shared tenets between CDE and CMLA.

Based on the above literature review, particularly the interrelations of CDE and CMLA, this study examines a group of pre-service language teachers' experiences in a teacher education course informed by CDE. Specifically, the study zooms in on the complex processes and conditions that facilitate or impede pre-service language teachers' CMLA development. Based on data from post-course interviews and relevant documents (e.g., forum posts and reflective

Table 3.1 Shared tenets of CDE and CMLA

Critical dialogic education (Kibler, Valdés, & Walqui, 2021)	Critical multilingual language awareness (García, 2017)
• Collaborative meaning construction between teachers and students from diverse linguistic and socio-cultural backgrounds	• Acknowledging the existence of bilingualism and possessing a plurilingualism mindset
• Putting social justice, power dynamics, and equity issues at the center of instruction to foster a critical stance	• Understanding the sociopolitical dimension of the language in relation to its histories and ideologies
• Giving voice to students, especially those socially disadvantaged minorities	• Accepting translanguaging as a legitimate language practice and a tool for meaning construction

essays), the study answers one research question: *To what extent and how did the pre-service language teachers develop their CMLA in the course in a Macau university?*

The Course with a CDE Focus

Informed by the principles of CDE (Karam, 2021; Kibler et al., 2021), the course, entitled "Introduction to Applied English Studies" and offered for a cohort of forty year-one university students, started with the history of English and its evolution, and then discussed the function and use of English for communicative purposes in diverse social settings. The socio-political dimension of English was also probed in relation to a range of critical factors such as gender, race, and social class. The course further delved into the reality and theory of English as a lingua franca (ELF), guiding students to understand and explore how English is learned and taught through intercultural communication. Relatedly, topics such as native-speakerism, translanguaging, and English-medium instruction were introduced to students to expand their knowledge about the presence and impact of English in daily life and disciplinary learning. Table 3.2 summarizes the key topics covered in the course.

Such diversified topics relating to the sociopolitical side of language could give voice to students in reflecting on inequitable power dynamics in the multilingual world (Karam, 2021). Moreover, throughout the eighteen-week course, the student teachers took part in a range of learning and assessment activities guided by the course instructor, including in-class participation, online forum learning, group presentation, and individual reflective essay.

Apart from the knowledge input about different topics delivered through lecturing facilitated by joint discussion and multimode resources, blended

Table 3.2 Main topics of the course

1.	The nature and history of English
2.	English use through the lens of pragmatics
3.	English language and gender
4.	English language and race
5.	English language and social class
6.	English as a lingua franca and intercultural communication
7.	English medium instruction
8.	Translanguaging in daily communication and language teaching

learning emerged as a highlight of the course, where the student teachers engaged in individual and collaborative writing on the Forum, followed by collective discussion. Together, those collaborative learning tasks were designed specifically in a dialogic way to provide student teachers with opportunities to challenge the "normality" of language-related social issues in a collaborative manner (Suh & Michener, 2019). Three forum tasks were organized based on different topics as shown in Table 3.3.

While the forum tasks allowed the student teachers to draw meaningful connections between the course content and their individual experiences and

Table 3.3 Forum discussion tasks

Individual forum task 1—What is English?
In this task, you are invited to share your reflection about the following three questions: 1. What did English mean to you before taking the course? 2. Did your understanding of English change through the past sessions in the course? If so, what changes have you experienced? How do you evaluate such changes? 3. What else do you still want to know about English? Please write a reflection between 300–500 words and post it on the forum. You are also encouraged to read and comment on others' reflections. Each of you needs to comment on at least three pieces of reflections posted by your classmates.
Individual forum task 2—Challenges and coping strategies in EMI learning
Write a short reflection to share the challenges you have encountered in your EMI learning and how you tried to cope with the challenges. Try to be analytical by discussing your thoughts, feelings, and self-evaluation regarding your EMI experiences.
Collaborative forum task 3—Promoting intercultural communication and learning in your university
In Session 8, you have read about international and Chinese students' perceptions and experiences about intercultural collaborative learning in a mainland university. In this task, you are going to reflect on and share your own views and stories about intercultural learning. Based on your discussion and personal experience in your current university and your previous schools, you need to work in groups (four to five students per group) and write a letter to our university management to share your views and give concrete suggestions on how to promote intercultural learning in your university. This is a collaborative task and each group thus needs to write one letter of around 400 words. The letter should be submitted by the group leader (or a group member) on the forum.

Table 3.4 Suggested topics for the final reflection essay

Topic 1: Is English a world language to you? Share your analysis and reflections.
Topic 2: What kind of English language teachers do you want to become and why?
Topic 3: What constitutes an effective English language curriculum in Macau local schools and why?

perspectives, they were also required to work in a group (four or five students per group) and give a formal academic presentation about a research paper assigned by the course instructor at the end of the course. The selected papers (e.g., Chen, 2023; López-Gopar, 2014) published in international journals such as *ELT Journal* and *RELC Journal* are directly concerned with the diverse issues of English language use and learning in the multilingual and multicultural world. In the group presentation, not only did they need to describe the study in detail regarding its research background and design, key findings, as well as implications, but they also needed to share their personal experience and reflections based on the research findings collaboratively. In this way, a classroom community was built for the student teachers in an "open exchange of ideas, jointly undertaken inquiry, and engagement with multiple voices and perspectives" (Haneda, 2017, p. 1).

The final assessment task of the course is an individual reflection essay (around 1200 words including references), in which the student teachers needed to discuss one or a few key issues based on the course content in an analytical and reflective manner. Table 3.4 shows the suggested topics provided for their reflective writing. The task aims to engage student teachers in critical and in-depth probing of English language use, learning, and teaching by summarizing, synthesizing, and interpreting what they have experienced and learned in the course.

Overall, covering a wide range of topics and featuring a collaborative and process-oriented design, the course engages student teachers dialogically and collaboratively with English not only in terms of its dynamic nature, rich history, and communicative function but also its socio-political dimension and embodied complex linguistic ideologies and values.

The Participants

Upon the completion of the course with the final grades released, research invitations were sent to all the course participants via email. Eight of them, named from S1 to S8, responded and joined the study on a voluntary basis.

The participants come from different geographic and educational backgrounds. Seven of them are Chinese, with one (S7) from the Philippines. All the student teachers spoke two or three languages (Chinese, English, and Filipino). Regarding their educational backgrounds, two student teachers (S5 and S6) studied in the Chinese mainland, four (S1, S2, S3, and S8) in Macau, one (S7) in the Philippines, and one (S4) in Singapore, before entering the university. Such a diversified sample might help generate a holistic understanding of the student teachers' course engagement and CMLA development (if any) to answer the proposed question.

Data Collection and Analysis

The data of the study consist of semi-structured interviews, students' online forum discussion posts, and their final reflection essays. Considering the role of the first author as the course instructor, individual interviews were conducted by the second and third author with each participant to explore their gains, challenges, and reflections in relation to the course content and activities with a particular eye on their understanding of English and its learning and teaching. Specifically, the participants were asked about their attitudes toward English before and after the course, their previous and current English learning experiences, and their changing opinions toward language teaching (if any). Each interview lasted around one hour and was conducted in Chinese except for one in English with the Philippine student S7. Apart from the interviews, the participants were invited to share the posts they made on the three forum discussion tasks and their final reflection essays (all in English). Such artifacts, which were generated through the students' ongoing course participation in relation to different topics about language use, can provide another perspective on the research question.

The interviews were transcribed and analyzed through a thematic approach (Creswell, 2014). By carefully reviewing the transcripts for multiple rounds, a range of initial codes was identified in light of the research question. Informed by the conceptual framework of CMLA, these codes were juxtaposed, merged, and refined, which gave rise to the major categories that reflected the participants' understanding of English and its function and nature. A cross-case comparison was then conducted, through which the categories from each case were compared and contrasted to form a holistic picture of the participants' cultivation of CMLA in the course. During the process of data analysis, the findings that emerged from the interview data were checked and validated with reference to the forum posts and reflection essays. In the end, three major themes arose from the dataset, that is, reconsidering English as a subject with rich history and culture, fostering a multilingual mindset with enhanced pedagogical thinking, and approaching English and its use with a critical view. The trustworthiness of the study was ensured through data triangulation and the first two authors' constant discussion and reflection in the data analysis process.

Researcher Positionality

The first author served as the teacher educator who designed and taught the course with a focus on student teachers' CMLA development. To reduce potential stress on the participants and minimize potential conflicts of interest, the interviews were conducted by the second and third authors. The interviews were carried out after the course ended with the final grades released. The participants were informed that their participation was voluntary and their views would be instrumental in the course revision and improvement. During the interviews, the second and third authors kept an open and inquiring position to induce genuine and reflective sharing by the participants. To increase the trustworthiness of the study, the authors employed multiple sources of data to ensure data triangulation and engaged in multiple rounds of discussions during data analysis until a consensus was reached.

Findings

Reconsidering English as a Subject with a Rich History and Culture

The data revealed that through the course informed by the principles of CDE, the participants fostered a clearer and more systematic understanding of the nature and use of English as a subject. Specifically, they reported that the course materials and teaching activities scaffolded their exploration of various facets of English from historical, cultural, and functional perspectives. For example, before entering university, S1 focused more on the practical side of English which could help him develop a career.

> Although I have chosen English education as my major, I didn't know much about English before. At that time, I thought English was about basic reading or speaking skills. And English was merely a tool for me to make a living.
>
> (Interview, S1)

However, as the course proceeded, S1 seemed to grasp more about the "deep side of English" (Interview, S1), as he wrote in the forum:

> I realized that English is not only a language but also a culture. There is a long history of English and English has experienced a very long evolution. Now what we are learning is an inheritance of culture. As we are going to become English teachers, I think we must know the story behind English.
>
> (Forum, S1)

The above quote demonstrates S1's new awareness of the multiple dimensions of English, which could be attributed to the course content on the nature, history, and evolution of English and refined CDE materials targeting global multilingual issues in students' daily lives (Kibler et al., 2021, p. 12). As a result, he realized "the necessity of knowing these things, just like when we study Chinese and the sociocultural aspects behind" (Interview, S1).

In addition, several in-class tasks were designed to support the participants' development of metalinguistic awareness and reflection on their own language-learning experience. For example, conducting the discourse analysis guided by the course instructor helped S2 detect the pragmatic side of language and explore how English functions in diverse professional and socio-cultural settings. As she recounted in the interview:

> Our analysis of a debate in a video about the trade war between China and the United States brought me a lot of ideas in class. In fact, a debate between two public figures is influenced by their positions and personalities. Someone's original ideas might be misunderstood or manipulated by another party in the debate. I took part in some English debates when I was in middle school, but I didn't realize that English has such a magical power of communication.
>
> (Interview, S2)

The excerpt indicated that through watching and analyzing a debate, S2 realized how English was used to index the speaker's stance and achieve specific communicative purposes. She added that "In the future, I think I can better use English to express something or persuade others" (Interview, S2). Similarly, S3 also introduced how he learned more about the culture and thinking behind English through the course:

> I remember one example of how a Chinese student communicated and cooperated with international students in teamwork. I found there were various problems caused by their different cultures and different ways of thinking. But

there were also good things. For example, they could learn from each other and offer new ideas from different perspectives.

(Interview, S3)

S3 commented that as a social product, English reflects different thinking modes across contexts and cultures. Later, he continued to reflect that "I realized that to be an English teacher, we need to cultivate students' critical thinking and their awareness of intercultural issues" (Final essay, S3). Thus, the student teachers' critical analysis of English and their cultivation of CMLA exerted positive impacts on their pedagogical thinking.

However, multilingualism as the core content of the course presented the participants with some difficulties because "topics relating to accent and race are totally new" for most of them (Interview, S1, S3, and S4). Initially, the participants encountered anxiety and frustration in classroom activities and forum writing. S4, for instance, candidly confessed that she "felt at a loss in reflecting on what English is during the forum discussion" because she "had never thought about such a question" (Interview, S4).

Fostering a Multilingual Mindset with Enhanced Pedagogical Thinking

The findings also indicated that the participants developed a mindset of multilingualism and plurilingualism, a critical component of CMLA as emphasized by García (2017). They came to acknowledge the important fact that English is not possessed by a single country but is shared by a large number of speakers in different parts of the world. More importantly, all languages are of value and should be respected and celebrated. S5 shared his reflection based on his group presentation task:

> We read and presented about a research project conducted in Mexico, where there are hundreds of indigenous languages gradually disappearing and being replaced by English. Many local people preferred to use English and discriminated against those who spoke minority indigenous languages. I think the project made us see each language equally. That is, there is no rule that English should be superior to my mother tongue.
>
> (Interview, S5)

While the project focused on the colonized and oppressed history of indigenous languages in Mexico, such a learning experience facilitated S5's recognition of the value of multilingualism and the legitimacy of various linguistic practices in their situated context. As he believed, "When we teach English, we must assume the responsibility to encourage our kids to be able to speak different languages confidently in their daily life" (Interview, S5). In a similar vein, S6 also discussed his awareness transition from seeing English as possessed by others to "I can own it."

> In the beginning, I didn't consider English an international thing. I just thought it was the language of the British and Americans. I didn't think I can own it. Now, I know that English belongs to its speakers. For example, the Chinese accent is not a bad thing at all. Rather, it represents a variety of English and a special Chinese flavor. It also represents my background.
>
> (Interview, S6)

Instead of regarding English as owned by British or American people, S6 reclaimed confidence in his accent while dismissing the insecure feeling of linguistic inferiority. Besides reinforcing the students' multilingual awareness, the course also impelled them to take a further step as pre-service language teachers. As S7 explained, she was empowered to "spread the idea" of multilingualism and encourage her future students to fully utilize their entire language repertoire.

> The course empowered me, helping me realize that I don't have to speak like a British or American. As long as I'm pronouncing English properly, with the right pronunciation, that's fine already. And the course made me see that I want to teach these things in the future, maybe not directly, but I would definitely spread the idea among my students.
>
> (Interview, S7)

Another aspect closely related to multilingualism is the concept of translanguaging, which was carefully explained with concrete examples and explicitly modeled by the instructor in the course. One of the participants, S5, then connected translanguaging with his own approaches to note-taking. He shared that "After class, I would reorganize my notes by using other languages I am more familiar with and drawing pictures on them" (Interview, S5). This showcased an ideal way for the students to appropriate and apply multilingual practices to their own studies and daily lives. S8 also drew on his own teaching experience to illustrate the usefulness of translanguaging:

> Translanguaging can be applied to our life or teaching. For example, this semester I helped my little brother improve his English. When explaining the

meaning of English words, I would read them in English first, and then explain with the help of Chinese and some pictures. I think this is very useful.

(Interview, S8)

The reflections of other students proved more pedagogical relevance. S6, for instance, acknowledged the necessity of nurturing the translanguaging capacities of students in his future language teaching. Drawing on his group presentation task, he elaborated,

The article presented by our group is about how an instructor employed translanguaging during instruction at a Turkish university. After our discussion and presentation, I believe that I can use similar approaches to translanguaging to make students better understand the content. We can make full use of the advantage that both students and professors are bilinguals who can speak two languages.

(Interview, S6)

The excerpt above also elucidated how group projects, as one of the CDE tasks, could not only help the participants develop their CMLA, but also stimulate their pedagogical thinking as prospective language teachers. As S6 recalled, "Since three of my group mates had Filipino backgrounds, there were a lot of intercultural exchanges during group projects" (Interview, S6). He stated that "my peers shared how having an accent might be seen as illiteracy in former colonies" and how this motivated him "to promote social change through education in future teaching" (Final essay, S6). Through participating in dialogic conversations with peers and group mates, the student teachers actively shared intercultural experiences and reflected on the potential of translanguaging as a teaching approach in their future language classrooms.

However, despite the reported benefits from their collaborative engagements, some student teachers also implied hardships during group work. Several participants mentioned that there were "free riders" who lacked engagement in group discussions and presentation preparation (Interview, S1, S3, S5, and S7). They showed frustration and disappointment toward those inactive group mates because it not only "led to unfair task allocation and increased the workload of other group members" (Interview, S5) but also negatively influenced the quality of their group projects.

Approaching English and Its Use with a Critical View

Another important aspect of their CMLA was a critical stance the participants embraced as they learned to unpack the power entanglements associated with

English in the socio-political reality, where certain linguistic practices were legitimized or marginalized. For instance, several student teachers pointed out gendered language use during forum discussions. In the below quote, S7 presented the differences between masculine and feminine linguistic features and argued that such socially constructed stereotypes should be eradicated:

> For example, women need to talk softly and men need to be masculine. These stereotypes just prevent people shine and obstruct their progress to become what they want to be. As a teacher, I think I have the responsibility to fight such a stereotype.
> (Forum, S7)

Similar to S7, S8 also shared his reflections on the issue of gendered language features as they were guided to analyze and discuss potential gender issues embedded in textbook materials provided by the course instructor:

> Gender stereotyping and male firstness are wrong gender representations in some local textbooks, which need to be amended to promote equitable gender values.
> (Final essay, S8)

Additionally, the student teachers developed a critical understanding of the relationship between languages and ideological issues as part of their CMLA. For example, S6 reported his enhanced understanding of language and identity through an in-class reading task. In the interview, he recalled the story of a Hispanic boy "who didn't want to speak Spanish and lost his cultural identity" (Interview, S6) introduced in the course. From the story, S6 came to see that the assimilation into the dominant language (i.e., English) community could exert a detrimental effect on the preservation of cultural heritage and identity of minority groups. Recognizing that language learning is also a process of identity building, he was determined to encourage his future students to "develop the habit of being skeptical and challenging what they hear to combat the colonial mentality and the myth of idealized native-speakerism" (Final essay, S6).

Relatedly, S2 wrote her reflection on "white English" in the forum discussion task:

> I once thought that English was just a language, yet it had a hidden dark background such as the "white" English. Why is it called "white" English? Why does accent matter to people? Why do people discriminate against non-native speakers? Why? The truth is we've been brainwashed our whole life. But the truth is: it's not about who is better at English or who has the best accent. It's about who delivered it the best, it's about respecting the culture, and it's about using it in the right way.
> (Forum, S2)

The racial label of "white English", according to S2, can reinforce hegemonic beliefs about language and obscure the existence and legitimacy of multilingualism. Therefore, she criticized the linguistic hierarchy of "while English" and proposed a more inclusive view of English use. Recognizing that non-native teachers should be empowered, she believed that an important mission of language teachers is to "promote diversity within schools and create a positive learning environment where everyone feels accepted and free to express their own ideas" (Final essay, S2).

To sum up, the above findings revealed the participants' development of CMLA as they learned to analyze how dominant ideologies could dictate the "privileged" or "marginalized" linguistic practices. However, since the course was delivered in English as the medium of instruction (EMI), some students found it difficult to adapt to such a teaching mode especially at the beginning of the course. S1 recalled that "I was not quite used to this kind of teaching" because "back in high school, our English course mainly focused on reciting grammatical knowledge, doing exercise, and preparing for examinations" (Interview, S1). Meanwhile, some participants reported difficulties in comprehending the course content and participating in classroom activities through English, especially when dealing with abstract topics touching upon language ideologies and power relations. As S4 shared, "These definitions and terminologies are very different from that of everyday language, and we need extra time and efforts to process and understand" (Interview, S4). These linguistic challenges thus indicated that the student teachers might need further language support in the course.

Discussion and Implications

The study shows positive evidence about the student teachers' development of CMLA through their engagement and reflection in a course informed by CDE. As argued by García (2017), teachers equipped with CMLA need to 1) understand language as the subject matter, 2) have an awareness of plurilingualism and the social construction of language, and 3) perceive ideological dimensions in language and its teaching. The three themes reported in our research findings align well with such a conceptualization of CMLA, illustrating the participants' expanded understanding of English, particularly with a critical dimension. Departing from their previous technical view of English as a subject matter (focusing on linguistic skills) and tool for communication, the student teachers came to appreciate the breath (e.g., its dynamic history and culture) and depth (e.g., its entanglement with complex power-related issues including gender and race) of English and its application.

More crucially, the participants' enhanced awareness prompted their critical reflections on their own language practices as language learners and teachers (Dubiner, 2018; Svalberg, 2007), thus casting light on their future learning and work in language education. For instance, their engagement with the issue of "native-speakerism" exerted a liberating effect on the participants as they transformed their self-perception from inadequate non-native English speakers to confident owners and users of English, and they planned to convey such an important message to their students in the future. Another example relates to the notion of translanguaging, which can serve as an effective and equitable approach to language teaching. Recognizing the potential of their multilingual backgrounds and practices as crucial assets in supporting meaning-making and academic learning (Yuan & Yang, 2023), the participants (e.g., S6 and S8) showed the willingness and tendency to integrate translanguaging into classroom practice to facilitate their students' language learning. This finding is similar to Ponzio and Deroo's (2023) study, suggesting that an explicit focus on translanguaging can be pedagogically beneficial for pre-service teachers in SLTE programs.

The student teachers' CMLA development was strongly mediated by the CDE elements embedded in the course arrangement, which not only provided relevant input covering various topics (see Table 3.1) and in diverse forms (e.g., lecturing, reading materials, and videos), but also created a meaningful dialogic space for student teachers' individual and collaborative reflections. Echoing the findings of Athanases et al. (2018) and Suh & Michener (2019), the study revealed that reflective tasks such as forum discussion and reflective writing offered opportunities for students' dialogic engagement, expanded pre-service teachers' perspectives of linguistic diversity and helped them foster a multilingual mindset. The findings also demonstrate the growth of student teachers' critical stances in both explicit and implicit manners (Kibler et al., 2021; Liu, 2017). On the one hand, ideological issues of linguistic bias, native-speakerism, and social justice were incorporated as important content topics for student teachers. On the other hand, an implicit critical awareness was instilled into the participants' minds by creating student-centered learning tasks and giving voice to student teachers of diversified linguistic and ethnic backgrounds. As a result, they could learn to foster ownership of multilingualism and translanguaging that is traditionally silenced in language classrooms.

Collaboration, as an important aspect of dialogic education, is also a pivotal element in cultivating student teachers' CMLA development. Drawing on their individual backgrounds and past experiences, student teachers can contribute their personal voices and literacy practices to the discussion of critical issues in the English language and learning and unpack the complex ideologies and power structures involved. Such a process illustrates the power of multivocality in CDE, where multiple voices were encouraged in group work and individual experiences were embraced as valuable assets for CMLA improvement. This might explain why the participants did not report the feelings of anxiety and vulnerability experienced by the research participants in Godley et al.'s (2015) study when engaging with similar issues, because the collaborative design generated a sense of security and support during the process of self-reflection and self-interrogation. Another reason might be attributed to the use of the online forum, which afforded time and space to help mitigate unease and even confrontation that might arise from the face-to-face discussion. Therefore, language teacher educators may need to consider how to diversify the forms of reflective practice in SLTE courses to help student teachers navigate potentially negative emotions and maximize their reflective learning.

However, the student teachers also encountered some obstacles in the course, which to some extent impeded their professional learning and CMLA development. One challenge arose from the participants' lack of familiarity with the learning content and task arrangement in the course. Having been immersed in a traditional mode of language learning dominated by memorization and mechanical drills, the participants might experience unease when being introduced to content about the pragmatic and critical dimensions of English or being asked to participate in forum writing and group tasks. Given that such input and activities are of great value to foster CMLA as reported by the participants, it is pivotal for language teacher educators to provide the necessary guidance, cognitively and affectively, to smooth their transition into the course and sustain their motivation. For instance, open sharing, explanation, and modeling can be helpful to help student teachers see the relevance and value of the course content in relation to their future work (Yuan et al., 2022), and specific instruction can also be given for student teachers when they form groups and engage in collaborative tasks.

Another prominent issue relates to the EMI mode, which turned out to be challenging for some participants who just entered the university. For instance, some participants reported difficulties in comprehending the course content and participating in classroom activities through English, especially when dealing with abstract topics pertaining to language ideologies and power relations. To address such a challenge, teacher educators may need to incorporate a language focus into classroom teaching, where they not only deliver content knowledge but also teach specific language to help student teachers understand and apply newly acquired knowledge in meaningful tasks. From the course instructor's perspective, while he intentionally provided linguistic support through various linguistic acts (e.g., occasional use of Chinese, pictures, and videos) to clarify meaning and promote understanding, limited pedagogical attention was paid to the participants' output in spoken (e.g., group discussion) and written forms (e.g., reflective essays) during the course. This suggests the need for more tailored language support in future courses to promote language-content integration (Yuan & Yang, 2023) in student teachers' course engagement and learning.

Conclusion

This study explores to what extent and how the pre-service language teachers developed their CMLA in a teacher education course guided by CDE. The findings reveal the cognitive growth of pre-service teachers with respect to their multilingual mindset, critical perspectives, and pedagogical thinking. Such growth was achieved through a series of carefully designed activities, the collaborative learning environment, as well as students' continuous reflections. The study presents empirical evidence of integrating critical dialogic learning activities into an SLTE course to support pre-service teachers' CMLA development, and such findings contribute to the scholarship of critical pedagogy and teacher education. However, several limitations of the study should be noted. First, despite the use of multiple sources of data, most of them were self-reported by the student teachers without the researchers' direct observations. Second, since the focal participants were selected on a voluntary basis, the process of sampling may contain potential selection bias and the results should be interpreted with caution. Future research can integrate language teacher educators' viewpoints and draw on observation data over a longer period of time to illuminate a more comprehensive picture of pre-service teachers' CMLA development.

References

Athanases, S. Z., Banes, L. C., Wong, J. W., & Martinez, D. C. (2018). Exploring linguistic diversity from the inside out: Implications of self-reflexive inquiry for teacher education. *Journal of Teacher Education*, *70*(5), 581–96. https://doi.org/10.1177/0022487118778838

Borg, S. (1994). Language awareness as methodology: Implications for teachers and teacher training. *Language Awareness*, *3*(2), 61–71. https://doi.org/10.1080/09658416.1994.9959844

Chen, R. T.-H. (2023). Teaching intercultural communication in an English as a lingua franca context. *RELC Journal*, *54*(3), 839–47. https://doi.org/10.1177/00336882221074106

Creswell, J. W. (2014). *Research design: Qualitative, quantitative, and mixed methods approaches* (4th Ed). Sage.

Deroo, M. R., & Ponzio, C. M. (2023). Fostering pre-service teachers' critical multilingual language awareness: Use of multimodal compositions to confront hegemonic language ideologies. *Journal of Language, Identity & Education*, *22*(2), 181–97. https://doi.org/10.1080/15348458.2020.1863153

Dubiner, D. (2018). "Write it down and then what?": Promoting pre-service teachers' language awareness, metacognitive development and pedagogical skills through reflections on vocabulary acquisition and teaching. *Language Awareness*, *27*(4), 277–94. https://doi.org/10.1080/09658416.2018.1521815

Dwomoh, R., Osei-Tutu, A. A., Chhikara, A., Zhou, L., Oudghiri, S., & Bell, T. (2023). Critical understanding of English learners: Experience and practice of educators in a professional development course. *TESOL Quarterly*, *57*(4), 1401–33. https://doi.org/10.1002/tesq.3200

Fairclough, N. (Ed.). (1990). *Critical language awareness*. Longman.

Gage, O. (2020). Urgently needed: A praxis of language awareness among pre-service primary teachers. *Language Awareness*, *29*(3–4), 220–35. https://doi.org/10.1080/09658416.2020.1786102

García, O. (2017). Critical multilingual language awareness and teacher education. In J. Cenoz, D. Gorter, & S. May (Eds.), *Language awareness and multilingualism* (pp. 263–80). Springer.

Gay, G. (2006). Connections between classroom management and culturally responsive teaching. In C. M. Evertson & C. S. Weinstein (Eds.), *Handbook of classroom management* (pp. 343–70). Lawrence Erlbaum.

Godley, A. J., Reaser, J., & Moore, K. G. (2015). Pre-service English language arts teachers' development of critical language awareness for teaching. *Linguistics and Education*, *32*, 41–54. https://doi.org/10.1016/j.linged.2015.03.015

Haneda, M. (2017). Dialogic learning and teaching across diverse contexts: Promises and challenges. *Language and Education*, *31*(1), 1–5. https://doi.org/10.1080/09500782.2016.1230128

Hawkins, M., & Norton, B. (2009). Critical language teacher education. In A. Burns & J. Richards (Eds.), *Cambridge guide to second language teacher education* (pp. 30–9). Cambridge University Press.

Iversen, J. Y. (2022). Pre-service teachers' narratives about their lived experience of language. *Journal of Multilingual and Multicultural Development, 43*(2), 140–53. https://doi.org/10.1080/01434632.2020.1735400

Karam, F. J. (2021). Re-envisioning the ESOL classroom through a virtues-based curriculum: Contributions to critical dialogic education. *TESOL Journal, 12*(3), e582. https://doi.org/10.1002/tesj.582

Kibler, A., Valdés, G., & Walqui, A. (2021). Introduction: A vision for critical dialogic education. In A. Kibler, G. Valdés, & A. Walqui (Eds.), *Reconceptualizing the role of critical dialogue in American classrooms* (pp. 1–22). Routledge.

Lindahl, K. (2019). Teacher language awareness development and its implications for new educators. *The New Educator, 15*(2), 85–100. https://doi.org/10.1080/1547688X.2018.1526356

Liu, K. (2017). Creating a dialogic space for prospective teacher critical reflection and transformative learning. *Reflective Practice, 18*(6), 805–20. https://doi.org/10.1080/14623943.2017.1361919

López-Gopar, M. E. (2014). Teaching English critically to Mexican children. *ELT Journal, 68*(3), 310–20. https://doi.org/10.1093/elt/ccu017

Lourenço, M., Andrade, A. I., & Sá, S. (2018). Teachers' voices on language awareness in pre-primary and primary school settings: Implications for teacher education. *Language, Culture and Curriculum, 31*(2), 113–27. https://doi.org/10.1080/07908318.2017.1415924

Lucas, T., De Oliveira, L. C., & Villegas, A. M. (2014). Preparing linguistically responsive teachers in multilingual contexts. In A. Mahboob & L. Barratt (Eds.), *Englishes in multilingual contexts: Language variation and education* (pp. 219–30). Springer.

Otwinowska, A. (2017). English teachers' language awareness: Away with the monolingual bias? *Language Awareness, 26*(4), 304–24. https://doi.org/10.1080/09658416.2017.1409752

Ponzio, C. M., & Deroo, M. R. (2023). Harnessing multimodality in language teacher education: Expanding English-dominant teachers' translanguaging capacities through a Multimodalities Entextualization Cycle. *International Journal of Bilingual Education and Bilingualism, 26*(8), 975–91. https://doi.org/10.1080/13670050.2021.1933893

Suh, S., & Michener, C. J. (2019). The preparation of linguistically responsive teachers through dialogic online discussion prompts. *Teaching and Teacher Education, 84*, 1–16. https://doi.org/10.1016/j.tate.2019.04.015

Svalberg, A. M. (2007). Language awareness and language learning. *Language Teaching, 40*(4), 287–308. https://doi.org/10.1017/S0261444807004491

Thornbury, S. (1997). *About language*. Cambridge University Press.

Wright, T. (2002). Doing language awareness: Issues for language study in language teacher education. In H. Trappes-Lomax & G. Ferguson (Eds.), *Language in language teacher education* (pp. 113–30). John Benjamins.

Wright, T., & Bolitho, R. (1993). Language awareness: A missing link in language teacher education? *ELT Journal, 47*(4), 292–304. https://doi.org/10.1093/elt/47.4.292

Yuan, R., & Yang, M. (2023). Towards an understanding of translanguaging in EMI teacher education classrooms. *Language Teaching Research, 27*(4), 884–906. https://doi.org/10.1177/1362168820964123

Yuan, R., Lee, I., De Costa, P. I., Yang, M., & Liu, S. (2022). TESOL teacher educators in higher education: A review of studies from 2010 to 2020. *Language Teaching, 55*, 1–36, 434–69. https://doi.org/10.1017/S0261444822000209

Part One

Commentary: How Critical Dialogic Education Can Contribute to Equity-Oriented Pedagogy and Curriculum

Megan Madigan Peercy

This collection of chapters is committed to offering a better understanding of how the critical, dialogic reframing of curricula and pedagogies can have an impact on both pre-service and in-service teacher practice with multilingual students. Specifically, these chapters help us to understand the possibilities of employing critical dialogic education (CDE; Kibler et al., 2021) to inform three of the big questions that we ask about teacher education as a whole, and teacher education for multilingual students specifically:

1. How should we prepare teachers?
2. What does teacher practice look like?[1]
3. What impact does teacher practice have on students?[2]

Through the use of the CDE framework, which emphasizes the following three principles:

- equity-focused classroom pedagogies that are dialogic, critical, and inclusive;
- explicit goals for pedagogical practice that aim to disrupt inequitable power dynamics and their impacts on underserved student populations; and
- a democratic vision that prioritizes marginalized youth's voices and participation (Kibler et al., 2021, p. 1, p. 5, p. 8);

these chapters explore these big questions, with varying foci. Yuan and colleagues and Turner and Fránquiz emphasize the first question, while this is in the background in Walqui's chapter. Walqui digs deeply into the second and third questions, while questions two and three are in the background for Yuan and colleagues and for Turner and Fránquiz. Together, these chapters help illuminate how CDE can contribute to equity-oriented pedagogy and curriculum used by TESOL professionals.

My Positionality

My work on the preparation of teachers to foster the success of multilingual students has focused for several years now on the ways in which teachers learn and develop through opportunities for collaboration—with one another, with teacher educators, with the curriculum, with students (e.g., Fredricks & Peercy, 2020; Peercy, 2018; Peercy & Martin-Beltrán, 2012; Peercy et al., 2015, 2016, 2020)—and on how to support their growth as humanizing practitioners (e.g., Fredricks et al., 2023; Hardy et al., 2023; Kidwell et al., 2021; Peercy & Chi, 2022; Peercy et al., 2022a, 2022b, 2023a, in press, forthcoming; Tigert et al., 2022). I firmly believe that equity and justice need to be at the center of teachers' pedagogy and curriculum, and that they need concrete support (instructional and systemic) to achieve this. As a White, middle-class, cisgender, heterosexual, able-bodied, English-dominant, Protestant female who has the privilege of making aspects of my non-dominant identities invisible unless I choose to reveal them (e.g., Peercy & Sharkey, 2022; Peercy et al., 2019), I recognize that I have an important responsibility to try to be a co-conspirator (e.g., Love, 2019; Spaulding et al., 2021) with communities and individuals who are not centered and who are devalued and underserved by our educational and research enterprise.

I strive to use critical, collaborative, pragmatic approaches to find ways to effect change in the pedagogies and curricula created for teachers of multilingual students, with the aim that these approaches have meaningful impact on the educational experiences of P-12 multilingual students (e.g., Peercy et al., 2022a, 2023a). While I have not previously drawn specifically on CDE in my work, I see many connections between CDE and my commitments to dialogic teacher education (e.g., Peercy et al., 2020, forthcoming) and to supporting teachers' humanizing practices. I am inspired to more closely examine CDE alongside other equity-oriented frameworks (such as humanizing pedagogy, culturally relevant/sustaining pedagogy, linguistically responsive teaching, social-emotional learning, and restorative practices; e.g., Tigert et al., 2023) to consider the affordances of CDE for the joint enterprise of making schooling better for multilingual students and their families and communities. I encourage all of us in this field to look carefully at the intersections of these frameworks so that

Commentary: How CDE Can Contribute to Equity-Oriented Pedagogy   91

we can marshal them to do our work in the ways that best serve multilingual students.

Next, I explore how the three chapters in this section employ CDE to ask significant questions about the pedagogies and curricula we use with multilingual students and their teachers, and share how findings from these chapters can contribute to our efforts in equity and justice-oriented pedagogies in our field.

Overview of the Chapters in This Section

Examining questions about CDE and pedagogy, Yuan, Wang, and Li investigate the ways in which student teachers in Macau develop critical multilingual awareness (CMLA) in a language teacher education course that was informed by critical dialogic education (CDE; Kibler et al., 2021). Turner and Fránquiz also use CDE to help them explore pre-service teachers' pedagogy. They use CDE as a framework employed in tandem with translanguaging theories, investigating how four elementary school pre-service ESL teachers in the Southwestern United States positioned themselves with respect to multilingual pedagogies over time. Walqui takes a curricular focus, considering how four in-service eighth-grade English language arts (ELA) teachers in Los Angeles, California, were able to shift to more critical approaches through the use of innovative curriculum that embedded sociocultural approaches and CDE. All of these chapters help reveal the ways in which CDE can be used to support more critical and just uses of curriculum and pedagogy in teacher education and in P-12 classrooms. Next, I provide a brief description of how each chapter leverages CDE to make contributions to TESOL teacher education.

How These Studies Leverage CDE to Contribute to TESOL Teacher Education

Yuan and colleagues describe their course, *Introduction to Applied English Studies*, as informed by the principles of CDE. Their study examines "to what extent and how the pre-service language teachers developed their CMLA[3] in a teacher education course guided by CDE" (Yuan et al., this volume, p. 84). The authors demonstrate that in this course, pre-service participants gained a deeper and more nuanced understanding of various facets of English from historical, cultural, and functional perspectives, coming to appreciate that English is more than just a collection of structures, and understanding the need to "cultivate [language learner] students' critical thinking and their awareness of intercultural issues" (Yuan et al., this volume, p. 12). According to this study, these pre-service participants also developed a multilingual mindset. For instance, Yuan and colleagues share that participants gained a deeper appreciation and respect for all languages, for multiple varieties of English, and for translanguaging, as well as considering the pedagogical implications of these perspectives. Finally, Yuan and colleagues note that pre-service teachers in their study began to engage a critical stance regarding the ways that English gets deployed, including gendered and racialized uses of English. The authors note the importance of reflective, dialogic, collaborative approaches to teacher education, such as online forum discussion and reflective writing, for helping pre-service teacher candidates to develop this more critical stance with regard to their own uses of English and the ways in which they would teach English. This study illustrates how a CDE perspective can offer a helpful structure for supporting pre-service teachers' development of critical perspectives through its critical and dialogic emphases.

Turner and Fránquiz argue that given the uptake of translanguaging as a theoretical framework, it is also critical to understand how translanguaging can be enacted pedagogically in teacher education, and in what ways pre-service teachers are engaging with, enacting, and being challenged in their attempts to hold more holistic views of language and language pedagogies. They examine how CDE might be used in tandem with translanguaging theories to challenge linguistic norms, studying how CDE might be used as a pedagogical tool to support educators' additive language practices and pedagogical perspectives. Specifically, they were interested in how four elementary school pre-service ESL teachers positioned themselves in a course that focused on developing pre-service teachers' "holistic and inclusive approaches to language and language pedagogies" (Turner & Fránquiz, this volume, p. 49). By engaging pre-service teachers in a final project that involved tutoring elementary multilingual students using an asset-based lens that supported the use of students' full linguistic repertoire, the authors aimed for pre-service teachers to challenge monolingual assumptions and ideologies. The authors were also interested in whether and how pre-service teachers might sustain these perspectives over time, and found that their ability to maintain a critical stance was context-driven. Importantly for the use of the CDE framework, the authors found that structures, norms, mentoring, and power dynamics all played a role in the ways in which the pre-service teachers might challenge linguistic norms in their field placements, and it was important for the authors to offer meaningful opportunities for the pre-service teachers to engage in critical, reflective dialogue about their evolving work as language educators. Thus, further pedagogical developments in CDE will benefit from emphasizing and attending to the context in which CDE is being used.

Walqui examines the use of a socioculturally grounded, spiraled English language arts (ELA) curriculum informed by CDE principles, that is designed to support teachers and multilingual students in engaging with language arts in a deeper and more linguistically challenging (and supported) way. The materials she and her team developed focus on the overarching question *"How have human beings across time and space interpreted their environment and tried to control it?"*, and they offer opportunities for teachers to better understand why they might teach in such a way, and what the theory behind such instruction is. The four in-service ELA teachers who participated in this work also received two days of professional development prior to implementation, and four coaching sessions during the implementation period. Walqui found CDE to be a helpful lens for understanding how teachers must rethink "both their pedagogies and their beliefs about students, as well as their assumptions about what 'good' classroom talk entails (Kibler et al., 2021)" (Walqui, this volume, p. 35). Specifically, she found that despite teachers' initial hesitance about the complexity of the new ELA materials provided, students were highly engaged and capable of reading the materials, as well as engaging in conversations about the material. Additionally, she noted that providing specific norms for student talk offered a helpful structure for high engagement and sustained conversation. Walqui also found that professional development for teachers was critical to implementing such a different approach: teachers were hesitant to let go of their prior instructional habits, such as requiring mastery of details and of multiple language skills at once, and they also needed time to develop their own understanding of the curricular materials, as well as plan how to use them.

Walqui found that the use of rich, demanding, and longer texts is possible with multilingual students who have been designated as long-term English learners, when appropriate support is provided for both teachers and students. Through her study, Walqui illustrates how critical dialogic engagement is possible when strong, iterative efforts are made to develop such materials; when teachers, students, and curriculum developers have the opportunity to offer feedback and refine materials; and when teachers and students are well-supported in using the materials. Her study contributes to our understanding of CDE's potential for supporting curriculum development and teachers' more critical stances in their approaches to classroom materials and considerations of the capabilities of multilingual students. Further examination of how CDE can support teacher development of a critical stance through approach to curriculum and high expectations for students will be quite valuable.

How These Studies Employ and Extend Our Understanding of CDE

When considering how these studies employ and extend our understanding of CDE, it is clear that using a CDE perspective (Kibler et al., 2021) can reframe teachers' and students' roles in classroom learning, while also offering important support to both teachers and P-12 students for more critical, dialogic engagement in curricula, classrooms, and pedagogies. These chapters help to expand upon prior work on critical and dialogic education (e.g., Bakhtin, 1986; Haneda, 2017; Haneda et al., 2017; Kibler et al., 2021; O'Connor & Michaels, 2007; Wells, 1999, 2000) by offering further insights regarding how these shifts can look in pre-service and in-service teacher education when CDE is applied as a framework. These studies also add to the body of work regarding the importance of dialogic interactions for supporting teachers' development and their capacity to enact humanizing, equity-oriented pedagogy (see also Peercy & Troyan, 2020; Peercy et al., 2020; Peercy et al., forthcoming; Peercy et al., in press).

Especially important in this section of the book is an understanding of CDE as an approach which offers principles that can support teachers in moving critical, dialogic mindsets to action through the reimagination of curricula and pedagogies. This is an area that still needs significant elaboration for teachers and teacher educators to successfully mobilize humanizing intentions and commitments (e.g., Faltis & Valdés, 2016; Fredricks et al., 2023; Peercy et al., 2022b, 2023b; Tigert et al., 2023). One way in which my colleagues and I have aimed to move equity-oriented mindsets to action is by identifying intersections between pedagogies of practice-based teacher education and humanizing pedagogies (e.g., Kidwell et al., 2021; Peercy et al., 2020, 2022a, 2022b; Tigert et al., 2022). As I elaborate upon below, my suggestions for future research related to the studies in this volume include additional examination and illumination of how teachers learn to pair CDE principles with pedagogical maneuvers, as Yuan et al. suggest here with their combining of CDE and CMLA, and as Turner and Fránquiz demonstrate with their integration of CDE and translanguaging pedagogies. Walqui illustrates how CDE principles get mobilized in curriculum and in teachers' practices when using innovative curriculum, as well as how teachers' perspectives on students' capabilities can shift when using curriculum informed by CDE principles.

Suggestions for Expanding Work on CDE

Next, recognizing that the data and analysis from the studies in this section represent only a portion of the work in which these authors are engaged, I offer some possible suggestions for how to continue to advance the use of the CDE framework in teacher education, across our field. These suggestions are based on the findings and implications of these chapters, and drawing upon my own research in dialogic and collaborative teacher education to advance humanizing, equitable approaches to education for multilingual students.

Some of the implications of the research of Yuan and colleagues include that reflective and dialogic approaches to teacher education appear to support pre-service teachers' capacity to view English teaching and learning from a critical, multilingual perspective that is more broadly accepting of the ways language is used in classroom settings. As the authors note, finding a number of ways to engage teacher candidates in reflective teacher education appears to be an important facet of their growth, and engaging pre-service teachers in a variety of opportunities to self-reflect and self-interrogate in safe environments is key. One way the authors engaged in self-reflective approaches was through interaction in online forums. Future research could examine additional ways to facilitate teacher self-reflection *and* self-*reflexivity*[4] through additional dialogic opportunities. These could include use of teacher rounds[5] that support boundary crossing and flattening hierarchies (Hall, 2022), sustained collaborative conversations about real problems of practice that offer humanizing spaces for teachers (Peercy et al., forthcoming), and fostering early career teachers' emerging identities as humanizing practitioners and advocates in peer support groups that focus on their experiences in the early years of teaching (Peercy et al., in press). These approaches may offer teachers additional needed agency and space to develop critical perspectives in their work as advocates and practitioners, as well as positioning them in ways that both humanize their experience as educators, and increase the potential for them to engage in humanizing practice. I see these as aligning in crucial ways with CDE principles of equity-focused pedagogies, the disruption of inequitable power dynamics, and prioritizing marginalized students' voices and participation. Examining data that illustrate the affordances and outcomes of these approaches to teachers' growth alongside CDE principles as a guiding framework could offer a meaningful way to discern whether teachers' professional development aligns with CDE's intended ends of dialogism, equity, and elevating marginalized students in their practice.

Furthermore, as Yuan and colleagues note, much of the data for this study came from pre-service teachers' self-reports. Expanding future inquiry to include direct observational data from the developing pedagogical understandings and practices of pre-service teachers who have been engaged in coursework that is underpinned by CDE will help us to better evaluate its impact on teacher education and practice, as will data regarding teachers' practices collected from the students, families, and communities (including community members and community organizations) where pre-service teachers teach. As Zeichner (2023) has recently noted, we will know much better the impact and importance of our equity-oriented work when we more directly involve a broader array of participant voices in our data collection and analysis.

As with Yuan et al.'s study, Turner and Fránquiz's work sheds light on the need for teacher education experiences to provide continual opportunities for critical dialogue and reflection. As some of our research has shown (Peercy et al., in press; Peercy et al., forthcoming), novice teachers can also provide these kinds of important supports *to one another* through collaborative conversations and peer support groups. Thus, it is valuable for teacher education to offer a variety of means for engaging in critical dialogue about equitable instruction for multilingual students, including examination of how translanguaging is being enacted (and challenged) in practice, across pre-service teachers' contexts and experiences, and considering how CDE might offer a framework for preparing teachers to engage in this work in their classrooms. Since the data shared in this chapter are primarily interview data that rely on the pre-service teachers' self-reports about their pedagogy, future research that examines observational data from the teacher participants' field placement classrooms (and into their early years of teaching) could expand our understanding of the pedagogical implications of their translanguaging stance. I suggest that examining pre-service teachers' and/or their mentor teachers' translanguaging and other practices that elevate the value of students' home languages in classroom interactions, alongside the three principles for CDE that Kibler and her colleagues highlighted, might further illuminate what needs to be better developed and understood in order to push this translanguaging stance into practice. As the authors note: "[by] generating spaces that are critical, inclusive, and dialogic, teacher educators and preservice teachers can work in communion over time, as they *together* identify and reimagine setbacks and roadblocks, both within and outside of ourselves"

(Turner & Fránquiz, this volume, p. 61). Knowing more about the ways that these groups can support a translanguaging stance in practice will help move our pedagogies with multilingual students in more deeply equity-focused and dialogic directions.

While the chapters by Yuan and colleagues and Turner and Fránquiz both help illuminate the ways that pre-service teachers *learn more critical and dialogic pedagogies*, Walqui helps us to see the possibilities of the *enactment of a more critical, dialogic curriculum* when it is put in the hands of in-service teachers, and they are supported in how to use the curriculum, as well as made part of an iterative curriculum redesign process. Her team's implementation of rich, spiraled ELA curriculum that included long and complex texts, and the deep engagement of multilingual students with the curriculum, are all tremendously encouraging moves toward more challenging and equitable educational experiences for multilingual students. Her work demonstrates the potential of CDE principles as a framework that can foster the development of rigorous, meaningful curriculum that supports the linguistic development and content knowledge of multilingual students. To further inform teacher education regarding how to support teachers in using critical and dialogic curricula, in future research it would be helpful to have more details regarding the professional development and coaching sessions in which Walqui and her team engaged. More information regarding their methods for this aspect of the study, as well as practical implications for the professional development of educators to use more critical and dialogic approaches, would be a welcome addition to the literature.

Therefore, as with the work by the other two studies highlighted in this section, I also recommend more observational data in the work by Walqui and her team (from the professional development and coaching sessions in this study), and in other studies like theirs, to offer even greater contributions to the research. Additionally, while the participation of teachers and students in the curriculum redesign process is tremendously valuable (e.g., Fredricks & Peercy, 2020; Peercy et al., 2015, 2017), I also urge future work that uses CDE to inform curriculum development, including the work by Walqui and her team, to consider including a wider range of stakeholders in the curriculum re/design process—including parents, families, community leaders, and community organizations (Zeichner, 2023)—to make it more fully critical and dialogic.

Finally, as I mentioned early in this commentary, it may be useful to explore how CDE—and the ways in which it can be applied to both the creation and analysis of curricula and pedagogies—intersects with, complements, and diverges from other critical and dialogic approaches to education, including humanizing pedagogy, culturally relevant/sustaining pedagogy, linguistically responsive teaching, social-emotional learning, and restorative practices (e.g., Tigert et al., 2023). A better understanding of the affordances of CDE and its intersections with these and other equity-oriented frameworks will help us all to more effectively do the work of preparing teachers and teacher educators for the kinds of concrete, specific approaches to developing and supporting advocacy that are currently missing in our teacher preparation (Faltis & Valdés, 2016). It may also allow us to better address the dearth of specific implications and actions for teacher education and practice that can be grounded in critical perspectives about language use being situated in relations of power (e.g., Hawkins, 2011; Hawkins & Norton, 2009; Peercy et al., 2023b). I suggest beginning with theoretical/conceptual work that allows us to examine the intersections between these equity-oriented frameworks, and identifying what these frameworks allow us to see and how they might allow us to challenge and change the pedagogies and curricula we use in K-12 and teacher education settings. Future empirical work could more deeply investigate the ways in which some intersection of these frameworks can inform classroom-based inquiry (including close examination of classroom observational data), as well as the impact such changes might have on teacher practice, teacher educator practice, and multilingual student learning outcomes.

Conclusion

Our field is in need of specific ideas that enrich our understanding of how to prepare critical, humanizing professionals who teach multilingual students (e.g., Peercy et al, 2022b). Working together and examining a variety of frameworks and their connection to practice, we will be able to strengthen our understanding of what teachers and teacher educators need to know and be able to do (e.g., Faltis & Valdés, 2016) to connect humanizing mindsets, such as CDE, with humanizing practices. As Cochran-Smith (2023) recently noted, teacher education is currently constructed as an "equity problem" (p. 128). These chapters help move our understanding forward regarding how teacher education can mobilize and leverage the CDE framework to prepare teachers in ways that help them to have not just equity-oriented mindsets, but move into equity-oriented practices in actionable ways. From the work shared in these chapters, we know using the CDE framework can help teachers to become more critical about what language is, to hold more holistic views of language—including the use of translanguaging pedagogies—and to develop capacity to use rich, demanding curricular materials. Such work does not happen overnight, but requires repeated and prolonged opportunities for teacher reflection, dialogue, collaboration, planning, and access to materials, as well as a commitment to developing systems and structures that allow for this (e.g., Smith et al., 2023). I argue that it is important for each of us to consider how we can be part of the solution.

In my own work, this will mean a commitment to finding sustainable ways for teachers to dialogically engage regarding research and praxis (e.g., Peercy et al., in press, forthcoming), as well as involving a broader array of collaborators (including community leaders, community members, families, and P-12 students) to continue to rethink and reframe the pedagogies and curricula in which we engage multilingual students. It will also mean identifying how to prepare teacher *educators* to engage in critical, dialogic work (e.g., Peercy & Sharkey, 2022; Peercy et al., 2023b; Souto-Manning & Stillman, 2020; Stillman & Beltramo, 2019). Finally, my work should include deeper advocacy to identify and challenge systemic barriers to critical, dialogic engagement with a broader range of partners, and to leverage the opportunities that such engagement could afford in our approaches to the education of multilingual students.

Notes

1 That is, how do they enact the preparation they receive, and what influences their practice?
2 In other words, what do students do, and how does that relate to teachers' practice?
3 The authors describe teachers' critical multilingual awareness (CMLA) as their "understanding of language as socially created and changeable, and thus entangled with linguistic hierarchies and power struggles experienced by individuals (especially linguistic minority students)" (p. 65).
4 Judy Sharkey and I have distinguished self-reflective from self-reflexive approaches, with self-reflexivity more explicitly and intentionally building from and supporting a critical and equity-oriented stance (e.g., Peercy & Sharkey, 2020, 2022; Sharkey & Peercy, 2018; Sharkey, Peercy, Solano-Campos, & Schall-Leckrone, 2022).
5 Teacher rounds are modeled after medical rounds, and engage educators in collectively observing other teachers during instruction with students, followed by debriefing (e.g., Del Prete, 1997; Goodwin et al., 2015; Gore et al., 2017).

References

Bakhtin, M. M. (1986). *Speech genres and other late essays* (M. Holquist, Ed.; C. Emerson & V. W. McGee, Trans.). University of Austin Press.

Cochran-Smith, M. (2023). What's the "problem of teacher education" in the 2020s? *Journal of Teacher Education, 74*(2), 127–30. https://doi.org/10.1177/00224871231160373

Del Prete, T. (1997). The "rounds" model of professional development. *From the Inside, 1*(1), 12–3.

Faltis, C. J., & Valdés, G. (2016). Preparing teachers for teaching in and advocating for linguistically diverse classrooms: A vade mecum for teacher educators. In D. H. Gitomer & C. A. Bell (Eds.), *Handbook of research on teaching* (5th ed., pp. 549–92). American Educational Research Association. https://doi.org/10.3102/978-0-935302-48-6_8.

Fredricks, D. E., & Peercy, M. M. (2020). Youth perspectives on humanizing core practices. In L. Cardozo-Gaibisso & M. V. Dominguez (Eds.), *Handbook of research on advancing language equity practices within immigrant communities* (pp. 107–28). IGI Global. https://doi.org/10.4018/978-1-6684-3690-5.ch065

Fredricks, D. E., Peercy, M. M., Tigert, J. M., & Hardy, M. (March, 2023). *Beyond "Fake it till you make it": Humanizing core practices*. Workshop presented at the annual meeting of the Teachers of English for Speakers of Other Languages International Convention. Portland, OR.

Goodwin, A. L., Del Prete, T., Reagan, E. M., & Roegman, R. (2015). A closer look at the practice and impact of "rounds." *International Journal of Educational Research, 73*, 37–43. https://doi.org/10.1016/j.ijer.2015.06.006

Gore, J., Lloyd, A., Smith, M., Bowe, J., Ellis, H., & Lubans, D. (2017). Effects of professional development on the quality of teaching: Results from a randomised controlled trial of Quality Teaching Rounds. *Teaching and Teacher Education, 68*, 99–113. https://doi.org/10.1016/j.tate.2017.08.007

Hall, W. H. (2022). "Leveling the playing field": Rounds in ESOL pre-service teacher education [Doctoral dissertation, University of Maryland, College Park]. ProQuest Dissertations Publishing.

Haneda, M. (2017). Dialogic learning and teaching across diverse contexts: Promises and challenges. *Language and Education, 31*(1), 1–5. https://doi.org/10.1080/09500782.2016.1230128

Haneda, M., Teemant, A., & Sherman, B. (2017). Instructional coaching through dialogic interaction: Helping a teacher to become agentive in her practice. *Language and Education, 31*(1), 46–64. https://doi.org/10.1080/09500782.2016.1230127

Hardy, M., Peercy, M. M., Fredricks, D. E., & Tigert, J. M. (March, 2023). *Knowing your multilingual students: Moving humanizing mindsets to action*. Workshop presented at the annual meeting of the Teachers of English for Speakers of Other Languages International Convention. Portland, OR.

Hawkins, M., & Norton, B. (2009). Critical language teacher education. In J. Richards & A. Burns (Eds.), *The Cambridge guide to second language teacher education* (pp. 30–9). Cambridge University Press.

Hawkins, M. R. (2011). Dialogic determination: Constructing a social justice discourse in language teacher education. In M. R. Hawkins (Ed.), *Social justice language teacher education* (pp. 102–23). Multilingual Matters.

Kibler, A., Valdés, G., & Walqui, A. (2021). *Reconceptualizing the role of critical dialogue in American classrooms: Promoting equity through dialogic education.* Routledge.

Kidwell, T., Peercy, M. M., Tigert, J., & Fredricks, D. (2021). Novice teachers' use of pedagogical language knowledge to humanize language and literacy development. *TESOL Journal, 12*(3), 1–17. http://doi.org/10.1002/tesj.590

Love, B. L. (2019). *We want to do more than survive: Abolitionist teaching and the pursuit of educational freedom.* Beacon Press.

O'Connor, C., & Michaels, S. (2007). When is dialogue "dialogic"? *Human Development, 50*(5), 275–85. https://doi.org/10.1159/000106415

Peercy, M. M. (2018). Mainstream and ESL teacher collaboration. In J. Liontas, M. DelliCarpini, G. Park, & S. Salas (Eds.), *TESOL encyclopedia of English language teaching, v.7* (section on teacher training and professional development) (pp. 4631–36). Wiley. https://doi.org/10.1002/9781118784235.eelt0889

Peercy, M. M., & Chi, J. (2022). "Oh, I was scaffolding!": Novice teachers' use of scaffolding as humanizing practice with multilingual students. In L. C. de Oliveira & R. Westerlund (Eds.), *Scaffolding for multilingual learners in elementary and secondary schools* (pp. 102–20). Routledge. https://doi.org/10.4324/9781003196228-9

Peercy, M. M., & Martin-Beltrán, M. (2012). Envisioning collaboration: Including ESOL students *and* teachers in the mainstream classroom. *International Journal of Inclusive Education, 16*(7), 657–73. https://doi.org/10.1080/13603116.2010.495791

Peercy, M. M., & Sharkey, J. (2020). Self-study in English language teaching: Emerging considerations about the intersection of teacher educators' identities and pedagogies. In J. Kitchen, A. Berry, S. M. Bullock, A. Crowe, H. Guðjónsdóttir, & M. Taylor (Eds.), *International handbook of self-study of teaching and teacher education* (2nd Ed.). Springer. https://doi.org/10.1007/978-981-13-1710-1_28-1

Peercy, M. M., & Sharkey, J. (2022). Who gets to ask "Does race belong in every course?": Staying in the anguish as white teacher educators. In A. Martin (Ed.), *Self-studies in urban teacher education: Preparing U.S. teachers to advance equity and social justice* (pp. 95–112). Springer.

Peercy, M. M., & Troyan, F. J. (2020). "Am I doing it wrong?": Critically examining mediation in lesson rehearsal. *Teaching and Teacher Education, 93.* https://doi.org/10.1016/j.tate.2020.103082

Peercy, M. M., Martin-Beltrán, M., Silverman, R. D., & Daniel, S. M. (2015). Curricular design and implementation as a site of teacher expertise and learning. *Teachers and Teaching: Theory and Practice, 21*(7), 867–93. https://doi.org/10.1080/13540602.2014.995486

Peercy, M. M., DeStefano, M., Yazan, B., & Martin-Beltrán, M. (2016). "She's my right hand": Teacher collaboration for linguistically diverse students' equitable access to curriculum. In J. C. Richards & K. Zenkov (Eds.), *Social justice, the Common Core, and closing the instructional gap: Empowering diverse learners and their teachers* (pp. 39–56). Information Age Publishing.

Peercy, M. M., Martin-Beltrán, M., Yazan, B., & DeStefano, M. (2017). "Jump in any time": How teacher struggle with curricular reform generates opportunities for teacher learning. *Action in Teacher Education, 39*(2), 203–17. https://doi.org/10.1080/01626620.2016.1248302

Peercy, M. M., Sharkey, J., Baecher, L., Motha, S., & Varghese, M. (2019). Exploring TESOL teacher educators as learners and reflective scholars: A shared narrative inquiry. *TESOL Journal, 10*(4). https://doi.org/10.1002/tesj.482

Peercy, M. M., Kidwell, T., Lawyer, M., Tigert, J., Fredricks, D., Feagin, K., & Stump, M. (2020). Experts at being novices: What new teachers can add to practice-based teacher education efforts. *Action in Teacher Education, 42*(3), 212–33. https://doi.org/10.1080/01626620.2019.1675201

Peercy, M. M., Tigert, J. M., & Fredricks, D. E. (2022a). *Core practices for teaching multilingual students: Humanizing pedagogies for equity.* Teachers College Press.

Peercy, M. M., Tigert, J., Fredricks, D., Kidwell, T., Feagin, K., Hall, W., Himmel, J., & Lawyer, M. (2022b). From humanizing principles to humanizing practices: Exploring core practices as a bridge to enacting humanizing pedagogy with multilingual students. *Teaching and Teacher Education, 113.* https://doi.org/10.1016/j.tate.2022.103653

Peercy, M. M., Tigert, J. M., Fredricks, D., & Hardy, M. (2023a). *Core practices for teaching multilingual students.* https://www.youtube.com/@corepracticesformlls.

Peercy, M. M., Troyan, F. J., Fredricks, D. E., & Hardy, M. (April, 2023b). *Calling for a humanizing turn in language teacher education: Problematizing content and language instruction.* Paper presented at the annual meeting of the American Educational Research Association. Chicago, IL.

Peercy, M. M., Fredricks, D. E., Tigert, J. M., Heard, S., Mallory, A., & Stutzman, A. (forthcoming). "Maintaining our integrity as teachers and human beings": How a dialogic research partnership created a humanizing space for early career teachers of multilingual students. In O. Uztuk & J. Curtis (Eds.), *Building a culture of research in TESOL: Collaborations and communities.* Springer.

Peercy, M. M., Sodani, D., & Hall, W. (in press). "Figuring out my end game": Supporting novice ESOL teachers' emerging identities as humanizing practitioners and advocates through peer interaction. In P. DeCosta & O. Uztuk (Eds.), *A sociopolitical agenda in TESOL teacher education.* Bloomsbury.

Sharkey, J., & Peercy, M. M. (Eds.). (2018). *Self-study of language and literacy teacher education practices: Culturally and linguistically diverse contexts.* Emerald Publishing. https://doi.org/10.1108/s1479-3687201830

Sharkey, J., Peercy, M. M., Solano-Campos, A., & Schall-Leckrone, L. (2022). Being a reflexive practitioner and scholar in TESOL: Methodological considerations. In E. R. Yuan & I. Lee (Eds.), *Becoming and being a TESOL teacher educator: Research and practice* (pp. 127–46). Routledge. https://doi.org/10.4324/9781003004677-9

Smith, C., Arnott, S., Battistuzzi, A., & Masson, M. (April, 2023). *A critical review of language teacher preparation and induction in Canada: Polishing a poisoned apple?* Paper presented at the annual meeting of the American Educational Research Association. Chicago, IL.

Souto-Manning, M., & Stillman, J. (2020). In the pursuit of transformative justice in the education of teacher educators. *The New Educator, 16*(1), 1–4. https://doi.org/10.1080/1547688x.2019.1698871

Spaulding, E. C., Adams, J., Dunn, D. C., & Love, B. L. (2021). Freedom dreaming antiracist pedagogy dreams. *Language Arts, 99*(1), 8–18.

Stillman, J., & Beltramo, J. L. (2019). Exploring Freirean culture circles and Boalian theatre as pedagogies for preparing asset-oriented teacher educators. *Teachers College Record, 121*(6), 1–38.

Tigert, J., Peercy, M. M., Fredricks, D., & Kidwell, T. (2022). Humanizing classroom management as a core practice for teachers of multilingual students. *TESOL Quarterly, 56*(4), 1087–111. https://doi.org/10.1002/tesq.3093

Tigert, J. M., Fredricks, D. E., Peercy, M. M., & Hardy, M. (March, 2023). *"Can I really apply this?": Humanizing pedagogies for multilingual students.* Paper presented at the annual meeting of the Teachers of English for Speakers of Other Languages International Convention. Portland, OR.

Wells, G. (1999). *Dialogic inquiry: Towards a socio-cultural practice and theory of education*. Cambridge University Press.

Wells, G. (2000). Dialogic inquiry in education: Building on the legacy of Vygotsky. In C. D. Lee & P. Smagorinsky (Eds.), *Vygotskian perspectives on literacy research* (pp. 51–85). Cambridge University Press.

Zeichner, K. (2023). The "Turn once again toward practice-based teacher education" revisited. *Journal of Teacher Education, 74*(2), 178–80. https://doi.org/10.1177/00224871231161459

Part Two

Reimagining the Roles of Teacher Candidates and Teacher Educators

"I Just Really Want to Focus on Expressing How Valuable Each Student Is": Impact of Collaborative Exploration of Problems of Practice on Teachers' Visions of Critical Dialogic Education

Heather M. Meston and Emily Phillips Galloway

Introduction

Students most impacted by the visible and not-so-visible currents of institutional power are often afforded the fewest opportunities to critically examine and question those currents (Adair, 2014). For teachers seeking to address this disconnect, critical dialogic education (CDE), which calls on learners and educators to co-construct knowledge around issues of social justice and collaboratively interrogate inequitable power dynamics through discussion, represents a powerful pedagogical tool for positioning learners as reflective change agents and authors of their own learning (Karam, 2021; Kibler et al., 2021). By focusing on critical learning mediated by language and interaction, CDE offers particular benefits for linguistically minoritized learners, who can "gain communicative and interactional expertise and challenge the linguistic and racialized norms and expectations that often limit their opportunities" (Kibler et al., 2021, p. 1).

These benefits may be particularly important for multilingual students with interrupted formal education (SIFE), who are still in the process of developing heritage and English language literacy, and who possess limited experience in formal educational systems (DeCapua & Marshall, 2011). Therefore, SIFE must simultaneously learn English, literacy, and the complex cultural norms of industrialized educational settings. And though SIFE possess a wealth of cultural, linguistic, and experiential assets, these assets are typically undervalued in American schools (DeCapua & Marshall, 2015), indicating a need to reframe the ways that SIFE are typically viewed and taught in classrooms. Given its focus on leveraging and expanding students' *funds of knowledge*, or the competencies and areas of expertise students have acquired across their lives (Gonzalez et al., 2006), and on using these funds of knowledge in the co-construction of meaning, CDE may offer one avenue for supporting SIFE as agentive learners empowered to question and push back on oppressive systems that position them as "lesser" (Kibler et al., 2021).

However, teaching is a complex endeavor, made more so when educators stray from teacher-centered instructional methodologies that dominate in US schools (Aukerman & Chambers Schuldt, 2017). Therefore, teacher educators hoping to support teachers' enactment of CDE cannot rely on traditional models of professional learning that emphasize the development of decontextualized "best practices" too often centered around certain ways of knowing, being, and speaking (Cochran-Smith, 2001). Rather, professional learning about complex pedagogies such as CDE must instead engage teachers as agentive practitioners refining their pedagogical judgment to meet the needs of specific students within their specific classrooms (Horn & Garner, 2022).

However, as Duffy (2005) explained when critiquing common forms of professional development offered (and often thrust upon) educators today:

> Training tends to emphasize passive assimilation of knowledge and compliance with experts' recommendations, which in turn causes teachers to construct the understanding that they are expected to be followers who should not "think-on-their-feet."
>
> (300)

We suggest that professional learning that calls upon participants to strive toward their *visions*, or the pedagogical ideals that teachers hold for their classrooms (Duffy, 2002; Vaughn et al., 2021), may prove more fruitful in positioning educators as agentive learners, teachers, and collaborators. We argue that, to enact a vision of equity- and agency-enriched instruction, teachers require opportunities to collaboratively analyze problems of practice in support of these goals. By implication, this kind of professional learning, which is highly individualized and contextualized, may offer particular affordances for teacher educators and coaches seeking to support educators in learning about CDE.

In this chapter, we describe our partnership with four in-service teachers of SIFE. These educators were all striving to enact and refine their visions of CDE, supported by collaborative analysis of problems impeding their aspirational teaching practice (hereafter called "problems of practice") in the context of a Critical Friends Group (CFG), a structured form of professional learning wherein participants question and propose potential solutions to problems of practice presented by collaborators. Participants' visions served as anchors to guide analysis around problems of practice related to implementing CDE in classrooms, and these analyses, in turn, served to shape educators' visions over time. This work is focused by the question: *How does collaborative exploration of problems of practice impact educators' visions of Critical Dialogic Education?*

Theoretical Framework

Critical Dialogic Education

Recent research has questioned how ostensibly dialogic classrooms may be failing to engage some learners as agentive, as, for example, when students from minoritized populations struggle to have their ideas accepted into classroom discourse spaces (Segal et al., 2017; Snell & Lefstein, 2018) or when students are divested of their right to silence (Lefstein et al., 2020). Practitioners of CDE attempt to alleviate these challenges by engaging students' funds of knowledge as valuable assets, by analyzing the dynamics of their classroom discourse to ensure equitable participation opportunities, and by privileging discussion that centers as topics of investigation students' own minoritized status and the systems that create the conditions for their marginalization (Kibler et al., 2021).

CDE has the potential to disrupt harmful hegemonic practices in support of equity and agency for all learners, particularly those from historically minoritized backgrounds. Dialogic learning has typically been defined in contrast to traditional "banking" pedagogies, which position learners as passive recipients of static knowledge (Freire, 1973). In general, these banking pedagogies tend to rely on a formalized curriculum dictated by those in positions of authority, creating little space for questioning the knowledge presented or the nature of knowledge itself (Freire, 1973). By contrast, CDE emphasizes inclusive, supportive, and reciprocal classroom norms (Alexander, 2020; Kibler et al., 2021; Lefstein & Snell, 2014), pushing back on institutional structures that marginalize certain voices or means of conveying ideas (Kibler et al., 2021; Alexander 2015), questioning and critiquing institutional knowledge in the exploration of multiple perspectives (English, 2016; Glick & Walqui, 2021), creating space for dialogic reflection (Glick & Walqui, 2021; Meston et al., 2022), and welcoming and celebrating learners' diverse funds of knowledge, recognizing their potential as rich resources for the deep co-construction of meaning (Kibler et al., 2021; Alexander, 2015). In enacting these values, educators strive to democratize classroom interaction, disrupt harmful educational norms, and support students as agents pursuing social justice.

For SIFE, CDE may have particular benefits. Indeed, this fact impacted our choice to pursue this project in the Southeastern United States, where populations of SIFE are rapidly growing (Gándara & Mordechay, 2017). For educators in these settings—particularly those with limited knowledge of the languages and cultures of students' origin countries—the task of providing CDE may seem particularly formidable (Breiseth, 2020). Educators have often had little formal preparation to recognize and leverage the assets these learners bring to the classroom. Furthermore, because SIFE students are often misdesignated as "remedial" in school systems, educators may be ill-prepared to surface these assets (DeCapua & Marshall, 2011). Unlike other students designated as English Learners, these students often bring educational histories interrupted by conflict (war, forced resettlement, genocide), which may have impacted their access to formal educational settings. Yet, these learners also bring significant assets— whether it be broader perspectives on global issues, insights into the lived realities of war and social strife, bilingual or biliterate skills or, as documented in the literature focused on Latine youth, experience learning in cooperative and collaborative settings—that can be utilized in CDE (Phillips Galloway et al., 2021). These valuable forms of cultural and social capital have not traditionally been valued or acknowledged in school settings, but are in CDE instruction (Gonzalez et al., 2006). CDE offers opportunities for SIFE students to leverage and develop these assets as they learn to engage in "deliberative democracy" (Segal et al., 2017, p. 21), which intentionally surfaces underrepresented voices and perspectives.

Visioning

But how can professional learning support teachers in achieving CDE's lofty goals? One alternative to professional learning prioritizing "best" practices are experiences that support educators' capacity to realize their visions, or the ideals toward which they aspire, coming to fruition at the intersection of lived experiences, personal ideologies, conceptions of pedagogy, passions, and social and cultural factors (Duffy, 2002; Parsons et al., 2014). Educators with strong, contextualized visions of their aspirational teaching as centering student agency, knowledge co-construction, equity, and the interrogation of power dynamics can draw on those visions as resources to support their own agency as thoughtful decision-makers navigating the constraints and affordances of their contexts (Darling-Hammond & Bransford, 2005; Hammerness, 2001; Parsons et al., 2014). Darling-Hammond and colleagues (2005) explain that educators with a clear pedagogical vision "know 'where they are going' and how they and their students are going to get there" (177). Teachers who spend time *visioning*, or engaging in the reflective practice of articulating and refining their vision of aspirational teaching (Duffy, 2002), may feel more empowered to push back on or work around situational constraints that hinder their capacity to enact CDE and other ambitious pedagogies (Vaughn, 2014; Vaughn & Parsons, 2012).

Visioning as a practice supportive of educators' agency is based in social constructivist theories (Scales, 2021; Vygotsky, 1978). Educators engaged in visioning shape and refine their visions to accord with their experiences and contexts, as they synthesize information from personal histories, knowledge, and passions, alongside alternative conceptions of teaching presented via involvement in professional learning communities (Scales, 2021). Here, we focus not on visioning as an independent practice, but rather on visioning as benefitting from the dynamic interactions around practice occurring in professional learning communities. This shifts the locus from a focus on individuals' visions to a focus on how visions are shaped and refined in interaction with others.

It is important to note that certain visions of teaching may reinforce social inequities (as when a teacher's vision centers students only using standardized American English); therefore, professional learning centered on teacher visioning has often focused on helping educators to refine their visions in support of equitable, agency-supportive instruction (e.g., Vaughn & Kuby, 2019). However, traditional vision-centered professional learning has typically been divorced from experiences that focus explicitly on collaboratively addressing problems of practice, as most visioning research has focused primarily on the visions that participants construct individually (e.g., Vaughn & Kuby, 2019). We argue that visioning in combination with collaborative analysis of problems of practice may offer powerful affordances in support of educator agency and pedagogical judgment centering equity, learning, and agency (Horn & Garner, 2022; Little & Horn, 2007; Vedder-Weiss et al., 2018).

Design

This qualitative study of professional learning around CDE took place during the spring of 2022. During that time, a CFG of four SIFE educators and two researchers met four times to collaboratively analyze, reimagine, and reframe problems of practice impeding their enactment of their visions of CDE. The process of designing this CFG was done in consultation with one of the teachers who had previously worked and written with the research team. CDE was proposed as a grounding theoretical framework for the professional learning experience because of its potential to center the agency and linguistic strengths of SIFE alongside their minoritized status and unique needs. SIFE face the formidable task of simultaneously learning the language of instruction, the content being taught, and the norms and practices of schooling in an unfamiliar societal context. By recognizing and leveraging the significant assets these learners bring to dialogic classrooms, educators can promote students' learning and agency (DeCapua & Marshall, 2011; Meston et al., 2022).

Design of the Professional Learning Experience

The CFG's first session focused on introducing CDE's goals and principles. These were presented as general goals and principles that could be applied to all learners, and educators were tasked with connecting these to their specific SIFE-designated learners. Given our limited time, we focused on four principles that we considered particularly foundational to CDE:

1. Students agentively co-construct meaning around authentic and relevant questions with peers and educators (Alexander, 2020; Kibler et al., 2021; Lefstein & Snell, 2014);
2. Respectful, supportive, inclusive, and reciprocal classroom norms support interaction (Alexander, 2020; Kibler et al., 2021; Lefstein & Snell, 2014);
3. Students and teachers consider diverse perspectives in questioning authoritative knowledge (Alexander, 2020; Kibler et al., 2021; Lefstein & Snell, 2014);
4. Students' linguistic resources and experiences, alongside their minoritized status, are viewed as assets and topics for dialogue (Kibler et al., 2021).

Using a Google Jamboard, a form of collaborative virtual whiteboard, participants brainstormed what each of these elements currently looked like in their own classrooms, their vision of these principles enacted within their own classrooms, and challenges that impeded these visions. Following this brainstorming session, educators concluded by engaging in visioning about CDE, responding to the prompt, "What is your vision for Critical Dialogic Education in your classroom? Where are you already achieving that vision? Where do you feel as though you still need to work toward that vision? What challenges do you foresee?"

The remaining sessions were designed to support educators working collaboratively to address problems of practice in pursuit of deep conceptual change (Horn & Garner, 2022). We drew upon a version of the Tuning Protocol provided by the National School Reform Faculty as a means of structuring engagement with problems of practice (for sample protocols, visit https://nsrfharmony.org/protocols/). This protocol is designed such that a presenter's problem of practice—one identified as impeding the realization of their vision of CDE—is the focus of one hour of deep analysis, as participants help the presenter to reconsider constraints, affordances, and the nature of the problem. To ground this experience in the work occurring in classrooms, we included in the problem presentation a short video clip (approximately five minutes) of a moment within the focal educator's classroom that seemed to highlight the problem under discussion. This rich representation created opportunities for participants to draw attention to constraints and affordances that may have gone unnoticed or unquestioned by the presenting educator. To conclude each session, participants were encouraged to refine their visions as needed (see Figure 4.1).

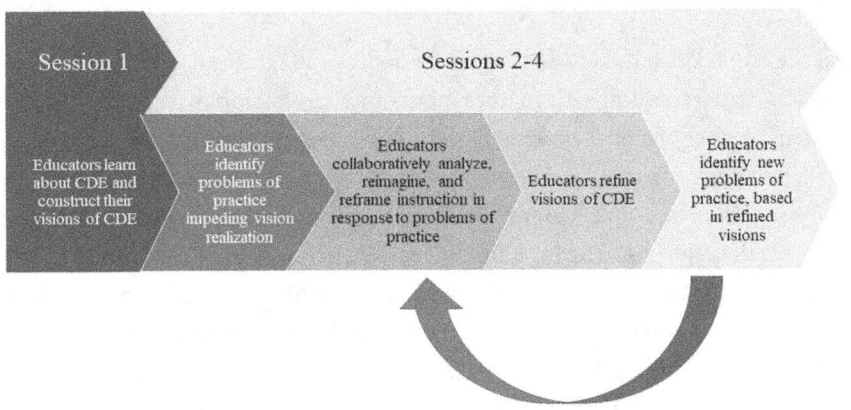

Figure 4.1 CDE and visioning professional development protocol.

Table 4.1 Participating educators

Educator	Grades taught	Subjects taught to SIFE	Total years of experience	Years spent teaching SIFE
Mattie	5–8	Literacy	5	3
Helen	6–8	Science and social studies	3	2
Ryan	9	Physical science and history/citizenship	6	4
Perla	9	English language development 1	10	3

Participants and Context

Participants included four secondary SIFE educators teaching in an urban district in the Southeastern United States (see Table 4.1). Participants were chosen purposively based on their active involvement in a larger study examining learning and agency in classes serving emergent bilinguals. In particular, these participants have demonstrated a commitment to continuous learning, and thus represented a strong cohort for this exploratory work. All participants were already acquainted through prior professional learning experiences that had explored dialogic and other forms of ambitious teaching. All CFG meetings took place via Zoom.

Data Collection and Analysis

Data were collected between April and May 2022. Data sources included artifacts and recordings from four-hour-long professional learning sessions, written teacher visions as articulated at the beginning and the end of the CFG, and semi-structured interviews conducted following the experience and centering reflection on specific critical moments impacting educators' learning. Each participant engaged in a single semi-structured interview wherein they were asked to reflect on their specific learnings within the CFG and to discuss the moments that they perceived as facilitating those learnings. These interviews were limited to thirty-five minutes or less out of respect for educators' time. Educators' written visions informed our understanding of changes experienced in pedagogical ideals over time; recordings from CFG sessions offered insight into moments catalyzing those changes, providing a more comprehensive view of how visions are co-constructed and negotiated in teacher-led professional learning; and interviews created spaces for participants to expand on important moments in the CFG.

Data were analyzed in two phases—an inductive and a deductive one. Initially, the first author open coded initial and final visions, focusing on what participants centered as important elements of visions and how those visions changed over time. The first author used a structured practice of memoing following coding of initial and final visions, focusing primarily on documenting changes between the two visions, as well as noting similarities and differences in the changing visions of different participants. The axial phase of coding entailed creating themes across these visions (Charmaz, 2014), with the end goal of discovering how participants' visions changed across the professional learning series. Five overarching themes emerged from this analysis. Participants' visions for CDE in their classrooms centered:

1. A learning ecology emphasizing respect and emotional safety;
2. Student agency in accessing and creating learning experiences;
3. Content, language, and literacy learning experiences that are simultaneously rigorous and accessible;
4. Educator and student critical stances emphasizing linguistic equity and questioning of authoritative knowledge;
5. Relevance in drawing on students' funds of knowledge and preparing for their futures.

As discussed in the findings section below, themes one, two, and three were primarily present in both initial and final visions, while themes four and five were primarily present only in participants' final visions.

Following this inductive coding, these thematic codes were applied deductively to transcripts of the CFG meetings and interviews (excluding Helen's, due to a technical difficulty), focusing on episodes in which participants were identifying or negotiating meaning around their affordances, constraints, instruction, problems of practice, or visions. The goal of this analysis was to understand which aspects of the CFGs contributed to those conceptual changes; therefore, although this analysis focused on applying codes created from the visions themselves, the first author remained open to other moments of meaning negotiation that might need new codes—for example, "Clarity in interactions with students" appeared repeatedly during CFGs as integral to visions of CDE, despite not being present in written visions. We attempted in our coding to explore instances where participants reframed or reimagined their affordances, constraints, problems of practice, or visions, exploring how the educators in this study afforded each other new conceptions of what equitable, ambitious teaching looks like in the SIFE classroom.

Following both phases of analysis, the second author then reapplied constructed categories across approximately 20 percent of the data set. Inter-rater overlap was calculated at 87 percent across codes. To further increase the trustworthiness of the findings and ensure accurate representation of participants' unique realities, the authors then engaged with member checking with the four participating teachers, by allowing each to read and comment on this paper. All members affirmed the interpretations included herein.

Positionality

We come to this work with perspectives informed by our experiences and identities. We are both White, primarily English-speaking education researchers and former middle school educators. This limits our understanding of what it means to navigate systems of linguistic and cultural hierarchy that may stymie the agency of SIFE. However, we have both researched and taught SIFE populations and share a commitment to supporting students as agentive learners and collaborators working toward more a just world. In particular, our experiences working toward social justice in linguistically restrictive systems shaped our decision to center visioning as a lens and anchor for our collaborative work with teachers; having both experienced the power of visions to support ambitious teaching in the face of constraints, we believed that visions might play a role in sustaining commitments to the principles of CDE.

Findings

In seeking to answer, *How does collaborative exploration of problems of practice impact educators' visions of Critical Dialogic Education?*, we first explore changes that occurred in participants' visions over the course of eight weeks and then move into discussing how those changes may have occurred.

How Participants' Visions Changed

The most significant change that we noticed across all participants' visions was an expansion: While all participants' original and final visions emphasized safe and respectful learning ecologies (theme 1), student agency in accessing and creating learning experiences (theme 2), and simultaneously rigorous and accessible content, language, and literacy learning experiences (theme 3), only participants' final visions emphasized these elements of dialogic meaning negotiation *as a means of supporting linguistic and other forms of equity (theme 4), creating opportunities for students to use their funds of knowledge as valuable resources for learning (theme 5),* and *providing students' opportunities to question and impact the world in support of social justice (theme 5)*. To demonstrate these changes in depth, we zoom in on two participants' visions: Perla's and Mattie's. These two participants were chosen because of the richness of their visions and the range of foci they represent—both Mattie's and Perla's initial visions centered the first three themes listed in Table 4.2, but Mattie's final vision particularly changed in its emphasis on students and teachers embodying critical stances (theme 4), while Perla's final vision had a greater emphasis on relevance in drawing on students' funds of knowledge and preparing for their futures (theme 5).

The primary difference between Perla's initial and final visions was a new focus on students valuing themselves and recognizing the value of their funds of knowledge. Her initial vision focused heavily on elements of dialogic education, but only mentioned students' funds of knowledge once ("using prior knowledge"), while her new vision emphasized "elevating the students as the expert in the room," so that students "see themselves as a valued wealth of information and background knowledge." Perla explained that these changes stemmed from discussions occurring during her opportunity to serve as a presenting educator:

> I was really impacted by some of the comments relative to having the students tap into their funds of knowledge about what they could have done personally in the story ... And so, I have just been thinking a lot about that and just thinking about my own evolution as a person and trying to value people in general for coming to the table in any situation with value and with wealth of life experience and whatever they have. I just think being a teenager is hard, being an immigrant is so difficult, being an unaccompanied minor with really no parent ... I think those things are really hard and I think it's easy to feel like you're not enough, you don't know the culture, like all of this deficit thinking for yourself. And so, I just really want to focus on paying attention to expressing how valuable each student is in a real personal way.
>
> (Interview, June 7, 2022)

Opportunities to critically examine her own teaching practices supported Perla's understanding of the resources her students had and the challenges they faced,

Table 4.2 Mattie's visions*

My vision for CDE ... is that visitors feel that they are observing a dinner table or perhaps even an academic roundtable rather than a discussion moderated by the teacher. In an idealized world, IRE [Initiate-Response-Evaluate] is nonexistant as students are the ones primarily generating the questions and then offering feedback on those same questions as they negotiate meaning-making with their peers. All voices, regardless of class or home language or ELP [English Language Proficiency], are valued equally and hold the floor with equal amount of time. Respect is not so much demanded as ingrained in the daily activities of what students are doing. *Students and the teacher are positioned on equal footing during the discussion, so students are empowered to embody a critical stance by questioning their own ideas/assumptions, the ideas of others, and even the statements of the teacher. The critical stance extends to awareness of language learning as students discuss the ways in which language has power and can be used to impact our world.*
Currently, students have expectations for respect. We decided on these norms for respect by participating in a desmos [an interactive educational technology site] at the beginning of the year and actually co-creating a rubric for speaking together as students and teachers. *When students interact with each other by employing these norms, they receive points on the school-wide behavior system, but I would like to move towards intrinsic motivation where students recognize that they are collectively contributing the betterment of the group by sharing their ideas and engaging with one another using respectful norms. I am still working to achieve this vision- students feel comfortable with me but not always with each other which limits their interactions with others who are perceived as different- especially those students who have rather significant differences in gender, culture, language, etc. As a result, students tend to rely on me as the teacher to facilitate conversations with their peers. I am working to balance cultural relevance with cultural competence- I am still not sure how much I should be pushing students in terms of navigating conversational norms that are counter-cultural in their homeland but essential to holding one's own in the US.*

*Additions present in final vision denoted by italics.

causing her to reconsider what meaningful dialogic interactions might look like in her room.

Mattie's vision from the beginning to the end changed in significant ways (see Table 4.2). Like Perla's, her vision originally focused primarily on the dialogic elements of CDE, emphasizing collaborative meaning-making, respectful interactions, and student questioning. Mattie's final vision included all these elements, alongside an emphasis on students "embody[ing] a critical stance by questioning their own ideas/assumptions, the ideas of others, and even the statements of the teacher," as well as discussing "the ways in which language has power and can be used to impact our world." She further questioned her own role as a teacher enacting CDE, contemplating what it means to balance cultural relevance with cultural competence.

In sum, participants' visions moved over the course of the CFG from emphasizing primarily dialogic elements of CDE, such as creating an emotionally safe space for discourse, promoting student agency, and designing rigorous and accessible learning experiences, to integrating these dialogic elements with more critical ones, such as cultivating critical stances and leveraging students' funds of knowledge as valuable assets. In the next section, we discuss how these changes occurred.

How Did These Changes Occur?

Throughout the final three meetings of the series, presenters identified three problems of practice impeding realization of their visions:

1. Mattie wished to explore how she might engage students in actively collaborating and dialoguing with each other, rather than relying on her as a mediator;
2. Perla wished to explore how she might support students' investment and active engagement in the learning of the classroom;
3. and Helen wished to explore how to achieve language equity in a class characterized by a single language majority and several linguistic minorities.

Because of time constraints, Ryan did not have an opportunity to serve as a focal educator.

As teachers collaborated to analyze, explore, and reimagine problems of practice in relation to their visions of CDE, they engaged in two primary strategies that seemed particularly impactful in moving them toward visions that reflected deep commitments to equity, responsiveness, and cultural, linguistic, and experiential relevance. To some extent, these strategies reflect the nature of the protocol, which centers questioning teachers' goals, practices, affordances, and constraints, and providing feedback on perceived strengths and areas for improvement. However, adding in teachers' visions of CDE as an anchor for these discussions created explicit opportunities to place in contrast and trace connections between overarching (rather than lesson-level) goals and pedagogical and interactional practices. These strategies are discussed below.

Using Targeted Questioning to Help Presenting Educators Identify Disconnects between Their Current Instructional Practices and Their Visions of Equity- and Agency-Supportive Pedagogy.

Throughout the professional learning series, educators drew on two particular types of questions: clarifying questions, designed to provide a clearer picture of instruction, classroom culture, and students, and probing questions, designed to engage the presenter in defining, reframing, or reimagining important elements of their instruction, interactions, and visions. Probing questions might, for example, ask a focal educator to consider what their goals are for a specific activity and how those goals fit into their larger aims as a teacher. Oftentimes, probing questions served as means of highlighting disconnects between teachers' stated visions of CDE as equity- and agency-supportive and their instructional practices. For example, below we see Ryan asking Perla to define how much of her classroom instruction consists of "teacher talk" (this excerpt has been shortened for space reasons):

> Ryan: What would you say the percentage of teacher talk versus student talk was … ? Reason why I asked that, is that … going from your vision, you were talking about really trying to push that student voice … so just reflecting on this one lesson in particular, what would you say the percentage of the lesson was the directions and reclarifications compared to the students actually talking and responding?
> Perla: … My vision of course is they're doing the talking, holding the learning, but I spend a lot of time teacher talking. I'd say a fat 60%, maybe more, you know.
> Ryan: What could have been a way that you could have reduced that 60-70% to just an even 50-50?
> Perla: Maybe … you know, thinking about slowing down the instructions—So if I said "Okay, we're going to look at the 'who' and then we do kind of a 'we do,' which is to tell each other what what's happening in this slide. And then we go to the next slide and maybe someone can tell me, you know it's kind of now the 'we do,' but I'm releasing it a little bit, now you tell me what this instructional slide is. Now you all tell each other what that slide is. So, when they speak the instructions, not only is that elevating their English, but then they're owning it, because then they suddenly they know what to do, right? If I'm always doing the talking, they're like, so what?"

Here, we see Ryan's targeted questioning making clear to Perla a disconnect between her instruction and her vision of equity- and agency-supportive pedagogy: Perla's vision of a classroom filled with student talk and ownership over learning was impeded by her own speech.

In other instances, participants used questioning to engage presenters in critically considering linguistic, cultural, or ideological barriers impeding the realization of their visions. For example, Helen, in response to Mattie's concern that students were speaking only to her rather than to each other, asked:

I'm wondering how much of how much of their reliance on a teacher could stem culturally? ... What needs to be explicitly taught of, like, 'In the United States, some teachers might not know the answer, some teachers want you to tell me what you think. I'm not going to respond.' I'm wondering like how much of this was their cultural background?

In responding to Helen's question, Mattie reflected that she had never before considered the role that cultural expectations of authority and questioning might play in her classroom interactions and considered how she might explicitly teach these expectations to broaden their access to US discourse norms while simultaneously respecting their cultures. This represents a particularly important learning for educators working with SIFE, whose limited experience in formal schools means they are often not privy to the "hidden curriculum" of these settings (Giroux & Penna, 1979). By making explicit these hidden norms, educators facilitate students' access to learning across their school experiences. And by respecting students' cultural norms, educators create emotionally safe spaces wherein SIFE can begin the vulnerable work of navigating flexibly between cultural norms.

Making Explicit Connections between Student Agency and Relevance to Students' Current Funds of Knowledge and Their Future Roles as Citizens and Agents of Social Change.

Although all participants stressed student agency as knowledge co-constructors in both initial and final visions, only in final visions was this vision of agency deeply entwined with recognition of the expertise learners bring from past experiences, alongside acknowledgment that developing agency prepares students for futures as empowered citizens and change agents. This topic was frequently discussed during the CFGs, as when Mattie struggled to engage students in speaking to each other during text-based discussions. The following interactions took place over the course of the CFG, as participants co-constructed and reimagined how uplifting students' funds of knowledge might be integral to developing their agency:

Heather: Is there any sort of connection between the types of questions ... and their willingness to speak to each other?
Mattie: Yes, a lot of times when there's connection-type questions, they're more willing to speak to each other, particularly because I think I am just useless to them in most of those things– like I don't know the slang, I don't know a lot about different things in their cultures, and so those things they have to really rely on each other to kind of negotiate a meaning ... I think bringing in that literacy element in English is a showstopper and not great.

Heather: I was thinking about where you're talking about connection questions, where it's like you can't offer anything. I wonder if there's a way you can leverage that in terms of texts? Can you find texts about things that only they know about? Where you can come in and be like, "Hey I have no idea about this topic, I have not lived this topic"? Maybe it's what it means to be a SIFE learner, if there's a text about that. But these things where you're like ... "You guys are the experts in this."

Perla: I want to bounce off of that text they know about, and even something, you know, as kind of like an entry questionnaire and what are you good at?–And then maybe you could possibly find something that one or a couple of them know about, and it could be a short, could be a paragraph or something, and maybe as a bell ringer ... Just to begin to honor them as the expert in the room.

In these interactions, we see participants reframing meaningful literacy activities as those that position learners as experts capable of agentively creating meaning by intertwining their funds of knowledge, their passions, and knowledge gleaned from texts. This is particularly important for SIFE, whose funds of knowledge are often undervalued and underutilized in school settings (Gonzalez et al., 2006). In other instances, participants considered how these discussions prepare students for futures where they use their voices to contest inequity and injustice, as when Helen suggested to Perla that she consider what students are willing to fight for as potential cornerstones of her curriculum. Across the CFG, targeted questioning to identify disconnects between visions and practice, alongside a particular focus on agency through the lens of funds of knowledge, led to changes in educators' visions. These changes emphasized classrooms as not only dialogic spaces, but critical dialogic spaces designed to empower students to question authoritative knowledge and use their funds of knowledge to serve as change agents.

Discussion

Perhaps the most important learning from this study is that visioning alongside collaborative exploration of problems of practice can have a powerful impact on SIFE educators' focus on linguistic and cultural responsiveness, student agency, and equity. From the end of the first session to the end of the fourth session (an eight-week gap), participating educators' visions universally showed immense growth in their focus on these elements. Teachers' final visions emphasized the resources students bring to the class's learning, raised questions regarding the challenges of balancing cultural and linguistic responsiveness with cultural and linguistic relevance, and highlighted opportunities to support students to impact the wider world around them. These learnings may be of particular relevance for SIFE educators, given the deficit beliefs that so many educators hold regarding SIFE, as well as the challenges SIFE face in navigating the hidden curriculum of schools.

We can presume that these changes were not due to the direct instruction provided during the first session, as participants wrote their original visions immediately *following* this direct instruction; therefore, we emphasize that the key work underpinning this change seemed to be in the interaction of visioning with collaborative exploration of problems of practice.

Indeed, while visioning is sometimes viewed as an individual practice, here, we see how educators in community were able to move the visions of their colleagues, pushing on the outer edges of their ideas about equity in ways that session one's direct instruction in CDE's principles did not. Perhaps it was the need to make visible their visions to colleagues, to put language to and contextualize the abstract phenomenon of CDE. This positions equity work as involving learning "the talk" in dialogic interaction with peers as part of the broader phenomenon of "walking the walk" in classrooms. For some teachers, this may have involved simply naming practices already animating their classroom community. For others, this naming of aspects of interaction that promote CDE may have pushed them to try new practices that had been introduced by peers. Because we were unable to collect classroom observational data, we cannot say with any certainty how these refined, equity-focused visions translated into instructional practice. However, we argue that it is likely difficult, if not impossible, to create a culturally and linguistically responsive classroom without an awareness and vision of what that might look like—that, given the enormous systemic and institutional barriers opposing the realization of such a classroom, particularly for SIFE educators, teachers with an end goal in mind are significantly more likely to achieve that goal than those who are moving blindly.

Our focus was on in-service educators but the work of visioning may also benefit pre-service educators, particularly those participating in practicum experiences. Like the teachers in this study, pre-service educators are often placed at different school sites and faced with creating equitable discussions. We propose that articulating visions, which are constantly subject to revision and refinement, might be a helpful touchstone for participants in education programs that aim to foster a habit of reflection. We can also imagine that working with these teachers to refine visions in communities over time, especially as they enter into their own classrooms post-graduation, may be a particularly generative activity for nurturing their capacity to foster equitable talk in classrooms.

Of course, this represents a small study with one group of educators—and, notably, a group of educators who were already thoughtful practitioners working to engage students in the negotiation of meaning in their classes—working across a relatively short period of time. Other groups of teachers, such as those with less experience with dialogic teaching, may prioritize different visions of CDE or discover alternative means of refining those visions within collaborative learning experiences. Further studies might consider expanding this work, to see what visioning in combination with collaborative exploration of problems of practice affords for more heterogeneous groups of practitioners or pre-service educators.

In conclusion, this work revealed that collaborative exploration of problems of practice enabled educators to notice elements of their practice that failed to align with their visions of CDE in their classrooms, and that exploring problems of practice through the lens of these visions resulted over time in refined, more equity-focused visions.

References

Adair, J. K. (2014). Agency and expanding capabilities in early grade classrooms: What it could mean for young children. *Harvard Educational Review, 84*(2), 217–41. https://doi.org/10.17763/haer.84.2.y46vh546h4l12144

Alexander, R. (2020). *A dialogic teaching companion*. Routledge.

Alexander R. J. (2015). Dialogic pedagogy at scale: Oblique perspectives. In L. Resnick, C. Asterhan, & S. Clarke (Eds.), *Socialising intelligence through academic talk and dialogue* (pp. 413–23). American Educational Research Association.

Aukerman, M., & Chambers Schuldt, L. (2017). Bucking the authoritative script of a mandated curriculum. *Curriculum Inquiry, 47*(4), 411–37. https://doi.org/10.1080/03626784.2017.1368353

Breiseth, L. (2020). More than a warm welcome: Supporting immigrant students in Dearborn, Michigan. *American Educator, 44*(1), 4.

Charmaz, K. (2014). *Constructing grounded theory*. Sage.

Cochran-Smith, M. (2001). The outcomes question in teacher education. *Teaching and Teacher Education, 17*(5), 527–46. https://doi.org/10.1016/s0742-051x(01)00012-9

Darling-Hammond, L., & Bransford, J. (Eds.). (2005). *Preparing teachers for a changing world: What teachers should learn and be able to do*. Jossey-Bass.

DeCapua, A., & Marshall, H. W. (2011). Reaching ells at risk: Instruction for students with limited or interrupted formal education. *Preventing School Failure: Alternative Education for Children and Youth, 55*(1), 35–41.

DeCapua, A., & Marshall, H. W. (2015). Reframing the conversation about students with limited or interrupted formal education. *NASSP Bulletin, 99*(4), 356–70. https://doi.org/10.1177/0192636515620662

Duffy, G. G. (2005). Developing metacognitive teachers: Visioning and the expert's changing role in teacher education and professional development. In S. E. Israel (Ed.), *Metacognition in literacy learning: Theory, assessment, instruction, and professional development* (pp. 299–314). Lawrence Erlbaum Associates.

Duffy, G. G. (2002). Visioning and the development of outstanding teachers. *Reading Research and Instruction, 41*(4), 331–43. https://doi.org/10.1080/19388070209558375

English, A. R. (2016). Dialogic teaching and moral learning: Self-critique, narrativity, community and "blind spots." *Journal of Philosophy of Education, 50*, 160–76. https://doi.org/10.1111/1467.9752.12198

Freire, P. (1973). *Education for critical consciousness.* Continuum.

Galloway, E. P., Hsin, L. B., Jensen, B., LaRusso, M. D., Hong, M. K., & Mankowski, K. (2021). Examining the role of learner and classroom characteristics in the later language learning of Latinx Youth and their classmates. *Journal of Applied Developmental Psychology, 77*, 101353. https://doi.org/10.1016/j.appdev.2021.101353

Gándara, P., & Mordechay, K. (2017). Demographic change and the new (and not so new) challenges for Latino education. *The Educational Forum, 81*(2), 148–59.

Giroux, H. A., & Penna, A. N. (1979). Social Education in the classroom: The dynamics of the hidden curriculum. *Theory & Research in Social Education, 7*(1), 21–42.

Glick, Y., & Walqui, A. (2021). Affordances in the development of student voice and agency: The case of bureaucratically labeled long-term English learners. In A. Kibler, G. Valdés, & A. Walqui (Eds.), *Reconceptualizing the role of critical dialogue in American classrooms: Promoting equity through dialogic education* (pp. 23–51). Routledge.

González, N., Moll, L. C., & Amanti, C. (2006). *Funds of knowledge: Theorizing practices in households, communities, and classrooms.* Routledge.

Hammerness, K. (2001). Teachers' visions: The role of personal ideals in school reform. *Journal of Educational Change, 2*, 143–63. https://doi.org/10.1023/A:1017961615264

Horn, I., & Garner, B. (2022). *Teacher learning of ambitious and equitable mathematics instruction: A sociocultural approach.* Routledge.

Karam, F. J. (2021). Re-envisioning the ESOL classroom through a virtues-based curriculum: Contributions to critical dialogic education. *TESOL Journal, 12*(3), e582. https://doi.org/10.1002/tesj.582

Kibler, A. K., Valdés, G., & Walqui, A. (Eds.). (2021). *Reconceptualizing the role of critical dialogue in American classrooms: Promoting equity through dialogic education.* Routledge.

Lefstein, A., & Snell, J. (2014). *Better Than best practice: Developing teaching and learning through dialogue.* Routledge.

Lefstein, A., Pollak, I., & Segal, A. (2020). Compelling student voice: Dialogic practices of public confession. *Discourse: Studies in the cultural politics of education, 41*(1), 110–23.

Little, J. W., & Horn, I. S. (2007). "Normalizing" problems of practice: Converting routine conversation into a resource for learning in professional communities. In L. Stoll & K. S. Louis (Eds.), *Professional learning communities: Divergence, detail and difficulties* (pp. 79–92). Open University Press.

Meston, H. M., Phillips Galloway, E., & Barrack, K. A. (2022). Co-constructing agency: Weaving academic discussion. *The Reading Teacher, 76*(1), 23–33. https://doi.org/10.1002/trtr.2111

Parsons, S. A., Malloy, J. A., Vaughn, M., & La Croix, L. (2014). A longitudinal study of literacy teacher visioning: Traditional program graduates and Teach For America corps members. *Literacy Research and Instruction, 53*(2), 134–61. https://doi.org/10.1080/19388071.2013.868561

Scales, R. Q. (2021). A cross section of teacher visioning. *Peabody Journal of Education, 96*(4), 423–35. https://doi.org/10.1080/0161956x.2021.1965415

Segal, A., Pollak, I., & Lefstein, A. (2017). Democracy, voice and dialogic pedagogy: The struggle to be heard and heeded. *Language and Education, 31*(1), 6–25. https://doi.org/10.1080/09500782.2016.1230124

Snell, J., & Lefstein, A. (2018). "Low ability," participation, and identity in dialogic pedagogy. *American Educational Research Journal, 55*(1), 40–78. https://doi.org/10.3102/0002831217730010

Vaughn, M. (2014). Aligning visions: Striking a balance between personal convictions for teaching and instructional goals. *The Educational Forum, 78*(3), 305–13. https://doi.org/10.1080/00131725.2014.912369

Vaughn, M., & Kuby, C. R. (2019). Fostering critical, relational visionaries: Autoethnographic practices in teacher preparation. *Action in Teacher Education, 41*(2), 117–36.

Vaughn, M., & Parsons, S. (2012). Visions, enactments, obstacles, and negotiations: case studies of two novice teachers enrolled in a graduate literacy course. *Journal of Reading Education, 38*(1), 18–25.

Vaughn, M., Wall, A., Scales, R. Q., Parsons, S. A., & Sotirovska, V. (2021). Teacher Visioning: A systematic review of the literature. *Teaching and Teacher Education, 108*, 103–502. https://doi.org/10.1016/j.tate.2021.103502

Vedder-Weiss, D., Ehrenfeld, N., Ram-Menashe, M., & Pollak, I. (2018). Productive framing of pedagogical failure: How teacher framings can facilitate or impede learning from problems of practice. *Thinking Skills and Creativity, 30*, 31–41. https://doi.org/10.1016/j.tsc.2018.01.002

Vygotsky, L. S. (1978). Socio-cultural theory. *Mind in society, 6*(3), 23–43.

5

Critical Reflections on Dialogic Education and Practice: A Duoethnographic Approach by Teacher Educators

Naashia Mohamed, Christine Biebricher, and Rosemary Erlam

Introduction

Teaching can be antidialogical, framing students without agency and as empty vessels that need to be filled. Such an approach does not engage students in the true liberatory purposes of education, as it is unauthentic, culturally disconnected, and oppressive (Freire, 1970). This "misguided system" (Freire, 1970, p. 72) does not provide space to actively engage in processing, adapting, or creating knowledge as it establishes a hierarchy that promotes educational inequity (Kohli et al., 2015), obscures the struggles of marginalized communities, and invisibilizes injustice (Philip et al., 2018). What is required, Freire (1970) argues, is a model of dialogic, problem-posing education where both teachers and students work together in a process of reflection, action, and knowledge creation that allows for liberatory transformation.

Critical Dialogic Education (CDE) centers the importance of classroom talk that is co-constructed, purposeful, respectful, and responsive to context, and aims to dismantle inequitable power dynamics and their effects on minoritized students through questioning ongoing practices and examining underlying biases that influence educational practice (Kibler et al., 2021). As schools and communities continue to become increasingly diverse, it has become more important for educators to self-examine their beliefs and biases, and develop critical consciousness of the systems of power and privilege in education. Like other settler countries, New Zealand has experienced increased linguistic, ethnic, and cultural diversity, particularly over the last few decades. This has reinforced the need to facilitate a cohesive society and underscored the crucial role that schools and teachers play in fostering social harmony. In this chapter, we adopt a duoethnographic approach to present how we, as teacher educators, use reflective, critical, and dialogic practices in the context of TESOL teacher education programs for practicing teachers in New Zealand.

While there is a growing body of research that explores critical pedagogies through a justice-oriented lens (e.g., Ennser-Kananen, 2016; Flores, Tseng & Subtirelu, 2021; Paris & Alim, 2017; Von Esch, Motha & Kubota, 2020), there is a paucity of studies on the experiences of teacher educators who agentively address inequities by incorporating a focus on developing teachers' critical consciousness. In this chapter, we present a duoethnography where we aim to navigate our professional experiences as TESOL teacher educators in New Zealand who use critical dialogic approaches for socially just teacher education. In duoethnography, two or more co-researchers collaborate, engage in direct dialogue, and share and explore differences and understandings around a predetermined subject (Garcia & Cifor, 2019; Norris & Sawyer, 2012). Through an exploration of our narrative reflections, we aim to show what motivates us to utilize critical and dialogic approaches in teacher education, and how we empower our students to be agentic and participatory contributors to classroom negotiations. We begin by briefly addressing "the dialogic turn" in education (Racionero & Padrós, 2010) and its role in encouraging greater criticality and challenging inequity. Second, we describe our positionalities and our teaching context to help situate the study. Next, we outline our approach to duoethnography, before describing how we engage in CDE. Finally, we discuss our challenges in practicing CDE, and offer implications on the benefits of engaging in duoethnography to collectively understand the educational reality and professional lives of teacher educators.

Dialogic Practices and Critical Pedagogy

The importance of culture, intersubjectivity, and dialogue has long been recognized as being crucial for learning and development (Bruner, 1996; Lee, 2016; Vygotsky, 1978). Centering dialogue in the classroom creates more opportunities for development in language and communication (van der Veen et al., 2017), in critical thinking (Teo, 2019), and transforms classroom relationships (Mercer & Howe, 2012), improves academic achievement (Mercer et al., 1999), and empowers students to become agents of social change (García-Carrión & Díez-Palomar, 2015). Going beyond the traditional view of dialogic approaches to education, where learning is seen as a joint co-construction of knowledge, Kibler, Valdés, and Walqui (2021) introduced CDE to call for the addition of an explicit moral dimension to classroom pedagogy. They highlight the need to raise critical awareness of power structures, inequities, and discriminatory practices that challenge learners from marginalized backgrounds by redefining teaching and learning on four fronts: the curriculum, language pedagogies, the roles of students, and the roles of teachers. Our study focuses primarily on the role of teachers by reflecting on how our lived experiences inform our practice.

In keeping with duoethnography, and with the aim of helping readers contextualize our stories, we now share some brief descriptions of ourselves and how we came to teach on the two programs that are the focus of this study.

Who We Are

Growing up in the Maldives, Naashia developed a passion for languages, learning English alongside Dhivehi as her primary languages, while gaining varying degrees of competence in languages such as Hindi, Arabic, and Sinhalese. Naashia was educated in English-medium schools in the Maldives and Sri Lanka. Despite exposure to other cultures from a young age, it was not until she lived in the UK to complete her undergraduate degree that Naashia became aware of how her race, language and religion marked her as different, describing this as a time when her "racial consciousness" was awakened. After teaching English at her former school in the Maldives, Naashia embarked on a Masters and a Ph.D at the University of Auckland. On completion, she returned to the Maldives to take up a position as head of the Professional Development Division at the Ministry of Education where she helped make professional learning more accessible for teachers in the Maldives. She subsequently led a national curriculum reform project, working with a range of stakeholders to create a curriculum that explores the skills and competencies needed for children to thrive in the twenty-first century. Several years later, Naashia was invited to contribute to the development of the first postgraduate program, a master's in Dhivehi Language and Culture aimed at teachers of Dhivehi, to be offered at the country's first and newly established University. This teaching role honed her interests in sociolinguistics, bilingual education, and social justice. Some years later, she returned to Auckland, New Zealand, when she was appointed as lecturer in TESOL at the Faculty of Education and Social Work.

Christine grew up in Germany and trained as a secondary school teacher of English, German, and Religious Education. She describes herself as always having been passionate about English. She also has expertise in French and Spanish. After a Masters in twentieth-century literature in the UK, Christine taught adolescents, where at times she felt she needed skills as a social worker, as well as those of a language teacher. Keen to have an intellectual challenge, Christine subsequently embarked on a Ph.D in English which also involved teaching at the University of Education Ludwigsburg. Her Ph.D completed, Christine obtained a position in Applied Language Studies at the University of Auckland, thus taking the big leap of moving to the other side of the world with her two daughters. Here she was responsible for designing and teaching a suite of undergraduate language teaching courses, developed primarily but not exclusively for cohorts of Malaysian teacher trainees. Christine learnt to adapt to the mixed cultural backgrounds of the students in her classes, and later, in another role as Program Director of International Languages Exchanges and Pathways (ILEP), she broadened her horizon when she worked with colleagues from a range of cultural and linguistic backgrounds and she was put into direct contact with New Zealand language teachers. Appointed as lecturer to the Faculty of Education and Social Work, Christine set up the Bachelor of Education in TESOL program, designed to allow both domestic and international students to gain expertise in English language teaching.

Rosemary is New Zealand-born, with grandparents and great-great-grandparents who emigrated from the UK. She attended school, and then University, in Auckland during the 1970s and 1980s. Her interest in languages grew from her experience of learning French and Latin at secondary school. She subsequently spent time in France, as an English language assistant and lectrice, and then in the UK where she taught French. On completion of her Ph.D at the University of Auckland, she was appointed to a position as lecturer in Applied Language Studies and Linguistics. In 2017, she took up a position in the Faculty of Education and Social Work, and subsequently took over program leadership of the Graduate Diploma in Teaching English in Schools to Speakers of Other Languages (GradDip TESSOL). In 2020, Rosemary was successful in getting approval to set up the new Postgraduate Certificate/Diploma in Teaching

Linguistically Diverse Learners (PGCert/Dip TLDL) program. Rosemary particularly enjoys the challenge of making second-language acquisition theory relevant to teachers and of witnessing how their new understanding and learning impacts on practice.

The New Zealand Context

New Zealand was first settled by Māori who migrated from Polynesia in the fourteenth century and subsequently by the British who started to arrive in significant numbers around the beginning of the nineteenth century. The signing of *Te Tiriti o Waitangi* (Treaty of Waitangi) in 1840, an agreement between the British crown and key Māori leaders, is considered New Zealand's founding document. It was followed, unfortunately, by a period in which there was a general aim to assimilate all non-British groups into the dominant culture, and where English became the dominant language.

However, over time New Zealand society has become increasingly culturally and linguistically diverse, accompanied by significant changes in attitudes toward all languages and cultures. The 1960s saw significant migration from the Pacific islands, encouraged by the government, due to high demand for labor. A watershed moment was the Māori language Act of 1987 which accorded te

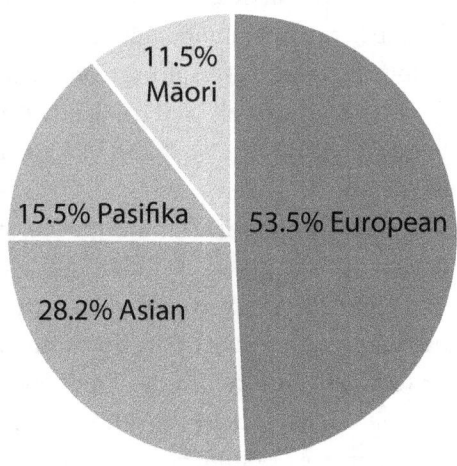

Figure 5.1 Population breakdown of Auckland from 2018 census data.

reo Māori official language status and saw the establishment of educational contexts where students could receive education in te reo Māori. At the same time, changes in immigration policy, which had hitherto privileged British immigrants, meant that country of origin no longer applied as a selection criterion. This led to significant Asian immigration and increasing "polyethnic diversity" (Smits, 2011, p. 99).

New Zealand has a population of 4.7 million (2018 census), with its biggest city, Auckland (around 1.6 million people), representing 33.4 percent of the total population. Auckland is considered "superdiverse" in that it is home to people from over 100 ethnicities who speak over 150 languages. According to the 2018 census (RIMU 2019) over 46 percent of Aucklanders identify as "other than European" (see Figure 5.1) compared to 30 percent of the remainder of New Zealand.

The Educational Context

This growing social diversity means there are increasing numbers of children at school (primary, intermediate, secondary) for whom English is the language of instruction, but not a first language. This is particularly true of Auckland, the context for the present paper.

The Ministry of Education (MOE) has responded to the challenge of meeting the educational needs of students from diverse linguistic and cultural groups in a number of ways. The 1993 curriculum acknowledged "awareness of the bicultural identity of NZ society and its multicultural composition" (MOE, 1993, p. 27) and emphasized the importance of ensuring that the "experiences, cultural traditions, histories and languages of all New Zealanders are recognized and valued" (Ministry of Education, 1993, p. 7). It also made a strong commitment to first language maintenance.

The 2007 curriculum also emphasized the importance of first language and culture, and inclusivity, but gave greater significance to the place of language in the curriculum for the learning of all students (Gray, 2012) stating that: "each learning area has its own language and languages" (MOE, 2007, p. 16). In order to access curriculum content, new learners of English needed assistance with the language that was typical of each disciplinary area, including "explicit and extensive teaching of English vocabulary, word forms, sentences, and text structures and language uses" (Ministry of Education, 2007, p. 16).

At a practical level, the MOE provides funding for students recognized as needing English language support, the demand for which has increased by about 10 percent every year. Another MOE initiative is to provide scholarships for teachers from all curriculum areas to complete qualifications that equip them to teach these learners. Scholarships are offered yearly to New Zealand registered teachers with at least two years of experience in state-funded school or early childhood education contexts. The University of Auckland is one of five providers and their programs, described below, form the context for the present study.

The GradDip TESSOL and the PGCert/Dip in TLDL

The GradDip TESSOL originated from the 1993 Diploma in TESSOL which was upgraded to Graduate Diploma status in 2003. In 2020, approval was granted for the GradDip TESSOL to be replaced by the PG Dip TLDL. During a period of transition, both programs were concurrently taught and the current study reports on the experiences of the authors during their involvement in both. The core focus of both programs was essentially the same, that of upskilling teachers in all curriculum areas so that they could empower English learners in their classrooms to achieve to their full potential. Because many teachers on these programs are mainstream teachers of maths, science, or other curriculum areas, and do not see themselves, therefore, as "English teachers" the decision was made, in designing the new program, to move away from the TESSOL terminology to that of *Teaching Linguistically Diverse Learners*. The name change was intended to emphasize an assets-based approach to teaching bilingual/multilingual learners, acknowledging their cultural and linguistic capital, funds of knowledge, and diverse languaging practices, rather than portraying students as lacking proficiency in English.

Methodology

We chose duoethnography as our methodological approach for this study, as its dialogic focus was suited to reflection on our dialogic practice as teacher educators. The process of duoethnography transcends mere self-narration and self-exploration to engage in cultural analysis and interpretation, allowing us to utilize our own histories, cultures, and experiences to broaden our understanding of others (Chang, 2008). Duoethnography is distinctive in its emphasis on the researchers as the site of research and on the interacting narratives (Breault, 2016). Researchers examine their lived experiences through a critical lens, question their constructed knowledge, and challenge each other to reflect on the different voices within each narrative. Recent studies of duoethnography (e.g., Sebok & Wood, 2016; Smart & Cook, 2020) illustrate how this approach enriches understanding of language teacher education, as new knowledge emerges through in-depth reflexivity and interaction between individuals who juxtapose their lived experiences to create a richer third space.

Our duoethnographic process in preparation for this study developed over a period of several months. We had formal and informal conversations about our professional experiences in relation to critical dialogic education and on how to capture these. After brainstorming aspects that might be included in our narratives, we decided to write our lived experiences based on prompts with an implicit focus on dialogic perspectives, suggested by the first author. They included considerations on how we position ourselves as teacher educators, crucial moments in our teaching, how we plan and work collaboratively as a team, and how our stance as teacher educators is reflected in our practice. We did not discuss how to approach these narratives but set a time by when we would share them. After distributing the first round of writing via email, we realized that our understanding of the role of the prompts varied between writing a focused response to each and using them as a springboard to broadly reflect on our experiences. Our narratives also displayed difference in how we had interpreted the prompts and what we emphasized. When we discussed our narratives, our primary approach for probing the topic of critical dialogic practice was interactive dialogue. Reading each other's lived experiences sparked further ideas and memories of what we each might include, leading us to another cycle of reflection and writing. Data generation was an iterative and cyclical process which was also intertwined with shared data analysis in each iteration of our narratives.

Our narratives still varied considerably not only in style but also in content, highlighting our different backgrounds, contexts, and experiences and complexities of being a teacher educator. "Differences" is one of duoethnography's tenets that allow us to reconceptualize our own values, beliefs, and perspectives. Duoethnography proved to be an ideal method for our study because differences provide space for a multiplicity of perspectives and are conducive to critical dialogue.

Once we had re-read our lived experiences, we came together to discuss and negotiate the potential themes we each perceived, based on our individual interpretations, to be present in our narratives. We then mapped out the structure of the chapter, allocating different aspects to each researcher. Below, we group our interpretations into two broad themes: how our lived experiences shape our practice, and how CDE embodies our teaching.

How Our Lived Experiences Shape Our Practice

Although our formative experiences and career trajectories have been very different, we all share a love of languages, an appreciation of cultural diversity, and a desire to prepare teachers to support plurilingual learners based on principles of inclusion. More importantly, our motivations emerge from critical self-reflection and dialogic interaction.

With her wealth of knowledge and experience in the field of second-language acquisition (SLA), Rosemary's focus is on making SLA theory accessible to teachers. Growing up in New Zealand in the 1960s, Rosemary experienced the privilege of a White middle-class upbringing but witnessed the challenges of Māori children with whom she attended school. Although unaware of it at the time, Rosemary acknowledges how the language and culture of Māori children were invisible in the school as they were expected to conform to the dominant culture. However, she recognizes that her cultural consciousness has evolved over time, and that she has a deeper appreciation of how individuals' values and worldviews may differ.

Rosemary recounts how in her teaching, one assignment required teachers to reflect on improvements that could be made at the school level, and to propose an action plan for positive change. In one incident, Rosemary recalls how a female teacher who identified as being from a Pacific background felt it culturally inappropriate to challenge the authority of her school leaders and indicated that this assignment was a roadblock for her. This incident made Rosemary aware of how her own privilege in questioning power structures may not be perceived as being equally applicable to individuals from other cultures.

Christine's experiences of teaching in Europe were highly dialogic. She enjoyed enthusiastic discussions among her students and welcomed students who challenged her opinions. When she began teaching in New Zealand, Christine realized that students from some cultures did not appreciate radical provocations or engage in challenging the lecturer's views. Working with students from these different backgrounds helped Christine become more culturally sensitive in terms of curriculum content and classroom pedagogy. Her insight into New Zealand schools, through her work with ILEP, helped Christine to relate to teachers' experiences and offer advice on how to support language learners in their classrooms. Christine uses her own personal experience of bringing up children bilingually as an immigrant in New Zealand to help teachers understand the links between the home language and one's identity and belonging. She feels that such moments of sharing opened teachers' eyes to different perspectives and possibilities.

Naashia's own schooling had promoted an English-only policy and emphasized silence over talk in the classroom. However, she recalls how opportunities to engage in interaction with peers and teachers were most rewarding for her learning. This personal experience of the power of classroom dialogue, combined with her teacher training, and many opportunities to observe schools and teachers in different international contexts led Naashia to realize that dialogic discourse formed the fabric of good teaching. Her experience as an immigrant and Woman of Colour heightened her awareness of inequities and injustices against marginalized groups, and she aims to apply social justice principles in her own teaching to disrupt deficit narratives in different ways.

Naashia recounts an incident in a lecture that focused on funds of knowledge, where a male teacher insisted that he was not learning anything new as he already practiced culturally sustaining pedagogies in his own teaching. He criticized the university's approach to cultural responsiveness as being tokenistic and in opposition to the pedagogy being promoted through our program. Naashia used the opportunity to praise him for his commitment to asset-based pedagogies and elicit ways in which he practiced this in his teaching. She highlighted how the strategies he reported using incorporated students' funds of knowledge in meaningful ways. She engaged the class in a discussion about tokenistic approaches to culture and how this can mask the forms of structural injustice that exist in schools. Through this discussion, Naashia was able to draw teachers' attention to how we need to move away from simply appreciating cultural diversity to recognizing and responding to the inequities that ELs face.

How CDE Embodies Our Teaching

Collaboration and Dialogue in Planning and Teaching

We see our practice and planning as a joint co-construction of knowledge. Christine and Naashia regularly co-taught a compulsory course of the program, each being responsible for one of the streams of the course. They had twice-weekly debriefing and planning meetings, once to plan for the upcoming session and once to reflect on teaching to ensure adaptation and contextual responsiveness. The reflections focused on what was successful, but also on what did not work, for example when a teacher prompt did not generate dialogue among students or when Christine and Naashia could not trigger critical reflection about students' own teaching contexts, or when they missed opportunities to draw on all their students' lived experiences and teaching expertise. As a result of those critical collaborative reflections, Christine and Naashia each made adjustments to teaching plans to engage students and themselves in increasingly dialogic practices during teaching sessions. They also kept in continuous dialogue about how to support the teachers with social and emotional issues outside the classroom and how and what to communicate about assignments to provide fair and consistent opportunities.

Similarly, when Rosemary and Naashia co-taught they also worked collaboratively in planning, teaching, and assessing learning. They shared individual planning sessions tapping into each other's strengths and complementing each other's expertise. In the moderation of assessments, dialogue between Rosemary and Naashia illustrated their focus on different aspects in assignments. For example, one typically focused on the strength of an argument or the quality of writing and the other looked closely at the expressed beliefs or values in the text, particularly with regard to reframing deficit perspectives. This awareness sparked critical reflection on their own positions and values which in turn led to more awareness of multiple perspectives in teaching.

When we developed the new postgraduate program, it was important to engage in dialogue to reflect on and decide on content for the core courses so as to ensure progression, coherence, and the relevance of each. In the following, we portray several examples from our teaching practice where we applied aspects of critical dialogic education.

For all our teaching we believe that learning is co-constructed and dialogic communication encourages our students to engage with multiple perspectives and voices (Kibler et al., 2021). We regularly invite students in online discussion forums to not just provide their own responses to a provided prompt, but to engage with perceptions of their peers. This often leads to learning from each other and critical self-reflection. For example, in one course we asked teachers to share practices of integrating and/or assessing English language learners, based on two readings. The following short excerpt shows the teachers reflecting and gaining new perspectives: Student A mentions that "We have found that READING the math test to our ESOL students helps to get a better picture of their math achievement," to which student B replies: "I like your strategy [name].

This comment makes me reflect on how accessible our Maths assessments are to our ELL learners." Student A continues the reflection with "It's good to ask the question 'What am I assessing, reading or maths knowledge?'". Student formal written feedback supports these notions, attesting that "collaborative discussion" that 'encouraged critical thinking" in "an environment where we could discuss and learn from each other" took place regularly.

We are also committed to listening to student feedback which we ask for halfway through the semester, as well as through the formal course evaluations conducted by the university at the end of each semester. For example, in one compulsory course, we asked about challenges, what students had enjoyed so far, and their suggestions on what could be changed to enhance their learning experience. We collated all anonymous feedback and made it available to the group to be transparent as to what students had enjoyed and where they saw challenges. We discussed this in the following session, encouraging group dialogue and reflection. For example, students were concerned about workload and suggested fewer compulsory weekly readings which ranged from two to four articles or book chapters. As full-time working professionals, students felt overwhelmed by the amount of expected readings. In acknowledging the nature of our classroom communities and in respecting the students' voices, we adjusted and reduced the course readings and/or provided summaries of readings. In addition, students felt the time and work required by one of the assessments were not reflected enough in the weightings. After critically reflecting on the students' arguments and the set assignment expectations, we negotiated between us where we each saw opportunities for adjustment and change to maximize student success. Aiming to be responsive to our teaching context, but without compromising the quality of the program, we changed the assessment weighting and expectations in the following year while also providing additional scaffolding to support learning.

Another example of how we engage in dialogue with students is when students on a new course voiced concerns of how assigned readings were typically discussed and presented in previous years, and Naashia challenged them to suggest an alternative way. A lively dialogue ensued in which students highlighted that the traditional practice had not been particularly helpful as they had felt pressured into a rigid pattern of sharing reading and writing summaries that allowed a few voices to dominate the discussion causing other students to feel excluded. Through a process of negotiation, we were able to agree on an alternative format which elevated previously marginalized voices and enhanced their sense of belonging as they felt more valued and heard.

In a similar way Christine listened to students who were uncomfortable with opening the class with personal statements, prayers, or anecdotes for students to engage with multiple perspectives, but also to get to know each other and create a learning community. While the practice was based on a dialogic approach and with the aim to be inclusive, some students expressed feeling uncomfortable and preferred to find out about each other on their own terms. Recognizing that, despite good intentions, the setting was not neutral, and the practice privileged some students as it marginalized others (Kibler et al., 2021), Christine encouraged students to express their different standpoints. After listening to each other's perspectives, the group, together with Christine, decided to change the practice.

CDE in Course Structure and Assessment

Aspects of CDE are embodied in the structure of our courses through our assessments. For example, in one assessment we expect the teachers to link what they have learnt with their practice, encouraging dialogue with theory, but also with their immediate teaching contexts and to initiate "first steps" for a change. In this assessment, we ask them to be "agents of change" in their teaching contexts. They identify an issue at their school that could be improved to enhance their students' learning experience, particularly for those who are marginalized. The teachers then design an action plan and outline first steps to bring about change. They listen to one another present these plans, and then they each write a critical reflection which they pass on to the presenter. When the written assignment is handed in, each teacher has to report on the critical feedback they received on how it may have changed their thinking/proposed plan. The assessment focuses on developing a dialogic stance where teachers engage with multiple perspectives, and where intellectually purposeful and respectful dialogue takes place (see also Kibler et al., 2021).

In the last two years, we also introduced regular online discussion forums as part of the course assessment to be inclusive of different learning styles and to provide alternative ways of engaging with the course materials. Teachers were expected to critically reflect on readings assigned to the weekly topics and teaching sessions. These reflections were initiated by a prompt we provided. While every teacher was expected to share their reflections with others on the forum, they were also expected to engage with what others had already posted to develop openness and awareness of multiple perspectives not just between the teacher and the reading, but also between the different teachers on the course.

Sparked by these reflections, teachers often shared some of their practices in relation to the reading. However, we do not assess the content discussed in the forum, rather the reflections. In the assessment guide we ask:

> Which aspects of the discussed course content and contributions from your peers on discussion forums have had an impact on your thinking and why? Reflect on whether those aspects had an impact on your teaching.

One of the readings discusses acculturation, assimilation, and liminality (Cunningham & King, 2018), concepts teachers were not necessarily familiar with, but when explained, could relate to either personally or through students in their classroom. The reading led to several posts, but we want to highlight one teacher's response (Student C) to illustrate how the reading sparked a cycle of critical reflection, action, and change of perception. Student C reflected that the reading

> was a real eye-opener for me in understanding how some English Language Learners or children born to migrant parents experience a feeling of "liminality" or cultural non-belonging in schools in Aotearoa [New Zealand]. I have revisited this reading several times to reflect on how to limit these experiences for learners in my classroom.

As a response to the reading, some teachers had shared in the discussion forum how they used maps of the world so students could position themselves and that this activity could give them a sense of belonging and of being valued in New Zealand. Other teachers talked about including different languages for classroom greetings to build every student's confidence with their heritage and culture. Based on her own reflections and the discussion forum's dialogue, Student C introduced a map of the world in her classroom and combined it with an inquiry into her students' individual cultural backgrounds to make them feel integrated and valued. She explained her intentions as follows:

> My intention with this activity was to give *mana* [prestige] to my students' heritage culture by allowing children to choose how it was represented (decorating the *waka* [canoe]) and to open up conversation. This did happen and *tamariki* [children] are often at the display asking each other questions and having open *korero* [conversation].

However, in her written reflection as part of the assessment, Student C questions herself and whether she had actually created a space where children could develop a sense of belonging. She critically reflected that by asking the students to position themselves on a map, she inadvertently made them choose one location, rather than acknowledging the complexities of identities and multicultural being, as she pondered: "I have realized some were potentially cast into this realm of 'non-belonging' by having to choose what they identify with the 'most', therefore potentially creating marginalization and that perhaps this activity had caused such feelings." As a consequence of this reflection Student C decided to explicitly discuss with her students that they did not have to feel connected only to one place: "We have, since then, connected our *waka* to other heritage places, including Aotearoa [New Zealand]. As well, we have explicitly discussed that many of us have shared heritages and it is difficult, and unnecessary, to place heritage or ethnicity in one place." This example illustrates the dialogue between teacher educators, teachers, and readings, highlighting the importance of critical dialogue with the potential to bring about change of perception and practice. It also shows how we encourage translanguaging so that everyone is comfortable using their full linguistic repertoire but in ways that do not impede understanding for others who may not share their named languages.

Discussion and Conclusion

The aims of this duoethnography were to explore our experiences and agency in incorporating CDE into our teacher education practice. What surfaces through this retrospective analysis of our teaching from a CDE perspective is the extent to which our own practices and identities shape the contextually bound design and application of our courses. Our findings highlight several implications.

From a methodological perspective, the process has highlighted for us the importance of working collaboratively and engaging in reflective practice, particularly with the intention of initiating change. We have gained valuable insight into how duoethnography can become a tool to enrich our agency, foster reflection, and develop critical support through shared understanding of an issue. We recommend teachers and teacher educators to engage in this act of collective self-introspection and professional learning that also helps to strengthen collegiality.

Our reflective narratives contained much more than can be included within the limits of this chapter. Although we have known each other professionally and worked together for several years now, journaling about ourselves helped us to discover more about each other, both personally and professionally. Our points of origin and the paths we took to reach this shared space may differ, but there are several intersections across our experiences and stories. We have each had different experiences of marginalization, and through sharing our stories we learned the significance of empathy and vulnerability in reflecting on our individual and collective trajectories. We recognize dialogue as a process of reflection and learning with potential to transform practice. Engaging in this conversation has also demonstrated our commitment to a more critically oriented pedagogy of teacher education (Hawkins & Norton, 2009) where we are jointly responsible with our students to reflect, learn, and grow through critical dialogue (Freire, 1970). Applied to our teacher education spaces, we see the value of fostering rich, critical discussions while nurturing empathy to build a caring learning community that is action-oriented to confront deficit perspectives.

Nevertheless, while acknowledging the need for cultivating more equitable systems of education, given the differences in our worldviews and identities, the process of doing that has varied between us. As Freire (1970) acknowledges, problem-posing dialogic education affirms us as being in the process of becoming; we are aware of our own state of incompletion. While we have championed diversity and encouraged cultural sensitivity, we perhaps need a more robust and unified approach to advocating for educational equity and preparing teachers to recognize and respond to underlying injustices faced by marginalized learners. Part of this is relevant to the terminology we use. Gorski (2016) critiques the use of terms like *culturally and linguistically diverse*, calling educators to shift the central focus from culture to the systemic conditions that underlie inequities. Rather than simply raising awareness of diversity, we need to envision strategies for change and develop a willingness to bring the real-life implications of inequity and injustice close enough to be meaningful.

Our reflective exploration raises important questions: How do we move forward to help teachers in our programs enable a future that is equitable for all learners? When we consider some minoritized groups in contemporary New Zealand society, the focus is on righting the current wrongs and taking action to build a more just future for them. At the same time, we have to acknowledge the injustices of the past, particularly in relation to Māori and Pacific peoples in this context and consider ways of putting right these past inequities. The challenge for us as educators, and for the teachers that we teach, is to hold both in tension. This is a challenge for the broader society, here in New Zealand, and across the world.

References

Auckland Council Research & Evaluation Unit. (2019). 2018 Census information results: Local board and special area information sheets. https://www.stats.govt.nz/tools/2018-census-place-summaries/new-zealand

Breault, A. R. (2016). Emerging issues in duoethnography. *International Journal of Qualitative Studies in Education, 29*(6), 777–94.

Bruner, S. J. (1996). *The culture of education.* Harvard University Press.

Chang, H. (2008). *Autoethnography as method.* Left Coast Press Inc.

Cunningham, U., & King, J. (2018). Ethnicity, and belonging for the children of migrants in New Zealand. *SAGE Open, 8*(2), 1–11. http://dx.doi.org/10.1177/2158244018782571

Ennser-Kananen, J. (2016). A pedagogy of pain: New directions for world language education. *The Modern Language Journal, 100,* 556–64. https://doi.org/10.1111/modl.1_12337

Educational Review Office. (2018). Responding to language diversity in Auckland. https://ero.govt.nz/our-research/responding-to-language-diversity-in-auckland

Flores, N., Tseng, A., & Subtirelu, N. (2021). *Bilingualism for all?: Raciolinguistic perspectives on dual language education in the United States.* Multilingual Matters. https://doi.org/10.21832/9781800410053

Freire, P. (1970). *Pedagogy of the oppressed.* Continuum.

Garcia, P., & Cifor, M. (2019). Expanding our reflexive toolbox: Collaborative possibilities for examining socio-technical systems using duoethnography. *Proceedings of the ACM-Human Computer Interaction, 3*(190), 1–23. https://doi.org/10.1145/3359292

García-Carrión, R., & Díez-Palomar, J. (2015). Learning communities: Pathways for educational success and social transformation through interactive groups in mathematics. *European Educational Research Journal, 14*(2), 151–66. https://doi.org/10.1177/1474904115571793

Gorski, P. (2016). Rethinking the role of "Culture" in educational equity: From cultural competence to equity literacy. *Multicultural Perspectives, 18*(4), 221–6. https://doi.org/10.1080/15210960.2016.1228344

Gray, S. (2012). Inclusive academic language teaching in New Zealand: History and responses. *Asia Pacific Journal of Education, 32*(3), 317–32.

Hawkins, M., & Norton, B. (2009). Critical language teacher education. In A. Burns, J. C. Richards (Eds.), *Cambridge guide to second language teacher education* (pp. 30–9). Cambridge University Press.

Kibler, A., Valdés, G., & Walqui, A. (2021). *Reconceptualizing the role of critical dialogue in American classrooms: Promoting equity through dialogic education.* Routledge.

Kohli, R., Picower, B., Martinez, A. N., & Ortiz, N. (2015). Critical professional development: Centering the social justice needs of teachers. *International Journal of Critical Pedagogy, 6*(2), 7–24.

Lee, D. C. (2016). Examining conceptions of how people learn over the decades through AERA presidential addresses: Diversity and equity as persistent conundrums. *Educational Researcher, 45*(2), 273–82. https://doi.org/10.3102/0013189X16639045

Mercer, N., & Howe, C. (2012). Explaining the dialogic processes of teaching and learning: The value and potential of sociocultural theory. *Learning, Culture and Social Interaction, 1*(1), 12–21. https://doi.org/10.1016/J.LCSI.2012.03.001

Mercer, N., Wegerif, R., & Dawes, L. (1999). Children's talk and the development of reasoning in the classroom. *British Education Research Journal, 25*(1), 95–111. https://doi.org/10.1080/0141192990250107

Ministry of Education. (1993). The New Zealand curriculum framework: Te anga marautanga o aotearoa. https://nzcurriculum.tki.org.nz/The-New-Zealand-Curriculum

Ministry of Education. (2007). The New Zealand curriculum for English-medium teaching and learning in years, 1–13. https://www.academia.edu/24415300/The_New_Zealand_Curriculum_for_English-medium_teaching_and_learning_in_years_1_13

Norris, J., & Sawyer, D. R. (2012). Towards a dialogic method. In J. Norris, D. S. Richard, & D. Lund (Eds.), *Duoethnography: Dialogic methods for social, health, and educational research* (pp. 9–40). Left Coast Press.

Paris, D., & Alim, H. S. (2017). *Culturally sustaining pedagogies: Teaching and learning for justice in a changing world.* Teachers College Press.

Peercy, M. M., Judy, Sh., Laura, B., Suhanthie, M., & Manka, V. (2019). Exploring TESOL teacher educators as learners and reflective scholars: A shared narrative inquiry. *TESOL Journal, 10*(4), e482. https://doi-org.ezproxy.auckland.ac.nz/10.1002/tesj.482

Philip, T. M., Souto-Manning, M., Anderson, L., Horn, I., Carter Andrews D., J., Stillman, J., & Varghese, M. (2018). Making justice peripheral by constructing practice as "core": How the increasing prominence of core practices challenges teacher education. *Journal of Teacher Education, 70*(3), 251–64. https://doi.org/10.1177/0022487118798324

Racionero, S., & Padrós, M. (2010). The dialogic turn in educational psychology. *Revistade Psicodidáctica, 15*(2), 143–62.

Randolph, J. L., Jr., & Johnson, S. M. (2017). Social justice in the language classroom: A call to action. *Dimension,* 9–31.

Sebok, S. S., & Woods, J. C. (2016). Using duoethnography to cultivate an understanding of professionalism: Developing insights into theory, practice, and self through interdisciplinary conversations. In R. Sawyer & J. Norris (Eds.), Interdisciplinary reflective practice through duoethnography (pp. 165–82). Palgrave Macmillan. https://doi.org/10.1057/978-1-137-51739-5_8

Smart, B., & Cook, C. (2020). Professional development through duoethnography: Reflecting on dialogues between an experienced and novice teacher. In R. Lowe & L. Lawrence (Eds.), Duoethnography in English language teaching: Research, reflection and classroom application (pp. 91–111). Multilingual Matters. https://doi.org/10.21832/9781788927192-007

Smits, K. (2011). Justifying multiculturalism: Social justice, diversity and national identity in Australia and New Zealand. *Australian Journal of Political Science, 46*(1), 87–103.

Teo, P. (2019). "Teaching for the 21st century: A case for dialogic pedagogy." *Learning, Culture and Social Interaction, 21*, 170–8. https://doi.org/10.1016/J.LCSI.2019.03.009

van der Veen, C., de Mey, L., van Kruistum, C., & van Oers, B. (2017). The effect of productive classroom talk and metacommunication on young children's oral communicative competence and subject matter knowledge: An intervention study in early childhood education. *Learning and Instruction, 48*, 14–22. https://doi.org/10.1016/j.learninstruc.2016.06.001

Von Esch, K. S., Motha, S., & Kubota, R. (2020). Race and language teaching. *Language Teaching, 53*(4), 391–421. https://doi.org/10.1017/s0261444820000269

Vygotsky, L. (1978). *Mind in society: The development of higher psychological processes*. Harvard University Press.

Toward More Inclusive Classroom Practices in the Turkish EFL Contexts: A Case Study on the Integration of Critical and Dialogic Approaches to Field Placement

Ayşe Kızıldağ and Işıl Günseli Kaçar

Introduction

Educational settings in the twenty-first century, with linguistically and culturally diverse learner/teacher profiles, put a heavy emphasis on the integration of critical and dialogic pedagogical practices. Dialogic approaches incorporate opportunities for students' co-participation and co-construction of thoughts, as well as their engagement in multifarious viewpoints and a boost in their self-awareness and respect for others. In addition, critical approaches motivate students to launch an inquiry into their established set of beliefs, new knowledge and non-inclusive "inequitable circumstances with a view toward social changes" (Kibler, et al., 2021, p. 16). Considering students' diverse cultural and linguistic backgrounds as affordances and assets in the learning process, critical and dialogic education (CDE) promotes inclusive and equitable practices. Such practices provide fertile learning spaces for students through multivocality. In other words, each student's participation in CDE with their own assets, unique opinions, and stances about the topic under discussion would provide productive spaces for active and inclusive learning. For example, hearing their differing and/or similar perspectives, synthesizing and analyzing various opinions, and expanding their own repertoires might form a basis for opening up multivocality in the participatory educational settings, thereby creating more inclusive learning spaces for students in teacher education programs, and for the children and adults they will teach in the future.

In fact, CDE lies at the heart of the study context, a practicum course and field placement for participating Turkish senior student-teachers enrolled in an undergraduate program in English Language Teaching (ELT) at an urban public university. A teacher educator, one of the authors of this chapter, supervised and co-worked with them during the implementation of the research. In the study, emphasis was placed on participants' critical inquiry into the power dynamics, inclusion, discrimination, equality, and equity regarding instructional materials and the delivery of instruction at their practicum schools. The concept of *inclusion* was operationalized as embracing all students regarding their learning styles and characteristics as well as individualizing and differentiating the instructional materials and the procedures to meet such needs.

Hence, this study addresses the question of how researchers incorporated critical and dialogic approaches to better prepare pre-service teachers for the needs of their English a Foreign Language (EFL) students, centering issues related to inclusion and equity. For this very purpose, we designed a cyclical model where the pre-service teachers can observe or notice, problematize, implement, and thus develop their own perspectives about inclusion and equity in classrooms during teaching English. In this three-stage model—we name it as *Notice-Problematize-Implement* (NPI)—participating student-teachers were actively engaged in critical and dialogic discussions between their peers and the university practicum supervisor (henceforth, PS) regarding the core topic of inclusiveness during their weekly class meetings on campus. As a result, this chapter elaborates on how the NPI model served as a means to incorporate critical and dialogic approaches into a TEFL field placement context.

Theoretical Framework

As a conceptual framework, the study adopted a CDE approach which calls for redefining the roles of learners and teachers (Karam, 2021; Kibler et al., 2021). From that lens, students are positioned as "knowers and researchers" capable of launching a critical inquiry into the already existing body of knowledge (Kibler et al., 2021, p. 17). In Freirean terms, students are asked to share "their knowledge of the 'world'—and all of the challenges and inequities it entails—to problematize the 'words' they are learning" (p. 17). Students assume an *agentic* role and are regarded as "legitimate and worthy conversation partners" in CDE (Karam, 2021, p. 5). Critical and dialogic teachers also constantly reexamine "their curricula, their instruction in the classroom, and their perceptions and positionings of students" (p. 5). As such, PS in this study facilitated dialogic discussions with the student-teachers, encouraging them to critically examine discriminatory and unjust pedagogical practices. Through negotiations, teachers acted as co-partners in creating engaging learning environments, tapping into students' personal experiences and their linguistically and culturally diverse backgrounds by providing tools for them to share their own views on issues both in and out of class from dialogic and multivocal perspectives. In fact, "multivocality (or the multiplicity of student voices and opinions in the classroom) is a central tenet of CDE" (Karam, 2021, p. 17). It is also important for teachers to promote student reflection on their own beliefs and their worldviews regarding the topic of discussion in and out of class. Thus, the study aims to explore how CDE, which is integrated into the Teaching English as a Foreign Language (TEFL) field placements, empowers student-teachers in the Turkish higher education context.

Context of the Study

This study was conducted in a small public university, at a faculty of education's ELT Department that adopts the nationwide standardized pre-service teacher education curriculum in Turkiye. The university was founded in 2006, and the department was opened later in the academic year of 2010–11. Each year, fifty EFL student-teachers are accepted to follow a one-plus four-year teacher education program. The first year is a preparation stage where trainees receive intensive four-skill-based general English language training. The second year is exclusively designed for academic English and beginners' level pedagogy courses like *Introduction to Education* and *Educational Psychology* and *Sociology*. The third year is when trainees are introduced to ELT methodology, first/second language acquisition, linguistics, and syllabus-curriculum design and analysis. The fourth and fifth years are allocated for in-depth ELT issues such as *Teaching English to Young Learners, Teaching English Language Skills, Literature and ELT, Assessment and Evaluation in ELT, Material Design, Development, Evaluation and Adaptation in ELT* with various specialized elective courses (*ELT Coursebook Analysis, Corpus Linguistics and ELT, Pragmatics and ELT*, etc.). The fifth year is also distinct with field placement when student-teachers are placed at a local school for two semesters.

Field placement is a collaborative process between the universities and the public schools while educating teachers at faculties of education in Turkish universities. Pre-service teachers registered at different teacher education departments are assigned to complete their practicum studies at a local compulsory school. There are three main participants: the PS, in-service teachers as the mentors, and the student-teachers (Koç, 2012). PS mainly supervises student-teachers during their on campus courses and advises them about the practicum procedures—including organizing the weekly schedules of student-teachers, informing the school, and introducing the student-teachers to the managers and the mentors of the schools (Turkish Ministry of National Education, 2020). Mentors are assigned to (a) work cooperatively with PSs for all the duties during the whole period, (b) supervise trainees to successfully complete these activities, (c) track the absenteeism of the trainees, and (d) manage the problems that might emerge during the period of field placement. As can be inferred, it is a top-down approach where PSs are expected to coordinate and control the process, and conduct communication with different agents during field placements. Finally, the third party in this process, student-teachers, is to attend to a six-hour-per-week practice teaching under the supervision of a PS and an English teacher mentor during twelve weeks each semester. Within a total of seventy-two-hour-practicum period at local schools, every student-teacher has to teach at least a ten-hour-long lesson per semester, four of which are observed and evaluated by the mentor and the PS together. In tandem, many observations with a special pedagogic focus are reflected on over weekly class sessions with their PSs back on campus during two class hours. At the end of the course, the mentor and PS assess and evaluate each pre-service teacher's performance and competence in line with a set of three-Likert-scale criteria. The emphasis in the field placement is on the professional development of the prospective teachers for practicing teaching skills including classroom management, classroom language, instructional routines, motivation, and feedback provision according to the assessment criteria provided by the Higher Education Council.

As for the twelve-year compulsory schooling system of Turkiye, each of the three levels (primary, middle, and high schools) lasts for four years. Currently, Turkiye has more than 19 million students enrolled at compulsory education who are taught by 1,139,673 teachers (National Education Statistics, 2022). Pre-school education is neither obligatory nor accessible for all the population across the country, though. Teachers are recruited by the ministry centrally as public officers after passing a written certificate exam and an oral test when they graduate. The medium of instruction in the compulsory school system is Turkish, except for foreign language courses in Arabic, English, French, German, Italian, and Spanish. Students take a national high-school entrance exam at the end of the eighth grade to choose the high school type (general academic, science, social sciences, technical and vocational, health, religion, and arts high schools) to which they would like to proceed for their further education. Being highly competitive, most middle schools focus on this exam in the eighth grade. High schools, equally, consist of four years during which students are educated in line with their personal and academic competencies. All the students who continue to tertiary education have to take another very competitive exam that has increased in popularity. For instance, on June 20, 2022, there were 923,237 graduates who took the test, which was 650,000 more than the previous year's number of test-takers (Hurriyet Daily News, 2022).

Implementing the NPI Model

The following procedures were implemented into the practicum course by the PS and involved engaging participating pre-service teachers with CDE through a developed model called NPI at each step.

Stage 1: Noticing

After observing participants' first practice teaching in the field placement, The PS realized that inclusive practices were not implemented by the student-teachers. Although the participants were instructed on inclusive practices when they were third-year students at the department, it was accepted as a natural phenomenon that they could not display such practices immediately. Therefore, the PS felt the need to draw attention to the issue of *inclusion versus exclusion* at schools during the post-practice teaching feedback sessions. In the discussions during these sessions, She highlighted that the all participants were teaching the whole class but not addressing particular learners while they were practice-teaching. She emphasized that the preservice teachers did not encourage all students to participate in the lesson. In fact, they only focused on those who were actively involved in the lesson. Furthermore, she pointed out that the participants did not integrate any pair and/or group work into their teaching tasks to ensure all students engaged in the lesson. Participants explored that it originated from the fact that they had not observed such practices at the practicum schools, either. Another expectation at this point is a common misbelief held by student-teachers that mentors are perfect role models to learn from and/or imitate. To deconstruct that misbelief, PS asked the participants to observe closely for collecting different types and incidences of non-inclusive classroom practices in the classrooms they attended; they were guided for what is happening or *not* happening about the issue at their practicum setting. Various samples were brought into discussions and they started analyzing the examples as well as trying to provide certain *instead-actions*. Though CDE does not foreground pre-planned structures, the PS stimulated the discussions to focus on participants' positioning for each case encountered via using "if I were the teacher, instead of X, I would do Y" structure, where X referred to the mentor teacher actions and Y to the student-teachers' own alternative suggestions. Although the participants were unfamiliar with CDE as the approach is not a part of the mainstream practicum tradition, The PS encouraged participants to find their voices and hear from each other, thereby promoting their multivocality. Finally, pre-service teachers themselves identified and categorized the cases of exclusion in terms of the type of learner, such as immigrants, those with learning disabilities, or unmotivated learners. They reported observing that their mentor teachers tended to take learners with special needs (e.g., learners with visual or hearing impairment) for granted and that the mentors did not incorporate differentiated instruction to cater for their learning needs. They also underlined that the unmotivated learners constituted a major part of the student population at practicum schools they attended. They pointed out that these students were likely to be excluded by their mentor teachers. What they mostly observed in classes was students who displayed off-task behavior and failed to focus on the lesson flow sitting aside and not participating. Such disengaged students were neither encouraged to take part in the classroom activities invited by the mentor for any activities nor approached outside the classroom to discuss the challenges they encountered in their learning process. The abovementioned examples highlight the non-inclusive attitude of the mentor teachers from the preservice teachers' perspective.

Stage 2: Problematizing and Modifying

Next was to identify the causes of non-inclusive practices at the practicum schools and provide adequate instructional modifications. The PS guided participants in screening the curriculum and the teaching materials by using the frameworks of Universal Design for Learning (UDL) and Bloom's Revised Taxonomy (BRT), which guided classroom processes for the individualization of learning as well as inclusion by addressing the needs of various learners.

UDL is "a set of principles for curriculum development that give all individuals equal opportunities to learn" (UDL, 2013). It provides valuable guidelines to design a flexible curriculum with different options for the presentation and evaluation of content, fostering inclusive learning spaces. Similarly, BRT helps teachers categorize different levels of cognitive outcomes from the lowest order of cognition (remembering) to the highest (creating) (Krathwohl, 2002). BRT, too, can assist in designing inclusive classes. Teachers can benefit from the taxonomy while setting learning outcomes and arranging the learning tasks/activities in line with an incremental level of cognitive difficulty and complexity, facilitating the achievement of the lesson objectives (Pintrich & Zusho, 2007).

Participants analyzed and evaluated both frameworks for implementing them into their future classroom practices by problematizing the curriculum and the teaching materials. They found many problems in the coursebooks used and modified the activities utilizing UDL and BRT.

Stage 3: Implementation

Participants prepared their lesson plans to remediate the issues they explored in stage 2. After in-class implementations, peer-to-peer and PS-to-trainee feedback sessions were conducted along with discussions on the written reflective reports on their teaching. This stage was significant for motivating reflexivity around how participants problematize the variables in the course materials that hinder inclusiveness and modify the activities to their theoretical stances. They were also encouraged to critically interact with The PS and their peers and analyze their positioning on the matters they derived at stages 1 and 2 of the whole NPI process.

Methodology

The study adopted an exploratory qualitative case study research design. Case studies are particularly beneficial in "enhancing our understanding of contexts, communities and individuals" (Hamilton & Corbett-Whittier, 2012, p. 4). Merriam (1988) defined a case study as "an intense, holistic description and analysis of a single instance, phenomenon, or social unit" (p. 21). In this study, the focus was on a group of EFL student-teachers' exploration of inclusion with the introduction of CDE in a TEFL field placement via the NPI model.

The study was conducted with ten senior EFL pre-service teachers as participants (one male, nine females; with an age range from twenty-three to twenty-five) in the Turkish context for six weeks during the second part of fall semester in the academic year 2021/22. They had a B2 and above proficiency level equivalent to 72 and above out of 120 in TOEFL iBT score (ETS, n.d.) in English with no prior classroom teaching experience. They were placed at two different local middle schools to observe and practice under the supervision of PS, the first author. Convenience sampling strategies and all the ethical guidelines were followed to obtain data. The group was already assigned to the PS by the department for the field placement at the beginning of semester; she invited them to the implementation of a particular model, NPI, and explained her reasoning. They openly and honestly showed their excitement for CDE to be implemented for the first time in the department and agreed to participate. Later in the middle of the semester just before starting the research, they were informed about the purpose and procedures of the study regarding what is expected from them in relation to CDE. The PS acted as a pedagogical mentor and facilitator for CDE, promoting the multivocality of the prospective teachers via the CDE discussions and research tasks, which would raise their awareness of how to foster inclusive and equitable classroom practices. She also explained that neither the NPI model nor the CDE research tasks were accounted for in the course score, giving the space of opting out whenever they felt so. Meanwhile, she acted as a participant observer with the student-teachers during weekly two-hour classes and practicum teaching sessions. She collected data while the second author supervised the whole research process. In the findings, the students are labeled as P1 through P10.

The data were gathered via three sources. First, CDE discussions were done on different aspects of EFL pedagogy during the practicum course such as participating teacher trainees' school observations, lesson plans and feedback from the PS, and their biweekly reflective journals for their practice teaching. All discussions within the CDE framework revealed participants playing an agentic role in launching a critical inquiry into their observations and experiences about the curriculum and classroom practices at the practicum schools. They also exchanged their different perspectives during discussion, which led to multivocality, that is, presenting their own views and enriching their professional repertoire for the issues emerging during field placement by hearing others' opinions. Second, a recorded online semi-structured interview was conducted at the end of the study by the PS. Each participant was interviewed for about half an hour to one regarding two main questions (a) how they benefitted from CDE during the six-week implementation period of the study particularly focusing on the critical and dialogic interactions between the self and peer, and the PS and (b) how and to what extent their experiences of CDE in the project raised their awareness and professional agency on inclusion in EFL teaching for their further professional career. The third data source was the researcher's field notes.

Classroom discussions were held and field notes were recorded in English, while interviews were done in the participants' mother tongue, Turkish, to allow expressing their thoughts at ease. Before starting analysis, discussions were transcribed, and interview data were translated separately. Then, back-translation was done for the interview data to re-align the comprehension and the interpretation of the meaning between the researchers.

Via content analysis, codes, categories, and themes were formed using inductive post-priori analysis, where codes come directly from the data (Miles et al., 2018). After completing this first cycle (Saldaña, 2021), the second cycle, called pattern codes, was done to group the codes into relevant categories and later to themes. Pattern codes are explanatory in nature and provide insights on the causes and relationships between the components of the research. For reliability and validity, both authors compared their independently analyzed findings to sustain consistency and discussed the areas of disagreement. Initial interrater reliability was calculated as a reliability measure, which was found to be 0.95. Later, both researchers arrived at a consensus through negotiating the problematic items.

As a result of the data analysis, two themes emerged: 1) fostering CDE through NLP and 2) engaging in critical and dialogic discussions. Codes under the first theme included noticing/identifying exclusive practices, analyzing and problematizing curricula, and developing individualized solutions for students. Codes under the second theme included benefits and challenges of engaging in critical and dialogic conversations around the field placement (e.g., benefits such as discussing inclusive practices and challenges such as grappling with difficult questions posed by the PS).

Data triangulation and member checking were utilized to ensure trustworthiness. Some of the participants were quite satisfied with the analysis of their personal accounts; some modified the researchers' interpretations of their data. For example, P7 elaborated more on his *incomplete pedagogic positioning* and even urged researchers to use the exact wording while interpreting his perception of CDE.

Findings

Overall, CDE seems to enhance participating pre-service teachers' displaying positioning and developing agency for professional issues regarding *inclusiveness* in classroom teaching as well as embracing critical inquiry and a growing awareness of theory-practice relations. Furthermore, participating pre-service teachers utilized CDE in two main themes such as sustaining inclusive practices and acquiring a critical and dialogic discourse in the field placement course. In other words, we see that participants benefitted from CDE as a means of developing inclusive teaching models and building a discourse to critically raise dialogic discussions.

Fostering CDE through The NPI: Sustaining Inclusive Pedagogy

The NPI was mainly developed for fostering CDE while participants were exploring the issue of sustaining inclusive practices and providing equal opportunities in EFL teaching for the disenagaged students who were observed to be ignored or excluded by the mentor teachers encountered at the practicum schools. Participants reported observing different cases of noninclusive classroom practices at the practicum schools, which involves diverse groups of students, such as immigrants and learning disabilities. In a classroom discussion during stage 1, when the PS previously assigned trainees to collect the sample cases, P3 referred to a learning-disabled student who was ignored by the mentor teacher constantly.

> PS: What did you observe as an example of exclusion in your practicum school last week?
> P3: The most significant one was that my mentor ignores X [student name]. Later I discovered he has been using medication regularly for his attention deficit. I talked to the mentor; she seems that she has neither has knowledge about the disorder nor interest in learning about it. She simply ignores the student in her classes.
> PS: Then, what would you suggest for such cases?
> P3: (…) If I were the teacher, instead of ignoring, I would investigate, explore his disorder in-depth. Also, I would definitely cooperate with the parents for his progress.
> PS: Good, then what is your lesson to be learnt from this observation?
> P3: Well, I realized that the course I have been receiving this semester on special needs of learners at schools is very important.

The excerpt above is an example of how dialogic interactions between PS and P3 lead to a critical analysis of the pedagogical classroom practices. The discussion above is a chain of analysis about a case on how inclusion is not realized at the practicum school due to the mentor's indifference toward a student with learning disability. PS probed for P3's describing the case of exclusion and seeking her positioning and action in such a similar case. Furthermore, PS asked for P3's critical reflections over this sample of exclusion for further professional learning, where P3 connected the case to another course she was attending, and apparently had awareness of how the course could contribute positively to similar cases when she became a full-time EFL teacher.

Another set of discussions was around the curriculum following the analysis of an assigned coursebook by the school administration. Participants were assigned to screen the coursebooks and problematize the activities in terms of embracing inclusive practices. In the following excerpt taking place during stage 2 of the NPI, the critical discussion between PS and P7 depicts the relations among the coursebook, mentor, and classroom teaching with reference to inclusive practices. P7 criticized the school praxis causing exclusion due to the mandated curriculum and thus coursebook activities. Furthermore, the mentor always completed those activities as individual work. Based on his observation of this practice, P7 reported raising his professional agency and realizing the importance of taking initiative and exercising pedagogic power over the teaching materials.

The following excerpt, taken from a classroom discussion with the PS, was a problematization of the coursebook activities that were organized to be implemented only individually. It also dealt with the mentor teacher who refused to modify the existing norms enforced via the curriculum. P7, then, proceeded to display his advocacy for group work that he believed would motivate timid learners and empower himself as a supporting teacher.

> PS: What is the problem here [pointing at the coursebook problem report]?
> P7: Activities are all to be done individually. Instructions don't include any pair or group work.
> PS: What do you mean? What does this mean for your problematizing of inclusion in the classroom?
> P7: My mentor depends very much on the coursebook used. She never modifies it to present varieties. What I mean is when the activities are all done individually and students do not work together or collaborate, some regular students participate only, and the teacher does not invite others who feel shy or intimidated somehow. You know, they need encouraging and supporting teachers. This is why these activities must be modified to include other learners, too.

A final step of how CDE was enacted was through the dialogic conversations on participants taking actions to eliminate exclusions in the practicum setting via their lesson plans and teaching practices. During another critical and dialogic session in stage 3 of the NPI, trainees discussed their own revisions of coursebook activities and how they took initiatives for modifying regular classroom teaching. In the following dialogic interaction between the PS and P1, she exemplified the theory-practice relations with regard to the revisions she made to the mainstream teaching praxis. These revisions were concerned with integrating differentiation and inclusiveness as a response to the problematized areas in the coursebook used at the practicum school. P1 rationalized her pedagogical modifications referring to the basic principles of UDL and BRT as well connecting them with the previous ELT methodology courses.

> PS: How do you think you mediated this problem [referring to her lesson plan and classroom practice]?
> P1: In the methodology classes we learnt including the students by making their learning individualized and personalized. We also covered UDL and Bloom's Taxonomy for making the classes inclusive and maximizing learning with critical thinking skills. With my revisions of the coursebook activities, first, I invited students to work together for the activity on page 24 and later analyze their own learning in the following activity individually.
> PS: How have these changes affected the exclusive practices that you have observed in this class so far?
> P1: Oh, it took a bit of extra time for me to organize them to group. I also realized that some of the groups had no idea about what they were going to do. I wanted some students in the groups to help the ones who needed scaffolding and guidance. I worked closely with some groups because they needed more explanations but I saw some groups were very busy communicating [with] each other. I think that was worth doing it. I included most of the students for the activity, even those students at the back … mostly idle ones at other times.
> PS: How about the individual work during the following activity?
> P1: That was for students' evaluating themselves, how much they understood the topic. What sports they like … which ones they don't. They checked their preferences. I particularly nominated those students at the back to share their ideas with us. My idea was them to speak out. I think this helped for their critical thinking, personalization, I mean.

The PS scaffolded P1 in the excerpt above with exploratory questions enabling her to elaborate on particular decisions she made about relating inclusion to UDL (*critical thinking skills*) and BRT (*evaluating themselves*). Through her questions, P1 revisited existing pedagogical decisions and started to engage in aligning her instructional practices and strategies with the principles of CDE, in particular the notion of personalizing instruction for varied learners.

Engaging in Critical and Dialogic Discussions: Benefits and Challenges within the Field Placement Context

During interviews, participant trainees were asked to describe how they engaged in the dialogic and critical discussions facilitated by the PS during the practicum class. Findings displayed pre-service teachers utilizing CDE for various purposes and benefitting from it to different extents. They mostly used the verb *criticize* and referred to it as a means to collect critical feedback from the instructor for their professional opinions, stances, and decisions in the following interview excerpts.

Dialogic discussions between the PS and the student-teachers were described as resourceful by the participants. They also found her challenging, provoking, and critical, as she posed many questions and even assigned new tasks instead of answering their questions directly. She even created a critical discursive space for pre-service teachers to reflect over performances and decisions behind the praxis. As seen below in P7's comments, he felt frustrated when he was challenged for the ideas he had stated on his reflective reports but also realized that this professional learning was a never-ending process.

> P7: You always asked for deeper and deeper analyses of what I did in my teaching. I sometimes think it can't go further and I explained it carefully enough. You ask many questions on the ideas I presented in my reports. I suddenly realize trivial things that I never find significant might be important, indeed. I understand how important it is to ask questions and try to answer them. But to be honest, I sometimes feel frustrated. It will never end to learn how to teach. Day by day I realize that teachers are lifelong learners.
>
> Original version:
>
> P7: Yaptığım derslerle ilgili her zaman daha derin analiz yapmamı istediniz. Bazen yeterince açıkladım ve daha fazla nasıl açıklanır ki, diye düşündüm. Raporlarımda sunduğum fikirlerim hakkında da çok soru soruyorsunuz. Aniden bana çok önemsiz gelen konuların aslında gerekli olduklarını farkediyorum, gerçekten. Ama dürüst olayım, bazen çok zorlanıyorum. İyi bir öğretmen olmayı öğrenmek hiç bitmeyecek gibi. Her geçen gün öğretmenlerin yaşam boyu öğrenciler olduğunu farkediyorum.

P9, similarly, characterized dialogic interactions with the PS as multi-layered when she received feedback on her teaching performance. While she was expecting to find the answers for the questions in her mind, PS was putting new tasks on the table. P9 emphasized that dialogues were opening new perspectives on the issues at hand. On the other hand, she also implied the tension of not being able to finalize learning about a single event because the PS invited her to consider other perspectives, which she described as a pedagogically enriching professional learning experience.

> P9: You mostly criticize and expect to learn my reasoning behind every item on my lesson plans. When I want to confirm whether I was going the right way in my teaching, you suggest a new perspective and ask me for doing further research about. When I feel like theoretically I understand your perspective I think that I explained well enough your questions on a certain issue, then, you draw my attention to a different angle at reviewing that issue.
>
> Original version:
>
> P9: Ders planlarımdaki her şeyin sebebini bilmek istiyorsunuz ve çoğunlukla eleştiriyorsunuz. Doğru yolda olup olmadığıma emin olmak isterken, yeni bir bakış açısı gösterip biraz daha okumamı öneriyorsunuz. Bakış açınızı kavradığımı ve konuyu anladığımı düşünüp sorularınıza doğru cevaplar verdiğimi düşünürken birden o konuya başka bir açıdan bakmamı istiyorsunuz.

However, P3 considered these chains of provoking dialogic interactions with the PS as beneficial and satisfying. She admitted that the conversations were overwhelming, but she also learnt to manage classifying information and the required tasks to be completed in her own time, suggesting the enactment of professional agency. She highlighted the connection between the dialogic conversations and extending professional development into her personal space at her own pace, thereby taking responsibility over her learning.

> P3: I always have found dialoguing with you is overloaded. I keep taking notes while listening to you ... some keywords to be researched further, some articles to be read later. I ask many precise but very short questions but you give full answers. I learnt how to categorize your messages. Some I took as homework for me; others food for thought. I think I have become a successful multitasker.
>
> Original version:
>
> P3: Sizinle bu konuları konuşurken her zaman yoğunluk hissettim. Sizi dinlerken notlarımı alıyorum ... mesela bazı anahtar kelimeleri, ya da makaleleri, sonra araştırıp okumak için. Kısa ama net sorularım var ama hep upuzun cevaplar veriyorsunuz. Cevaplarınızı ayrıştırmayı yeni öğrendim. Bazı bölümleri kendime ev ödevi olarak ayırıyorum, bazılarını motto olarak. Sayenizde multitask olmayı öğrendim.

PS's field notes of practicum discussions suggested a sense of urgency in compensating for a lack of consistency between the approaches espoused by the teacher education program and the mentors' practices. In this sense, the volume of information shared may have worked against dialogism, although the student found the information beneficial.

On the other hand, some participants considered the dialogic conversations in the field placement among the pre-service teachers (rather than with PS) to be confusing. They described the discussions about their teaching performances and even advice on alternative actions to be accomplished in classes was difficult for two reasons: either because of peers' misinterpretations of their teaching or rationales for it, or because of their lack of response to requests for feedback. Some complained that the peers were not taking full responsibility of dialogic interaction. In the following excerpt from the interview with P10, she problematized the content of the interaction with her peers after she had completed practice teaching, suggesting that they critiqued her pedagogy without listening to her rationale. She added, however, that she did find value in her peer's suggestion.

> P10: For example, one of my peers critiqued the way I used the worksheet I prepared. She suggested another technique but I already did it that way. I sometimes feel some of my friends can't follow what I mean.
> PS: Then what does this tell you?
> P10: I think the way we communicate was not clear enough. We should have clarified our points much better. I feel I have a good reason for employing a particular activity but perhaps, I should have done the other way around.
> Original version:
> P10: Örneğin, bir arkadaş hazırladığım worksheeti eleştirdi. Başka bir teknik söyledi ama zaten onun dediği şekilde hazırlamıştım. Bazen ne demek istediğimi anlamadıklarını düşünüyorum.
> Ders Hocası: Peki bu durum senin için ne ifade ediyor?
> P10: Bence, iletişim biçimimiz eksik. Ne demek istediğimizi daha net açıklamalıydık. Bir etkinliği kullanırken mantıklı iyi bir nedenim olduğundan eminim, belki de, diğer türlüsünü yapmalıydım.

In a similar manner, P4 stated that she could not enhance the conversations with peers to a dialogic level while seeking advice for reflective reports and lesson plans. Receiving no or somewhat incomplete responses from the peers seems frustrating for the participant.

> P4: A few times, I shared my reflections and lesson plans with my groupmates on our WhatsApp group chat. I naturally waited for their opinions but received hardly any feedback. I even asked again on our face-to-face meetings. Yet, nothing changed. It is sad that I have always been ready to review theirs when they cared mine at all!

Original version:

P4: Bir kaç defa ders planlarımla reflectionlarımı WhatsApp grubumuzdan paylaştım. Cevap bekledim ama neredeyse hiçbir dönüş olmadı. Yüzyüze görüşünce de sınıfta sordum. Yine aynı. Her zaman elimden geleni yapıp onlarınkine yorumlar yaptım; onlar benimkini görmezden geldiler, çok üzücü!

The participants were supposed to conduct de-facto peer review processes after each class teaching they completed during the practicum. They were provided with a peer-review form including both a 5-Likert scale and open-ended commentary sections, which opened up the bi-directional dialogic professional communication. Additionally, they were encouraged to give feedback for their lesson plans before they implemented them in class sessions at the practicum schools. However, the two excerpts above indicate that dialogic interaction attempts of the participants were somewhat inhibited by misinterpretation or perceived indifference, which interfered with the progress of the CDE development in peer communication.

Discussion

The aim of this chapter was to explore how the NPI model contributed to the enactment of CDE for inclusive pedagogies during a TEFL field placement of a group of Turkish EFL teacher trainees. The multi-layered interactions indicated that CDE opened pathways for teacher agency through reflective and critical discussions over professional matters in ELT. It is not surprising regarding the function of field placements in teacher education and how they can contribute to teacher learning (Cleak & Wilson, 2019), formation of professional identity and agency development (Kayi-Aydar et al., 2019). Moreover, participants' professional positioning via critical discussions on inclusive pedagogies and becoming aware of multiple perspectives through their field observations and interactions with PS, the mentors, and the peers at local schools (Chick, 2015) enabled a degree of multivocality. At this point, Karam's (2021) putting multivocality at the heart of CDE seems to emerge in our study with reference to participants seeking to learn, understand, and act upon different views, which include those of their mentors, their practicum classroom students, their PS, and each other. In fact, during the TEFL field placement, participants encountered noninclusive learning environments where teacher-fronted/teacher-centered instruction was implemented and where practicum schools failed to offer equal opportunities for classroom participation and student engagement. It is through participating in critical and dialogic reflections that participants displayed alternative pathways for mainstream classroom practices. Kumaravadivelu (2012) also highlights the significance of a context-sensitive second language teacher education by pointing out programs encouraging trainees to develop their own attitude, knowledge, skill, and thus autonomy that their contexts require. In fact, teacher educators in the pre-service teacher education contexts need to emphasize the importance of adopting a context-bound, location-specific pedagogy based on a thorough understanding of linguistic, political, and sociocultural features in learning environments (Kumaravedivelu, 2012). In light of the findings, teacher educators might want to invest in raising pre-service teachers' awareness toward "the sociocultural reality that influences identity formation in the classroom" and toward the development of a holistic perspective that unites learners' linguistic and social needs (Kumaravadivelu, 2001, p. 544). It is also important to keep in mind that classroom pedagogies might entail power relationships and tend to generate and sustain inequalities in society. In this respect, having a strong sense of sociopolitical consciousness for pre-service teachers or learners in diverse settings possess might serve as "a catalyst for a continual quest for identity formation and social transformation" (Kumaravadivelu, 2001, p. 525).

However, sustaining the quality and the process of critical and dialogic discussions was not free from challenges, and it was not a smooth pathway to realize a clear frame of CDE with and among pre-service teachers. According to participant descriptions on how dialogic interactions were established during field placement, they were not entirely satisfactory. Indeed, although some students found that the teacher's role supported their professional learning and development, they were also frustrated by extended questioning and the volume of information provided. Regarding dialogic interactions with the PS, participants' finding the discussions overwhelming might be a result of disconnects between the mentors' practice and that of the teacher education program, which led to the PS's feeling obliged to compensate.

Moreover, peers were reported to inconsistently take the full responsibility of acting as dialogic partners to each other at some stages of the field placement, either through miscommunication or unresponsiveness. This might be interpreted as having inhibited self-confidence due to the lack of professional experience, potential language, and required competency, but cultural norms and habits might also be another indicator for such behaviors (Hofstede, 2011). Turkish culture accepts teachers as the sole authority according to the paternalistic leadership model (Baykal, 2019), and thus, peer review is either very subtle or not realized throughout the compulsory education (Cemaloglu & Duran, 2018; Gülmez, 2022). As participants in Turkish higher education contexts tend to perceive themselves as having equal power, they may not be willing to take an active role in critical and dialogic peer discussions outside the classroom context. Thus, it is crucial to motivate the pre-service teachers in the teacher education programs to put forward their unique perspectives, irrespective of the power dynamics that exist among them.

Conclusion

Through the current study, we gained some critical insights on how CDE could be enacted in a TEFL field placement, and collected some concrete examples of how and why some aspects of CDE went well but not others. While findings from this study suggest that dialogic and critical discussions with student-teachers within the context of a field placement helped them reflect and propose how they can be more inclusive educators, the potentials of CDE were sometimes diminished without a functional triangulation where all the agents of the field placement, that is, teacher trainees, PSs and mentors, were involved in negotiated interaction. This lack of triangulation could be attributed to the fact that CDE is not a mainstream tradition of Turkish field placement schemes. The first author as the main data collector and participant observer implemented the whole research procedure and demonstrated a satisfactory understanding of CDE. However, when other spaces and agents in a community of practice seemed to provide insufficient dialogic interactions, the PS overloaded trainees by more critical questions, which was potentially frustrating. Nevertheless, the NPI is still a positive beginning to promote CDE in the study context.

The current NPI version can be extended to include all the partners like other PSs in the department and the mentors at practicum schools during the field placement. Therefore, another recommendation to develop such a scheme utilizing CDE for empowering each agent is sharing further and constant dialogic implementations responsibly by all parties within the practicum context. Then, it becomes more agreeable to accept CDE as a departmental policy for not only professional but also personal growth of the agents involved in the field placement. Overall, though small-scaled, this study showed a clear participant embracement of CDE through demonstrating active participation at each step of the research, where such engagements can be interpreted as promising and yielding. Future studies can investigate the adoption of critical and dialogic approaches not only within the field placement context, but also throughout the entire teacher education program.

References

Baykal, E. (2019). Turkish type leadership: Sabri Ulker example. *The Journal of Social Science, 3*(6), 425–38. https://doi.org/10.30520/tjsosci.590000

Cemaloglu, N., & Duran, A. (2018). Teacher leadership perceptions in Turkish culture: A qualitative analysis. *Journal of Education and Training Studies, 6*(11), 45–59. https://doi.org/10.11114/jets.v6i11a.3800

Chick, M. (2015). The education of language teachers: Instruction or conversation? *ELT Journal, 69*(3), 297–307. https://doi.org/10.1093/elt/ccv011

Cleak, H., & Wilson, J. (2019). *Making the most of field placement* (4th Ed.). Cengage Learning.

ETS. (n.d.) *Setting score requirements.* Accessed April 3, 2022. https://www.ets.org/s/toefl-essentials/score-users/scores-admissions/set/

Gülmez, D. (2022). Teacher leadership and the Turkish context: The impact of the structural characteristics of the school and teacher leadership culture. *International Journal of Educational Management, 3*(4), 515–26. https://doi.org/10.1108/IJEM-02-2022-0061

Hamilton, L., & Corbett-Whittier, C. (2012). *Using case study in education research.* Sage.

Hofstede, G. (2011). Dimensionalizing cultures: The Hofstede model in context. *Online Readings in Psychology and Culture, 2*(1), 1–26. https://doi.org/10.9707/2307-0919.1014

Hurriyet Daily News. (2022). *Results of university exams to be announced on July 20.* https://www.hurriyetdailynews.com/results-of-university-exams-to-be-announced-on-july-20-174706

Karam, F. J. (2021). Re-envisioning the ESOL classroom through a virtues-based curriculum: Contributions to critical dialogic education. *TESOL Journal, 12*(3), e582. https://doi.org/10.1002/tesj.582

Kayi-Aydar, H., Miller, E. R., Varghese, M., & Vitanova, G. (Eds.). (2019). *Theorizing and analyzing language teacher agency.* Multilingual Matters.

Kibler, A., Valdés, G., & Walqui, A. (2021). Introduction. In A. Kibler, G. Valdés, & A. Walqui (Eds.), *Reconceptualizing the role of critical dialogue in American classrooms: Promoting equity through dialogic education* (pp. 1–22). Routledge.

Koç, E. M. (2012). Idiographic roles of cooperating teachers as mentors in pre-service distance teacher education. *Teaching and Teacher Education, 28*(6), 818–26. https://doi.org/10.1016/j.tate.2012.03.007

Krathwohl, D. R. (2002). A revision of Bloom's taxonomy: An overview. *Theory into Practice, 41*(4), 212–8. https://doi.org/10.1207/s15430421tip4104_2

Kumaravadivelu, B. (2001). Toward a postmethod pedagogy. *TESOL Quarterly, 35*, 537–57. http://dx.doi.org/10.2307/3588427

Kumaravadivelu, B. (2012). *Language teacher education for a global society: A modular model for knowing, analyzing, recognizing, doing, and seeing*. Routledge.

Merriam, S. B. (1988). *Case study research in education: A qualitative approach*. Jossey-Bass.

Miles, M. B., Huberman, A.M., & Saldaña, J. (2018). *Qualitative data analysis: A methods sourcebook* (4th Ed.). Sage.

National Education Statistics. (2022). *Formal education 2021/2022*. Retrieved January 23, 2023, from https://sgb.meb.gov.tr/meb_iys_dosyalar/2022_09/15142558_meb_istatistikleri_orgun_egitim_2021_2022.pdf

Pintrich, P. R., & Zusho, A. (2007). Student motivation and self-regulated learning in the college classroom. In R. P. Perry & J. C. Smart (Eds.), *The scholarship of teaching and learning in higher education: An evidence-based perspective* (pp. 731–810). Springer.

Saldaña, J. (2021). *The coding manual for qualitative researchers* (4th Ed.). Sage.

Turkish Ministry of National Education. (2020). *Uygulama öğrencilerinin millî eğitim bakanlığına bağlı eğitim öğretim kurumlarında yapacakları öğretmenlik uygulamasına ilişkin yönerge [Practicum regulations for pre-service teachers to practice at schools of Ministry of National Education]*. Retrieved January 10, 2023, from https://oygm.meb.gov.tr/meb_iys_dosyalar/2020_07/13135500_Yonerge.pdf

UDL. (2013). *About UDL*. Retrieved July 7, 2022, from http://udloncampus.cast.org/page/udl_about

Part Two

Commentary: Reimagining the Roles of Teacher Candidates and Teacher Educators: How Identities, Voices, and Power Are Taught and Learned

Camille Ungco and Manka Varghese

The introduction of the concept and set of practices which are referred to now as *Critical* Dialogic Education (CDE) as proposed by Kibler et al. (2021) add a very important layer to the ideas and practices already associated with Dialogic Education by "questioning power structures that govern classroom dialogue and bringing equitable pedagogies to life" (Karam, 2021, p. 2). While CDE as originally conceived guides equity-focused classroom pedagogies for K-12 language learning, CDE is taken up by these three chapters in relation to dialogic, critical, and inclusive practices within current teachers', teacher candidates', as well as teacher educators' learning. Kibler, Valdés, and Walqui (2021) foresaw the need for teacher educators, teachers, and teacher candidates to also experience CDE as part of their own learning and preparation. Kibler et al. wrote: "We agree with arguments that dialogic environments support students' academic, linguistic, and intellectual development, but we extend such ideas to argue that **critical perspectives on dialogic education, both for researchers and practitioners, must be our starting point**" (2021, p. 1, emphasis added).

In attending especially to power differentials, as teacher educators and teacher education researchers ourselves, we put significant emphasis in terms of how learning is shaped by identity, shapes identity, and how the larger process of learning can be viewed as a form of identity formation (Daniels & Varghese, 2020; Varghese, 2006; Varghese, 2017; Varghese & Snyder, 2018) in our own work. The assumption, therefore, in our work is that in order to be critical teachers and critical teacher educators, teacher identity has to be accounted for, examined, and developed within teacher education programs and spaces (Daniels & Varghese, 2020; Snyder Bhansari et al., 2022; Ungco et al., 2022). In this vein, it seems important for both of us to briefly describe our own identities, our relationship to each other, as well as how some of our work relates to critical dialogic education within teacher education, to more effectively and authentically frame our commentary of the three chapters.

We are both teacher educators, a graduate student and a faculty advisor at the University of Washington in Seattle, and also both Asian diasporic immigrant women of color. Camille was a US public school elementary teacher, an English language teacher in Indonesia, and is currently working on her doctoral program. Her work focuses on anti-colonial practices in teacher education. Manka was also an English as a Second Language (ESL) teacher for a number of years before moving into a tenure line faculty position twenty years ago where her work has been focused on reducing harm and improving experiences for multilingual students through teacher education as well as for racialized multilingual teachers. Both of us have been working together for four years in an elementary teacher education program at the University of Washington (UW) College of Education. We collaborate on the identity-based strand which runs throughout the program as well as co-teaching a class focused on intersectionality (for students and for teacher candidates). In addition to teaching, we have been theorizing and writing about our collaborative work together and with others (Ungco, Snyder Bhansari, & Varghese, 2022; Varghese, Snyder Bhansari, & Ungco, in press). Our critical dialogic work with each other within teacher education guides our commentary.

As the chapters in this section suggest, CDE at the practitioner level is necessary for teacher educators, current teachers, and teacher candidates because it challenges and re-envisions what we might think of as traditional teacher education practices. Each author team in this section described how they created and grappled with dialogic, critical, and inclusive practices in teacher education: Mohamed, Biebricher, and Erlam's chapter (this volume) on themselves as teacher educators, Kızıldağ and Kaçar (this volume) with teacher candidates, and Meston and Galloway (this volume) with current teachers. What was striking in terms of the similarities and connections between each chapter was that all the authors were involved in promoting CDE with the teacher candidates or teachers they were working with and were also attempting to use or study how CDE was being used with the teacher candidates and teachers for their professional development. In this commentary, we articulate the connections and differences we identified across chapters, and keeping the following four themes in mind as they are relevant to how CDE is drawn on for TESOL teacher candidates, teachers, and teacher educators:

1. Accounting for identities, lived experiences, and contexts
2. Re-envisioning classroom talk
3. Collaborating and decentering authority
4. Learning equity and justice

Accounting for Identities, Lived Experiences, and Contexts

Although CDE does not explicitly call for the engagement of teacher and student identities, we explain our perspective of the importance of that in our introduction, especially as we reimagine the roles of teacher candidates, teachers, and teacher educators. In the introduction to their chapter, Mohamed, Biebricher, and Erlam (this volume) write that "as schools and communities continue to become increasingly diverse, it has become more important for educators to self-examine their beliefs and biases, and develop critical consciousness of the systems of power and privilege in education" (p. 5). Because of this goal in their chapter, the authors were the most intentional in constructing their respective study designs around their own identities as teacher educators in their chapter. However, the authors of all three chapters were intentional in highlighting, folding in and in some cases, constructing their own and their participants' teaching and learning contexts to align with the "contextual responsiveness" common to dialogic teaching (Kibler et al., 2021, p. 9).

In most explicitly discussing their own identities and contexts as teacher educators Mohamed, Biebricher, & Erlam (this volume) focus their findings around the following two themes: "how our lived experiences shape our practice, and how CDE embodies our teaching" (p. 135). The methodology used in this study of duoethnography is one with which "researchers examine their lived experiences through a critical lens, question their constructed knowledge and challenge each other to reflect on the different voices within each narrative" (p. 134), and in sharing their narratives, the three teacher educators were involved in "interactive dialogue" around their lived experiences and their practices as teacher educators. They write that although their lived experiences were very different, they all learned that they "share a love of languages, an appreciation of cultural diversity, and a desire to prepare teachers to support plurilingual learners based on principles of inclusion." Moreover, in discussing student assignments, they also write about how they learned that two of the teacher educators, Erlam and Mohamed, focused on different aspects of a particular assignment and by dialoguing with each other, realized that the former was more focused on the argument and the quality of the writing, and Mohamed looked more at the values expressed, paying attention to whether deficit perspectives were being exploited. Within this chapter, although not explicitly stated, it was clear to us that Mohamed is the only author and teacher educator of color and specifically wrote about her lived experiences related to that and how that "heightened her awareness of inequities and injustices against marginalized groups." Although the authors wrote about learning their sharedness and differences through their duoethnography, it was, however, not clear how the three authors engaged with each other in terms of their different intersectional identities and in learning around justice-related matters in language education. This was especially important since at the end of the chapter the authors acknowledged the following: "the need for cultivating more equitable systems of education, given the differences in our worldviews and identities, the process of doing that has varied between us," and that they desired to help prepare teachers build more equitable futures for their minoritized students in New Zealand (p. 142).

Although the authors in the other two chapters did not explicitly address their own identities or that of their participants as much, the contexts of each study were relevant to how they practiced CDE and how their participants responded to it. It should be mentioned that Meston and Galloway briefly address their identities and lived experiences as related to the focus of their study, SIFE (Students with Interrupted Formal Education) and teachers of SIFE. They mention their limitations as "White, primarily English-speaking education researchers and former middle school educators" but also mentioning that "we come to this work with perspectives informed by our experiences and identities," these being their experiences having researched and taught SIFE (p. 116). The most salient example, however, of how context was foregrounded in considering teacher educator and teacher candidate roles was in the study by Kızıldağ and Kaçar (this volume) which took place in Turkey. A significant conclusion made by the authors is that the mentor encouraging a more critical dialogic approach may not have been as well received by the teacher candidates because they were uncomfortable with it and used to a transmission model of learning in the context of Turkey. In other words, as Kettle and Luke (2012; as cited in Kibler et al., 2021, p. 6) argue, "an explicitly critical dialogic approach is problematic in certain terms, in that traditions of critique may be less culturally familiar and comfortable for some students than for others." In a different way, the contextual aspects which seemed to be most relevant for the Meston and Galloway chapter were the relationship they had with one of the teachers who recruited other teachers with similar commitments. This helped shape the dialoguing the teacher educators/researchers were able to construct with the teachers and among the teachers, in their study.

The fact that all three chapters took place in different countries and at least in two chapters—the ones by Mohamed, Biebricher, and Erlam and Kızıldağ and Kaçar—the authors made these spatial contexts integral to their arguments around re-envisioning roles for teacher candidates, teachers, and teacher educators. In the earlier paragraph, we discussed the challenges Kızıldağ and Kaçar wrote about the context of higher education in Turkey in terms of teacher candidates' receptiveness around critical dialogic education. Mohamed, Biebricher, and Erlam situate their study in the historical injustices against the Maori and the multilingual policies of New Zealand, and one of the strong threads in their chapter is around pushing and re-envisioning teacher candidates in terms of their justice orientations. Although Meston and Galloway's study and their participant teachers are situated in an urban Southeastern United States, what they center is that like them, their teachers are focused on SIFE in their CDE professional development. They specifically mention that CDE's "benefits may be particularly important for multilingual students with interrupted formal education (SIFE), who are still in the process of developing heritage and English language literacy, and who possess limited experience in formal educational systems" (p. 107).

In making a final note about the relevance of contexts in re-envisioning the roles of teacher candidates, teachers and teacher educators through CDE, it feels important to end with the following quote by Kibler et al. (2021, p. 9), which leaves us with a useful set of questions to ask about the studies (where the "students" would be teacher candidates, teachers, and teacher educators) in these chapters, as well as studies any of us choose to engage with "the notion that discourse is responsive to and inextricable from its contexts of use is also shifted in CDE, in this case toward a recognition that any context necessarily privileges some students as it marginalizes others: no settings are neutral."

Re-envisioning Classroom Talk

Guided by the identities and lived experiences, in one chapter more than the others, and by contexts of their participants, the three studies are connected through their re-envisioning of a traditional teacher education practice: "classroom talk." In each of the chapters, the participating teachers, teacher candidates, or teacher educators experience a version of classroom talk to learn about CDE, reflect on their dialogic teaching practices and learnings, as well as enact these practices with each other. Classroom talk is one of two key components of CDE-based pedagogies: "a critical dialogic perspective that is firmly grounded in a questioning of the 'necessary good' of classroom talk" (Kibler et al., 2021, p. 7). The authors ask us to re-envision classroom talk, but in TESOL teacher education contexts. Each chapter engaged with a form of classroom talk that is both shaped by and shifts the roles of teacher candidates, current teachers, or teacher educators. These three multivocal teacher education practices present possibilities to account for identities, collaborate, and decenter authority, as well as learn equity and justice.

To create opportunities for multivocal discourse and learning, the authors designed or re-envisioned a practice of classroom talk. Here is the name and definition of each chapter's multivocal pedagogy or classroom talk:

- *With teacher educators*—Duoethnography: "two or more co-researchers collaborate, engage in direct dialogue, and share and explore differences and understandings around a predetermined subject (Garcia & Cifor, 2015; Norris & Sawyer, 2012)" (Mohamed, Biebricher, & Erlam, this volume, p. 128)
- *With teacher candidates*—Notice-Problematize-Implement (NPI): "participating student-teachers were actively engaged in critical and dialogic discussions between their peers and the university practicum supervisor regarding the core topic of inclusiveness during their weekly class meetings on campus" (Kızıldağ and Kaçar, this volume, p. 148)
- *With current teachers*—Critical Friends Group (CFG): "a structured form of professional learning wherein participants question and propose potential solutions to problems of practice presented by collaborators" (Meston & Philips Galloway, this volume, p. 109)

The chapters' new visions for classroom talk within teacher education are dialogic-based, meaning each of these practices are "co-constructed, intellectually purposeful, adaptive, respectful, and responsive to context" (Kibler et al., 2021, p. 5). While traditional dialogic teaching practices are multivocal, it is important to note that not every practice of classroom talk, traditional or reimagined, truly embodies CDE.

As we discussed in the section above, teacher education practices, guided by CDE, need to account for the identities, lived experiences, and contexts of teacher candidates, teachers, and teacher educators. In recognizing that "no settings are neutral" through CDE, we noticed that each chapter's unique take on classroom talk offered both possibilities and limitations for who participates in multivocality and how (Kibler et al., 2021, p. 9). CDE posits that multivocal learning spaces are not bound by consensus or closure: "pedagogy and research in dialogic traditions such as CDE invite this multivocality without seeking to unify or resolve it" (Kibler et al., 2021, p. 186). Since each chapter offers a design for classroom talk where the teachers, teacher candidates, and teacher educators are all engaging in dialogue, we now look into how these new visions of classroom talk grapple with CDE's approaches to multivocality and its impact on TESOL teacher education.

Practices of classroom talk can potentially shift the expectations and roles of student teachers within teacher education programs. Kızıldağ and Kaçar (this volume) enacted classroom talk through a practice they named the "Notice-Problematize-Implement" (NPI) cycle. The NPI cycle provided opportunities for teacher educators to teach teacher candidates about CDE while mutually participating in CDE practices. To complete the NPI cycle, ten participating Turkish student teachers each shared a challenge of inclusion from their ELT student-teaching placement. The student teachers then experienced three stages of processing and problem-solving with both their one teacher educator and their peers during university-based coursework as well as within their student teaching placements. As we discussed in the first section, Kızıldağ and Kaçar encountered challenges with utilizing CDE practices because of Turkey's ongoing relationship with the traditional transmission model of learning. The NPI cycle, as a version of classroom talk, may not have thoroughly supported teacher candidates with their own enactments of CDE practices; however, the chapter initiates an international reckoning with the complexities of critical dialogic teacher education pedagogies.

Kızıldağ and Kaçar's version of classroom talk demands for the roles of teacher educators and teacher candidates to change. While the NPI cycle consisted of many opportunities for teacher candidates to participate in dialogue with one another as well as with their teacher educator, the classroom talk practice instead had teacher candidates feeling "frustrated by extended questioning and the volume of information provided" (Kızıldağ and Kaçar, this volume, p. 163). Additionally, teacher candidates had mixed experiences with their peers' input or participation in these dialogues because peer to peer learning is not highly valued in Turkey at this time. The NPI cycle, as a version of classroom talk in teacher education, calls for a change in how teacher educators and teacher candidates perceive their own roles as learners and teachers in TESOL teacher training.

Teacher candidates' roles can shift to recognizing one another as sources of knowledge since this is the aim for CDE practices when used with their own

K-12 students. Teacher educators need to both relinquish their traditional role as the only authority of teaching and enact classroom talk practices that sustain this role transition. One possible practice of shifting teacher educators' roles is explored in Meston and Galloway's chapter, which we discuss further in our fourth section. Instead of continuing to perpetuate hierarchical learning in teacher training programs, teacher educators can honor and value peer to peer learning—even colleague-to-colleague learning as shown in Mohamed, Biebricher, and Erlam's duoethnography practice. Kızıldağ and Kaçar's re-envisioning of a classroom talk practice in teacher education demonstrates how CDE pedagogies can reimagine the roles of teacher educators and teacher candidates to support peer to peer learning.

Collaborating and Decentering Authority

While Kızıldağ and Kaçar call for a shift in the roles of teacher educators and teacher candidates, they also signal a need for examining the ways in which classroom talk practices equitably engage learners in teacher training that is both dialogic and collaborative. The chapters show us that transforming teaching and learning roles within TESOL teacher education ultimately leads to confronting power and authority within these same programs. The second key component of pedagogies that enact CDE is "a proactive vision that seeks to give voice to students and disrupt inequitable power dynamics inside and beyond classrooms" (Kibler et al., 2021, p. 7). We return to our focus on the chapters' new visions for classroom talk in teacher education because the dialogic practices can support both collaborating and decentering authority among teachers, teacher candidates, and teacher educators.

Classroom talk within teacher education does not necessarily need a designated "classroom" space but rather a commitment to dialogic collaboration between learners. We return to Mohamed, Biebricher, and Erlam's chapter because they utilized duoethnography to create a version of classroom talk used amongst themselves as teacher educators. To facilitate duoethnography, these authors participated in an iterative cycle that consisted of formal and informal conversations, collaborative brainstorming, individual narrative writing, sharing these narratives via email, rewrites followed by rereading, and culminated with co-writing their chapter. This process took several months. Mohamed, Biebricher, and Erlam re-envisioned classroom talk as a practice that is more committed to time rather than space, that integrates various multimodal mediums of dialogue and, as they found, creates a "space for a multiplicity of perspectives" (this volume, p. 134). This chapter suggests that ongoing and intentional spaces of dialogues are needed to continue learner-to-learner collaboration, especially among teacher educators as the learners.

Continued dialogic collaboration across learners supports decentering authority within teacher training. Kızıldağ and Kaçar wanted to decenter the teacher educator as the authority figure through the NPI cycle and instead support teacher candidate collaborative learning. Mohamed, Biebricher, and Erlam's use of duoethnography aligns with CDE teaching practices that disrupt this authoritative power because the practice allows for multiple voices to collaborate and even co-reflect without assessment or conclusions. Mohamed, Biebricher, and Erlam found that their shared teacher educator narratives varied in form, content, and complexity. However, they did not see these variables as a limitation to their discussions, citing how "'differences' is one of duoethnography's tenets that allows us to reconceptualize our own values, beliefs and perspectives" (this volume, p. 134). Duoethnography, as a pedagogical practice, encouraged collaborative learning amongst a space for only teacher educators. None of the three authors took up an authoritative role amidst their iterative dialogic practice, instead recognizing how they were mutually learning from one another. For these teacher educators, classroom talk practices do not always need a physical space but rather a commitment to consistent collaboration while decentering authority amongst learner to learner dialogue. In Meston and Galloway's chapter (this volume), teacher educators helped decenter authority through collaborative participation in a critical friends group (CFG).

Learning Equity and Justice

Classroom talk, guided by CDE, needs to be responsive to identities and contexts, shift roles between learners, decenter authority, and be critical about whose voices are included. Meston and Galloway (this volume) re-envisioned classroom talk to be an ongoing space for teacher collaboration with teacher educators within the context of a critical friends group. These authors brought together four US teachers and placed them in their version of classroom talk—a Critical Friends Group (CFG). Each participating in-service teacher had designated time within the recurring CFG meetings to thoroughly share one problem of practice followed by an in-depth CDE-guided processing and problem-solving discussion with the other teachers. CFG meetings were led and participated in by only the collaborating teachers. Meston and Galloway supported teachers in creating and working toward their own visions, rather than reusing traditional teacher education practices with "passive assimilation of knowledge and compliance with experts' recommendations" (this volume, p. 108). The participating teachers shared their tensions with supporting SIFE through dialogic practices. Additionally, teachers offered questions and possible solutions to one another. They utilized their respective teaching experiences and contexts as well as their collective expertise without needing to negotiate power dynamics from a "more expert" teacher educator or otherwise authoritative source. CFG was multivocal, consistently supported peer-to-peer learning, and reimagined the roles within teacher education because the practice centered dialogic collaboration and allowed teachers to act as problem-solvers.

CFG's collaborative structure is also an example of how classroom talk can decenter authority in TESOL teacher education, as we explored in the previous section. This CDE enactment leads peer-centered discussions toward learning equity and justice in teacher education. The CFG teachers also reminded one another to center practices and components of CDE in their meetings and to center the needs and identities of their respective SIFE students. Meston and Galloway designed this practice of classroom talk based on the notion that teachers who "[engage] in the reflective practice of articulating and refining their vision of aspirational teaching" with one another are more likely to learn and enact critical practices such as CDE pedagogies (this volume, p. 111). Teachers had the recurring opportunity to collaboratively analyze problems of practice with each other. They learned to center equity and justice practices by enacting these practices with one another. Through CFG, teachers were able to collectively learn with and from each other and prioritize equitable strategies for dialogic education. Consequently, teacher educators moved from being the sole expert, a tension in Kızıldağ and Kaçar's chapter, to instead using their own programmatic agency and resources to create a truly CDE-based space for teacher learning.

CDE practices, as seen through the three classroom talk designs, used multivocal dialogue to support teacher candidates, teacher educators, and teachers in learning equity and justice in TESOL teacher education. Kızıldağ and Kaçar created the NPI cycle to initially teach students teachers how to problematize and solve noninclusive ELT teaching practices. Rather, the authors and participants began discussions on disrupting hierarchies in teaching and learning. They recognized inequitable practices were happening in their own spaces of learning. Mohamed, Biebricher, and Erlam's chapter, a manifestation of their duoethnography dialogue, ended with more questions than conclusions in relation to language teaching for Maori and Pacific peoples as an extension of bigger discussions on Indigenous sovereignty and justice. Finally, meant to focus on teaching practices for SIFE contexts, Meston and Galloway's CFG emphasized that teacher education needs to enact both experiences for learning and practicing CDE: "Perhaps it was the need to make visible [teachers'] visions to colleagues, to put language to and contextualize the abstract phenomenon of CDE. This positions equity work as involving learning 'the talk' in dialogic interaction with peers as part of the broader phenomenon of 'walking the walk' in classrooms" (this volume, p. 123).

Conclusion

Within each of these studies, the researchers recognized that it was not enough to learn about CDE through instruction. Current teachers, teacher candidates, and teacher educators needed to shift their practices, roles, and relationships to both learn about and experience CDE amongst themselves. Each chapter's responsiveness to learner identities, lived experiences, and contexts, as well as their respective reimagining of classroom talk articulated a facet of CDE. The NPI cycle highlighted the need for traditional roles of teacher educators and teacher candidates to change within the structure of teacher preparation programs. Duoethnography showed us how commitment to consistent collaborative dialogue and reflection is necessary for colleague-to-colleague learning. Finally, CFG meetings demonstrated how teachers need to recognize and utilize their own expertise while also continuing to develop their pedagogies for equity and justice amongst one another.

While the practices of classroom talk begin to reimagine the roles of teacher candidates and teacher educators, the author teams also expressed caution when utilizing classroom talk in TESOL teacher education. CDE practices can exclude teacher learners without proper instructional facilitation and equitable relationship building. Scheduling constraints and inaccessible methods of dialogue among teacher learner participants can create pauses and disruptions in dialogues. CDE provides a space and a way of learning, processing, and problem-solving inequities in classroom practices; however, teacher educators and teacher training program leaders need to use their authority and power dynamics to create more accessible and equitable structures for truly critical dialogic learning practices.

We looked at how the chapters re-envisioned practices of classroom talk to ultimately reimagine roles and relationships between current teachers, teacher educators, and teacher candidates. Also, it is not lost on us that each of these chapters was co-written, including our very own commentary. These chapters then push us to consider how classroom talk for TESOL teacher education can extend beyond the teacher learning spaces—the university classrooms, the program leadership and course instructor meetings, and the continuing teacher professional development meetings—to also spaces for research and writing while centering CDE?

References

Bhansari, R. S., Park, C., Varghese, M., & Daniels, J. (2022). Forging teacher educator identities: Embracing friction through critical reflexivity. *The New Educator, 19*(4), 1–15. https://doi.org/10.1080/1547688X.2022.2151675

Daniels, J. R., & Varghese, M. (2020). Troubling practice: Exploring the relationship between Whiteness and practice-based teacher education in considering a raciolinguicized teacher subjectivity. *Educational Researcher, 49*(1), 56–63. https://doi.org/10.3102/0013189X19879450

García-Carrión, R., & Díez-Palomar, J. (2015). Learning communities: Pathways for educational success and social transformation through interactive groups in mathematics. *European Educational Research Journal, 14*(2), 151–66. https://doi.org/10.1177/1474904115571793

Karam, F. J. (2021). Re-envisioning the ESOL classroom through a virtues-based curriculum: Contributions to critical dialogic education. *TESOL Journal, 12*(3), e582. https://doi.org/10.1002/tesj.582

Kettle, M., & Luke, A. (2012). The critical meets the cultural: International students' responses to critical, dialogic postgraduate education in a western university. In S. Sovic & M. Blythman (Eds.), *International students negotiating higher education: Critical perspectives* (pp. 104–23). Routledge.

Kibler, A., Valdés, G., & Walqui, A. (2021a). Introduction: A vision for critical dialogic education. In A. Kibler, G. Valdés, & A. Walqui (Eds.), *Reconceptualizing the role of critical dialogue in American classrooms: Promoting equity through dialogic education* (pp. 1–22). Routledge.

Kibler, A., Valdés, G., & Walqui, A. (2021b). Conclusion: Next steps for critical dialogic education: Conceptualizing and implementing a student-centered vision. In A. Kibler, G. Valdés, & A. Walqui (Eds.), *Reconceptualizing the role of critical dialogue in American classrooms: Promoting equity through dialogic education* (pp. 185–93). Routledge.

Norris, J., & Sawyer, D. R. (2012). Towards a dialogic method. In J. Norris, D. S. Richard & D. Lund (Eds.), *Duoethnography: Dialogic methods for social, health, and educational research* (pp. 9–40). Left Coast Press.

Ungco, C., Bhansari, R. S., & Varghese, M. (2022). Challenging epistemologies of objectivity through collaborative pedagogy: Centering identity, power, emotions, and place in teacher education. *Northwest Journal of Teacher Education, 17*(3), 29. https://doi.org/10.15760/nwjte.2022.17.3.29

Varghese, M. (2017). Drawing on cultural models and figured worlds to study language teacher education and identity. In S. Mercer & A. Kostoulas (Eds.), *Teacher psychology in SLA* (pp. 71–85). Multilingual Matters.

Varghese, M., Bhansari, R. S., & Ungco, C. (in press). Collectivizing our care: Offerings for holistic well-being in teacher education for multilingual teachers of color. In A. Feryok (Ed.), *Language teacher identity and well-being*. Multilingual Matters.

Varghese, M. M. (2006). Bilingual teachers-in-the-making in Urbantown. *Journal of Multilingual and Multicultural Development, 27*(3), 211–24. https://doi.org/10.1080/01434630608668776

Varghese, M. M., & Snyder, R. (2018). Critically examining the agency and professional identity development of novice dual language teachers through figured worlds. *International Multilingual Research Journal, 12*(3), 145–59. https://doi.org/10.1080/19313152.2018.1474060

Part Three

Reimagining Online TESOL Teacher Education: Creating Dialogic and Critical Online Spaces

Creating a Dialogic Online Space for Preparing Critically Reflective TESOL Educators

Guofang Li and Yue Bian

Introduction

With the increasing global migration, classrooms in the United States and worldwide are becoming more racially, linguistically, and culturally diverse. Discordant with the rapid influx of multilingual learners in PK-12 schools over the past few decades, teachers in the United States are found to be underprepared to address the cultural and linguistic diversities in their classrooms (Coady et al., 2011; Durgunoğlu & Hughes, 2010; Li et al., 2019). The shortage of qualified general education teachers and specialists in teaching English to speakers of other languages (TESOL) contributes to the persistent opportunity gaps and educational inequities between minoritized multilingual learners and their monolingual, dominant-language-speaking peers, which have been exacerbated by the Covid-19 pandemic (Li et al., 2021; Mahnken, 2022). To help multilingual learners fulfill their language and academic potentials, researchers have articulated dimensions of knowledge, skills, and dispositions that teachers need to be equipped with in the initial teacher preparation and ongoing professional learning (e.g., de Jong et al., 2013; Fillmore & Snow, 2002; Li, 2018; Lucas & Villegas, 2013). In addition to developing pedagogical knowledge of teaching language and teaching academic content through language, researchers also advocate for preparing critically reflective teachers with social justice orientations, who "challenge the linguistic and racialized norms and expectations that often limit multilingual learners' opportunities" and strive to dismantle the "inequitable and discriminatory ideologies, institutional structures, and social practices" (Kibler et al., 2021, p. 1).

Brookfield (2017) defined teachers' critical reflection as an ongoing, intentional self-interrogation of teaching assumptions. According to Brookfield (2017), "classrooms are not limpid, tranquil, reflective eddies cut off from the river of social, cultural, and political life" (p. 10). Rather, they are always intruded upon by structures and forces presented in the wider society. Critical reflection allows teachers to examine how education processes, interactions, and decisions are framed by such power structures and dominant ideologies. It also pushes teachers to challenge the hegemonic assumptions and practices of teaching that normalize, legitimize, and reproduce the way power dynamics operate in classrooms, schools, and the broader educational system (Brookfield, 2017). Critically reflective teachers are thus those who are willing and prepared to critique, interrupt, and transform existing patterns and processes of schooling to improve the learning of all, not only the privileged few (Down, 2006).

Dialogue, defined as "an act of communication in relationship that shapes one's orientation to others and the world" (Freire & Shor 1987, p. 323, as cited in Rule, 2004), has long been embraced by educational researchers as a means to empower students to become independent, critical thinkers and active citizens of a pluralistic, democratic society (Kibler et al., 2021). Freire (2005) emphasized the reciprocity of dialogic learning and critical reflection, arguing that "true dialogue cannot exist unless the dialoguers engage in critical thinking," which allows dialoguers to "perceive reality as process, as transformation, rather than as a static entity" (p. 92). It is through dialogic learning that people reflect together and act critically to transform reality (Freire & Shor, 1987, as cited in Rule, 2004).

Kibler et al. (2021) extended the discussion of critical and dialogic education to the field of second language education. Besides facilitating dialogic learning that is co-constructed, intellectually stimulating, and responsive to contexts, the authors emphasized questioning, recognizing, and disrupting power dynamics that marginalize or even exclude multilingual learners from active and agentic participation in classroom discourse. Teachers adopting critical and dialogic pedagogies need to attend to unequal structures and practices in and beyond their classroom communities and empower all students to become legitimate contributors to dialogic learning.

Advances in educational technology, digital resources, and particularly remote learning have urged researchers to examine the affordances and constraints of enacting dialogic learning and teaching in an online space. Farooq and Benade (2019) argued that while dialogue may be compromised because of the asynchrony and time lag in online communications, Web 2.0 technologies such as threaded discussion forums, blogging and microblogging (e.g., Twitter), Wiki projects, social networking, and video sharing (e.g., YouTube) (Lipika, 2016), make dialogue in the online learning environment approximate to real-time interactions (Farooq & Benade, 2019). Those technologies allow more than just receiving information but also sharing, communicating, collaborating, content building, and knowledge co-construction among users (Farooq, 2019). The "anywhere, anytime" mode of communication and the low-risk learning environment may also be attractive to students (Delahunty, 2018; Farooq, 2019).

In sum, there is an urgent need for preparing critically reflective teachers for multilingual learners and the advancement of educational technologies makes it feasible to address this need in an online space. In this chapter, we document how two teacher educators created a critically reflective and dialogic online learning space for teacher candidates to self-interrogate assumptions, acquire knowledge about multilingual learners and families, and develop a beginning repertoire of teaching multilingual learners and share lessons learned through these endeavors.

Methods

We followed Stringer's (2014) proposal of action research, an inquiry conducted by practitioners in their own educational settings to improve their practice and advance students' learning, that includes iterative cycles of *look* (identifying an issue and gathering information), *think* (analyzing the information and devising solutions), and *act* (implementing and evaluating solutions).

The Look Cycle: Between 2006 and 2013, we observed and collected anecdotal information about teacher candidates' limited preparation for supporting multilingual learners across institutions where we worked/studied. Course instructors shared challenges in incorporating more content and experiences about teaching multilingual learners. Teacher candidates complained about their limited training and thus lack of confidence and competence in supporting multilingual learners. These accounts of challenges pointed to an urgent need to enhance teacher preparation for multilingual learners.

The Think Cycle: Between 2013 and 2015, we conducted a mixed-methods study, collecting and analyzing interview and survey data from 57 course instructors and 433 teacher candidates about their perspectives and experiences of learning to teach multilingual learners in the Teacher Education Department at a state university in the United States. This department offered three teaching licensure options: elementary education, secondary education, and special education. Candidates could also add teaching minors such as TESOL, early childhood education, reading, etc.

The Act Cycle: Based on the data collected, we developed six online modules to promote teacher candidates' critical and dialogic learning on challenging the deficit framing of multilingual learners and enacting asset-based, equity-focused teaching (Flint & Jaggers, 2021). In 2015, we piloted the modules in a six-week online TESOL teaching laboratory course with twenty-two secondary TESOL candidates. Student work in the modules and meta-reflections on their learning experiences were collected as evidence for evaluating the effectiveness of the modules.

Our Positionality

Li was a faculty member in a teacher education department and Bian was a doctoral student when developing and piloting the modules. Both researchers were immigrants who came to North America from China for better educational opportunities. Li came from a low-SES background in her home country and was able to pursue higher education due to equal access to quality education and dedicated teachers who helped transform her academic trajectory. Even though she is now in a privileged position as a university professor, she approaches her research with a strong equity stance for disadvantaged students. Bian was a high-school English teacher in China after graduating from college. Experiencing how little institutional support and resources she and her colleagues received at her school, she went to the United States for graduate study with research interests in supporting prospective and in-service teachers in working with multilingual immigrant students. Our shared experiences as language learners, language teachers, and now language teacher educators, as well as our ongoing reflective conversations and our commitment to enacting justice-oriented and asset-based instruction, inspired the current study.

Hearing the Voices of Teacher Educators and Teacher Candidates

To understand and change the status quo of teacher preparation for multilingual learners in the focal program, we conducted two mix-methods studies on the perspectives and experiences of course instructors and teacher candidates, which later informed the development of six TESOL online modules that could be incorporated into the teacher education courses across content areas.

Perspectives of Teacher Educators

We conducted semi-structured interviews with twenty-three course instructors who were representative of the program faculty's demographics and content areas and surveyed all instructors ($N = 57$) (see Li et al., 2018). Data revealed huge variations in the instructors' expertise in teaching multilingual learners, which impacted how they designed curriculum and learning experiences in their courses. Few instructors had first-hand K-12 teaching experiences with multilingual learners; only two had a TESOL endorsement while others learned through self-education, professional development received as former teachers, teaching international students, and communicating with colleagues.

Several problems were identified with instructors' practices. First, discussions about multilingual learners were often blurred by broader conversations on supporting diverse learners or students with disabilities. A *pan-diversity* approach that treated "diversity as inclusive of all forms of differences without explicitly attending to any form of difference" (Li & Jee, 2021, p. 127) overlooked the necessity of preparing teacher candidates to address multilingual learners' unique needs in learning language and content simultaneously. Second, instructors tended to prepare candidates to plan and teach in general education classrooms with English monolingual students as their target population and then to think about how to "provide accommodations" for diverse learners. Teaching multilingual learners was often perceived as an afterthought. Third, content about multilingual learners was not systematically nor intentionally built into the curriculum but emerged from incidental classroom conversations. Teacher candidates' access to preparation for multilingual learners was improvised, depending on whom they had as course instructors or whether those issues were brought up by themselves and peers. Course instructors wished for more hands-on, practitioner-oriented readings and resources that could be readily incorporated into the existing curriculum.

Perspectives of Teacher Candidates

We surveyed 433 teacher candidates regarding their knowledge and experience with multilingual learners before and after they entered the program, perceived preparedness in different knowledge domains, and recommendations for program improvement. We then interviewed thirty-five TESOL and non-TESOL teacher candidates (see Li et al., 2019). Survey data revealed that 69 percent of participants grew up in linguistically homogeneous communities with little prior knowledge and exposure to multilingual speakers until college. While candidates expressed aspiration for developing a repertoire of teaching multilingual learners, 69 percent ($N = 299$) did not feel they had received adequate preparation in the program. Non-TESOL candidates (72 percent) were more likely to report unpreparedness than TESOL candidates (54 percent); they also scored lower in perceived knowledge and self-efficacy for teaching multilingual learners, as well as attitudes toward multilingual learners and families. The differences in readiness, perceived knowledge, and self-efficacy demonstrated the necessity to ensure all teachers, not just TESOL candidates, have access to specialized preparation in teaching multilingual learners.

Teacher candidates reported readings, group discussions, and lectures as the most common learning formats. Discussions on multilingual learners, if ever happened, were often skimmed over in one or two class periods. Candidates perceived such learning as superficial, decontextualized, and impractical. Candidates viewed hands-on, field-based learning experiences, such as service learning, classroom visits and observations, and student teaching/tutoring, as the most helpful. Unfortunately, direct interactions with multilingual learners were not guaranteed nor systematically structured, varying based on the linguistic demographics of their placement schools. More than a third of participants reported zero connections to multilingual learners throughout the program.

Teacher candidates expressed that they wanted "more"—more time on addressing multilingual learner topics and content across courses in the curricula, more interactions with multilingual learners and families, more concrete strategies for language and content teaching, more examples and modeling of best practices, more first-hand learning experience in the field, more coaching from site-based mentors, and more resources for continuing professional learning. These recommendations on content and resources became the foci of the modules, which we discuss in detail below.

Critically Reflective and Dialogic Learning in the Modules

In response to teacher educators and candidates' call for more resources and support, we designed six online modules (Table 7.1) that could be incorporated into teacher education courses with a field component (e.g., service learning, pre-internship student teaching, teaching internship) across content areas in both elementary and secondary education programs. To support course instructors' use of the modules, we included a section *Notes for Instructors* in the

Table 7.1 TESOL module summary

Module title	Initial engagement activity	Readings (see Appendix for a full list of module readings)	Multimodal learning materials	Discussion forum	Reflective essay	Exit ticket
Module 1: Understanding the Challenges that Prevent Multilingual Learners to Succeed	Dialogue with a multilingual student at the teaching placement or with an international student on the university campus about challenges they have experienced being labeled as "English language learner" or "non-native speaker of English"	Carlo et al., 2004; Fry, 2008	Two interview videos out of eight about multilingual learners' experiences in the general education classrooms	Jigsaw videos with classmates, discuss challenges faced by multilingual learners, and make connections between the videos and readings	Discuss how teachers can address the challenges experienced by multilingual learners and become change agents and advocates at their schools	Complete an exit ticket about students' experience in the module and recommendations for improving the content and format of the module
Module 2: Understanding the Learning Experiences of Multilingual Learners in Connection to School, Home, and Community Contexts	Conduct mini research of the ESL program at the teaching placement: dialogue with the ESL teacher to collect data about the program model, student demographics, and the curriculum and pedagogy used in the program	Moughamian et al., 2009; Gándara & Orfield, 2012; one chapter from Li, 2008	Two short videos of two multilingual learners sharing their experiences in the ESL programs	Share findings from the initial engagement activity about the ESL programs at the placements, analyze the effectiveness of the programs using course readings as references	Analyze the students and families depicted in Li's (2008) chapter, focusing on parents' cultural beliefs about schooling and education, involvement in their children's schoolwork, and barriers to more parental engagement at school	Complete an exit ticket about students' experience in the module and recommendations for improving the content and format of the module

Module title	Initial engagement activity	Readings (see Appendix for a full list of module readings)	Multimodal learning materials	Discussion forum	Reflective essay	Exit ticket
Module 3: Engaging Multilingual Families	Watch a video (Colorín Colorado, 2012) about a family literacy project supporting Spanish-English bilingual parents develops strategies to become literacy models at home	Brown, 2014; Mid-Atlantic Equity Consortium, Inc., 2016	Six short interview videos of immigrant parents, ESL teachers, classroom teachers, and a school principal first—about their perspectives and experiences in engaging multilingual families	Brainstorm principles, practices, and possible challenges of engaging and empowering immigrant families	Develop an action plan for fostering family-school partnerships to collaboratively support the learning and well-being of multilingual learners.	Complete an exit ticket about students' experience in the module and recommendations for improving the content and format of the module
Module 4: Teaching Strategies for Working with Multilingual Learners: Inclusive and Differentiated Instruction	Dialogue with the mentor teacher at the placement regarding their practices and perceived challenges for implementing inclusive and differentiated instruction	Buteau & True, 2009; Thamminen, 2013 Optional readings: Baecher et al., 2012; Rogers & Helman, 2009	Teaching Channel, n.d.a	Share lessons learned from dialoguing with mentors, reflect on takeaways from the readings and video, and discuss strategies for implementing inclusive and differentiated instruction in their future classrooms	Analyze a lesson plan candidates recently developed and discuss revisions they will make in the lesson aiming for supporting multilingual learners with diverse cultural and language backgrounds and English proficiencies	Complete an exit ticket about students' experience in the module and recommendations for improving the content and format of the module

Module title	Initial engagement activity	Readings (see Appendix for a full list of module readings)	Multimodal learning materials	Discussion forum	Reflective essay	Exit ticket
Module 5: TESOL Teaching Strategies in Content Classrooms	Dialogue and reflect with three classmates about their mentor teachers' practices in teaching different content areas with multilingual learners and the challenges of teaching content and language simultaneously	Gersten, 1999; Haynes, n.d; Select one from the four articles: Baecher, 2011; Brown, 2007; Lee & Buxton, 2013; Murrey, 2008 Optional readings: Haynes & Zacarian, 2010; Hernández, 2003; Pawan & Craig, 2011	four videos (Chambers, 2008; Keshav, n.d.; SouthernEdDes, 2012; Teaching Channel, n.d.b) that demonstrate techniques for teaching each of the four content areas	N/A	Modify a lesson that teacher candidates recently taught and discuss changes they will make to better support multilingual learners' content learning and academic language development	Complete an exit ticket about students' experience in the module and recommendations for improving the content and format of the module
Module 6: Putting It All Together	N/A	N/A	N/A	N/A	Option1, *Child Study*: identify a multilingual learner at the teaching placement, observe and interact with the student to collect data, and develop a plan for supporting the academic learning and wellbeing of the learner and for engaging their family Option 2, *Learning Summary*: summarize takeaways from the previous five modules and discuss the impact on beliefs and practices for working with multilingual learners, families, and communities	Final reflection survey of students on (1) perceived knowledge and preparedness for working with multilingual learners and (2) suggestions for enhancing learning experiences in the modules

overview of each module, outlining rationales on the module design, suggested student population (e.g., best for students taking 100-level/introductory education courses), and module logistics (e.g., prerequisite knowledge, reading sequencing, group configurations, possible discussion topics/questions). While attending to candidates' feedback about providing more practical knowledge for teaching multilingual learners, we were also cautious of peripheralizing equity and justice by overemphasizing the technical aspects of teaching and reducing learning to teach down to developing certain core practices (Philip et al., 2019). We intentionally designed learning opportunities for candidates to engage in dialogic and critical reflections on how classroom learning and teaching of historically marginalized groups, in our case multilingual learners, were shaped by broader systems of privilege, oppression, and social hierarchies. In the section below, we present a summary of the content and learning experiences we designed for each module, and discuss how we nurtured a dialogic space for preparing critically reflective future TESOL educators.

We followed Freire's (2005) advocacy for problem-posing education achieved through dialogic pedagogy with the explicit goal of transforming reality. In the first three modules, we posed "the problems"—structural challenges experienced by multilingual learners at micro-(society), meso-(home-school-community), and micro-levels (family) (Bronfenbrenner, 1977) that hinder their success at school and in society. Candidates engaged in inquiries on how they were part of a problematic system that perpetuated oppression, inequity, and injustice. To help candidates see the significance, relevance, and urgency of addressing those problems, we interviewed multilingual learners, parents, teachers, and administrators from local schools and included the video recordings as learning materials. In the next two modules, candidates reflected on how they could solve the problems and transform reality in and beyond their classrooms. Per the request of candidates on practical pedagogical knowledge of *teaching* multilingual learners, we introduced strategies of inclusive and differentiated instruction and teaching language and content simultaneously in general education classrooms. The last module was designed for candidates to synthesize and reflect on their overall learning in the previous five modules, make connections between the online modules and their field experience, and develop an action plan for supporting a specific multilingual student at their placement.

Brookfield (2017) argued that to practice critical reflection, teachers need to examine their views and actions through four lenses: theory and research, students' eyes, colleagues' perceptions, and personal experiences. In each module, we created opportunities for teacher candidates to engage in critical reflections with themselves, students, peers, module instructors/facilitators, and community members through dialogic learning. First, in the initial engagement activity, candidates had guided dialogues with stakeholders at their teaching placement or in the community about issues addressed in the module. Then, candidates engaged in dialogic and reflective learning in a discussion forum (see discussion topics of each forum in Table 7.1) where candidates made a post and responded to their classmates' posts to critically reflect on what they learned in the initial engagement activity and make connections to the readings (see the reading list in the Appendix). *Exploratory talks*, that is, posts that examined and contested ideas in pursuit of joint construction of new understandings (Delahunty, 2018), were encouraged and mediated by module facilitators. Candidates served as each other's *critical friends* (Brookfield, 2017) who offered a sympathetic ear to classmates' feelings and emotions, asked questions that spurred learning and the exchange of ideas, and fueled insights on understanding and solving new and familiar problems. At the end of each module, candidates constructed an action-oriented reflective essay to synthesize the module content and applied it to real-world learning-to-teach tasks. Candidates also completed an exit survey to share feedback on improving the content and format of the module.

To promote candidates' engagement in dialogic learning in virtual spaces, we enacted the following two strategies. First, effective student interaction during online learning requires clearly articulated participation requirements and guidelines (Delahunty, 2018; Pawan et al., 2003). We included a syllabus and overview of each module outlining module objectives, content, structure, assignment guidelines, and expectations for participation. We explicitly defined exemplary online discussion posts as those that (1) build a focused argument on issues addressed in the modules referencing course materials, (2) critically build on peers' ideas and raise new and relevant questions/perspectives for simulating and sustaining further discussions, and (3) draw on personal/professional experience and relevant course materials/literature to question, challenge, and push back ideas. Those definitions encouraged candidates to move away from "independent talk" and engage in more "cumulative" and "exploratory" talks (Delahunty, 2018, pp. 17–8). Second, we increased "teaching presence," defined as "instructor overt facilitation," which is pivotal in guiding students toward a higher level of online learning (Pawan et al., 2003, p. 125). Four doctoral students, including author 2, served as the module facilitators and each worked closely with a small number of candidates. Facilitators actively participated in discussion forums as the students, asking for clarifications, raising questions, directing candidates to more resources, and providing feedback. Through providing ongoing guidance and modeling on participation, we supported candidates to engage in collective dialogic inquiries as opposed to individual presentations of positions.

Piloting the Modules and Learning Outcomes

After developing the six modules, we identified a secondary social studies teaching methods course to pilot the modules and receive constructive feedback from teacher candidates. This course was an appropriate venue because the course (1) included online teaching laboratory sessions where we could integrate the modules, and (2) required candidates to spend four hours every week at their teaching placement which met the field experience expectation of the modules. Twenty-four secondary teacher candidates who were pursuing a TESOL endorsement completed the modules as a one-credit (six two-hour sessions) online teaching laboratory course. All candidates were English-monolingual, and twenty-two out of twenty-four were white. Candidates' discussion posts and responses, reflective essays, and feedback provided in the exit tickets were thematically analyzed as bases for a preliminary evaluation of the modules. Analyses showed that participating candidates demonstrated increasing critical awareness of the intersectionality of language and educational inequity and a growing understanding of the complexity of teaching multilingual learners. Candidates also reported that community-engaged learning materials and iterative cycles of reflective dialogues with different stakeholders helped them become more intentional in learning to teach multilingual learners during the field experience.

Kibler et al. (2021) argued that critical dialogic teaching sets "explicit goals for pedagogical practice that aims to disrupt inequitable power dynamics and their impacts on underserved student populations" (p. 5). We believe the first step in doing so was to increase teachers' critical awareness of power and privilege and how a lack of such awareness May impact multilingual learners and families. Student work in the modules revealed that candidates have demonstrated more empathy and more understanding of the structural inequities and challenges faced by multilingual learners, and gained an affirming view of immigrant families that recognized their transnational and cross-cultural experiences as assets instead of problems to fix.

For example, when discussing barriers to family involvement in school programs, as opposed to blaming families for not caring about their children's education as we observed in the interviews before the modules, one candidate in the discussion forum of Module 3, *Engaging Multilingual Families,* pointed out that "it is difficult to advocate for your child when the school administration can't understand you and doesn't understand your culture." Similarly, when discussing actions that teachers can take to increase family engagement, rather than showing the white saviorism mindsets to "save" immigrant families from not understanding the norms and expectations of U.S. schools, candidates emphasized the importance of learning about immigrant families' culture, language, and "what THEY [families] want for their children" (Module 3 discussion forum). Candidates were also cautious about imposing U.S.-centric parenting practices on immigrant parents. One candidate reminded her classmates in the Module 3 discussion forum:

> I think that by making parents aware of what might be expected of them in the US, but not pushing it upon them, and giving them information and making yourself available to the parents should they need to talk with you is a step in the right direction.

Dialogic learning opportunities embedded in the modules such as the initial engagement activities that pushed candidates to converse with different stakeholders and the discussion forums allowed candidates to acknowledge that communication and collaboration with immigrant families are not a one-way lecturing on how to be parents in the United States but learning about families' backgrounds and perspectives, collecting their feedback, and providing support, resources, and accommodations accordingly. In addition, the modules enabled candidates to see the complexities of working with multilingual learners by providing guiding questions to encourage them to engage in critical dialogues, particularly with peers and mentor teachers at their placements to better understand how education processes, interactions, and decisions can be impacted by power structures and dominant ideology in real school settings. These critical dialogues enabled the candidates to develop the critical realization that teaching multilingual learners is more than teaching the language in the language classroom, as one candidate mentioned in a discussion forum when commenting on interview videos of two elementary teachers:

> The ESOL profession requires a lot of effort to create support systems to help students on their journey to learn English … ESL teachers have the challenges of navigating administration, laws, and policies when it comes to assessing and educating English language learners, they have to construct educational environments in which all students have the opportunity to learn English. ESL educators have the additional work of bridging the "school-to-home" gap …

On top of all these, educators have to adhere to state standards and prepare students for standardized testing and academic success. To quote my mentor from [TESOL practicum course], "it's a tough job."

Students' reflections demonstrated a growing understanding of what TESOL educators' work embodies and how their work is mediated by factors outside the classrooms, including top-down national and state educational policies (e.g., policies that reinforce monoglossic language ideologies), historical and current educational initiatives (e.g., standards and high-stakes testing), as well as district and school administration and culture. As Arias and Wiley (2013) argued, it is important for candidates to develop a meta-awareness of how external forces are an essential backdrop to teachers' practices.

Besides, candidates reported the local relevance of learning materials enhanced their understanding of the course content and engagement in dialogic interactions. In particular, they found the interview videos recorded at local schools helpful in hearing genuine voices from the community, visualizing what they read in the course texts, making connections to personal experiences, and applying the content in their future classrooms. One candidate claimed in the final reflective essay of Module 6, *Putting It All Together*, "This course gave examples of real ELLs, their experiences, their challenges, and their culture. Listening and reading about these ELLs has really opened my eyes to the different students that I could have in a future classroom."

Watching videos of local students and teachers reminded candidates of the important conversations they had during their field placements and motivated them to engage in authentic and meaningful exchanges of personal experiences. For example, in one video, an ESL teacher from a local high school, Ms. T, shared her experience of visiting immigrant families. Some candidates recognized the teacher, with whom they connected during student teaching. They then engaged in dialogues using specific examples from the field to help each other contextualize and understand the issue of family engagement discussed in the module. The dialogue started with one student, S, who made connections between Ms. T and his mentor teacher's practices, and argued both established lines of communication between school and home. Another student, R, commented on his post:

> I also mentioned Mrs. T's home visits [in my post]. When I first heard her talk about these, I thought they were such a great idea to get more involved in the students' lives, but the more I think about it, the more I realize that it was probably more for the parents than the students. Being able to get to know

the person who is teaching your child another language and probably spending more time with them is going to be important for peace of mind.

The comment and connection that R made inspired S to give a specific example he observed Ms. T did, as he replied:

> I agree with your interpretation of Mrs. T's home visits. They seem to be very reassuring for the parents of her ESL students [...] For example, one of the students that I worked with for our differentiated instruction lab was in her class. I was able to employ a tactic to help support his work time for his English class. Mrs. T took a picture and texted it to this student's mother to show how hard he was working. She was thrilled.

A third student, J, then joined the dialogic reflection, while affirming the two classmates' perspectives, added her insights on supporting families beyond home visits:

> I agree, R, parent involvement is KEY in supporting ESL students. In my post I talked about visiting the families in their homes but I think that families participating in the classroom is an excellent way to get parents not just involved in their own student's education but in the education of the community. I think it would be cool to get parents of different students connected to one another so that they can maybe build support systems and community.

The example shows that when bringing that empirically generated knowledge back to the online dialogic space, teacher candidates were more likely to go beyond having "serial monologues"—presentations of positions that were independent of each other (Pawan et al., 2003, p. 135)—but to build off each other's ideas and make the online discussions a dynamic process of collaborative inquiry. Candidates commented that in-depth and focused dialoguing with classmates and others allowed issues addressed in the modules to surface from different angles. In the final reflective essay of Module 6, *Putting it All Together*, one candidate shared:

> One thing that I truly enjoyed about the [course] was that I was able to interact with fellow students who had a TESOL minor ... It was nice to be able to see others' viewpoints on videos and readings because they often saw things differently than I did. The discussions really forced me to apply what I had learned from the modules, and I was then forced to reflect on what I had learned while reading my classmate's discussion post.

Candidates' work revealed that through dialogic and critical reflective learning, they were more likely to be committed to enacting classroom practices that are "grounded in the lives of students," "critical," "anti-racist," "pro-justice," and culturally and linguistically sustaining (Down, 2006, p. 88).

Lessons Learned and Moving Forward

Since piloting the modules in 2015, the two authors have been engaging in ongoing conversations about supporting more teacher candidates in becoming critically reflective educators of multilingual learners. In this final section, we discuss lessons we have learned about nurturing a dialogic space for TESOL teacher candidates. We also make recommendations for preparing critically reflective teachers through dialogic learning in virtual spaces.

Lesson #1: Helping Teacher Candidates "Look/See" Differently

Brookfield (2017) reminded us that reflection itself is not necessarily critical unless it serves the distinct purposes of "illuminating power" and "uncovering hegemony" (p. 9). Developing and piloting the modules enabled us to see the significance of preparing teacher candidates to recognize how schooling has served to normalize and reproduce linguistic and cultural assimilations and unequal resources and opportunities for multilingual learners. We, therefore, advocate that the first step of preparing critically reflective TESOL educators is to support candidates who were in dominant and privileged positions to *"look and see"* differently, to develop the critical meta-awareness of the long-standing structural injustice and oppressions experienced by multilingual learners and families on a daily basis as many of them had never experienced these inequities themselves.

To help candidates "look and see" differently, we recommend the following learning opportunities that we found effective in the modules: (1) examining how the taken-for-granted pull-out ESL program model has been operationalized to alienate and stigmatize multilingual learners and perpetuate opportunity gaps, (2) analyzing the impact of the mismatch between home/community and school cultures on multilingual learners' well-being and learning in and beyond schools, (3) (self-)interrogating educators' implicit biases and how the biases may hinder family engagement and empowerment, and (4) developing pedagogical knowledge and skills on inclusive and differentiated instruction, ensuring that multilingual learners are attended to in general education classrooms and do not lose valuable content learning time. We also want to remind fellow teacher educators that we cannot distill learning to teach multilingual learners down to certain sets of core practices but help candidates intentionally look and see "the ways in which historicized injustices manifest in systems of power that play out in local classroom practice as part of disciplinary-based teaching and learning" (Calabrese Barton et al., 2020, p. 477).

Lesson #2: Nurturing a Relational Space for Teacher Candidates to "Think/Act" Differently

Dialogic learning is a joint effort in co-constructing knowledge as learners hear different voices, negotiate, and build upon each other's ideas (Kibler et al., 2021). With their renewed perspectives on multilingual learners and their families, teacher candidates need a safe space to engage in critically reflective conversations with themselves, peers, students, and teachers at their placements. To nurture a safe space for online dialogic and reflective learning, we recommend scaffolding learning experiences in the sequence of *communication, reflection, and transformation* (Freire, 2005), as our students' feedback testified to the clarity and effectiveness of such a structure. Candidates can start with an initial engagement activity through which to dialogue with people significant to the education of multilingual learners such as students, classroom teachers, and ESL specialists. Candidates can then engage in dialogic and critical reflections with peers in the discussion forum to make sense of what they learn from the initial engagement and module materials. Candidates conclude their learning cycle with a transformation-focused reflective assignment that asks them to discuss changes they would make to dismantle the unequal system and empower multilingual learners and families.

In addition, we recommend constant communication and negotiation with teacher candidates and adjustment of the online learning experience (Lee & Brett, 2015). In our modules, we included exit surveys at the end of each module and after completing all the modules, which gave us valuable information based on which to make modifications to the module content and format. For example, some candidates vocalized their concern with excessive time (compared to the course designation as one credit) spent on completing the module learning materials and assignments. We then in later modules included more jigsaw of the readings in the discussion forums and supplementary materials at the candidates' choice to read them now or for future references. While adjusting online learning experiences may not be as flexible as face-to-face classes, teacher educators can differentiate instruction by offering alternative pathways for approaching their learning in the online spaces, such as providing optional readings, choices of assignments, pace and sequencing of completing the modules, etc.

Lesson #3: Action Research as a Promising Pedagogical Tool of Professional Inquiry

Finally, this paper is a reflection of our experiences of *look, think, and act* in improving the preparation of teacher candidates for multilingual learners. Our collaborative experiences of enacting "problem-posing education" (Freire, 2005) suggest that action research is a powerful tool for professional inquiry to improve our own teaching practices and the quality of teacher candidates' learning experiences. In moving forward, we need to include dialogues and collaborations with other teacher educators and teacher candidates to engage in the next or new rounds of *look, think, and act* to help transform not just individual courses but a whole program. As we move toward the post-pandemic stage, new challenges and issues (e.g., Covid-induced academic slide, remote learning challenges, unequal access to educational technologies, and socioemotional learning needs) confronting multilingual learners have emerged (see Li & Sun, 2023). More than ever before, teacher educators (as well as teacher candidates) need to engage in locally grounded, collaborative, problem-solving inquiries (such as this action research) that promote relational dialogues and critical reflective practices to identify persistent and emerging problems, gather information and devise solutions, and take actions to transform their practices.

References

Arias, M. B., & Wiley, T. G. (2013). Language policy and teacher preparation: The implications of a restrictive language policy on teacher preparation. *Applied Linguistics Review*, 4(1), 83–104. https://doi.org/10.1515/applirev-2013-0004

Bronfenbrenner, U. (1977). Toward an experimental ecology of human development. *American Psychologist*, 32, 513–31. https://doi.org/10.1037/0003-066X.32.7.513

Brookfield, S. D. (2017). *Becoming a critically reflective teacher*. Jossey-Bass.

Calabrese Barton, A., Tan, E., & Birmingham, D. J. (2020). Rethinking high-leverage practices in justice-oriented ways. *Journal of Teacher Education*, 71(4), 477–94. https://doi.org/10.1177/0022487119900209

Coady, M., Harper, C., & de Jong, E. (2011). From preservice to practice: Mainstream elementary teacher beliefs of preparation and efficacy with English language learners in the State of Florida. *Bilingual Research Journal*, 34(2), 223–39. https://doi.org/10.1080/15235882.2011.597823

de Jong, E. J., Harper, C. A., & Coady, M. R. (2013). Enhanced knowledge and skills for elementary mainstream teachers of English language learners. *Theory into Practice, 52*(2), 89–97. https://doi.org/10.1080/00405841.2013.770326

Delahunty, J. (2018). Connecting to learn, learning to connect: Thinking together in asynchronous forum discussion. *Linguistics and Education, 46,* 12–22. https://doi.org/10.1016/j.linged.2018.05.003

Down, B. (July, 2006). *Developing critically reflective teachers in "wacky" times.* Making teaching public: Reforms in teacher education. Proceedings of the 34th Annual Australian Teacher Education Association Conference, Fremantle. https://researchrepository.murdoch.edu.au/id/eprint/3358/1/Developing_critically_published.pdf

Durgunoğlu, A. Y., & Hughes, T. (2010). How prepared are the U.S. preservice teachers to teach English language learners? *International Journal of Teaching and Learning in Higher Education, 22*(1), 32–41.

Farooq, S. (2019). *The critically reflective practice of online educators: Constructing a dialogic pedagogy in virtual learning environments.* http://hdl.handle.net/10292/12623

Farooq, S., & Benade, L. (2019). Constructing a dialogic pedagogy in virtual learning environments: A literature review. *New Zealand Journal of Teachers' Work, 16*(1), 7–13. https://doi.org/10.24135/teacherswork.v16i1and2.292

Fillmore, L. W., & Snow, C. (2002). What teachers need to know about language. In C. T. Adger, C. E. Snow, & D. Christian (Eds.), *What teachers need to know about language* (pp. 7–53). Delta Systems Co., Inc. & The Center for Applied Linguistics.

Flint, A. S., & Jaggers, W. (2021). You matter here: The impact of asset-based pedagogies on learning. *Theory into Practice, 60*(3), 254–64. https://doi.org/10.1080/00405841.2021.1911483

Freire, P. (2005). *Pedagogy of the oppressed* (30th-anniversary Ed., Myra Bergman Ramos, Trans.). Continuum.

Freire, P., & Shor, I. (1987). *A Pedagogy for liberation: Dialogues on transforming education.* Macmillan Education.

Kibler, A., Valdés, G., & Walqui, A. (2021). Introduction: A vision for critical dialogic education. In A. Kibler, G. Valdés, & A. Walqui (Eds.), *Reconceptualizing the role of critical dialogue in American classrooms: Promoting equity through dialogic education* (pp. 1–22). Routledge.

Lee, K., & Brett, C. (2015). Dialogic understanding of teachers' online transformative learning: A qualitative case study of teacher discussions in a graduate-level online course. *Teaching and Teacher Education, 46,* 72–83. https://doi.org/10.1016/j.tate.2014.11.001

Li, G. (2018). Moving toward a diversity plus teacher education: Approaches, challenges, and possibilities in preparing teachers for English language learners. In D. Polly, M. Putman, T. M. Petty, & A. J. Good (Eds.), *Innovative practices in teacher preparation and graduate-level teacher education programs* (pp.215–237). IGI Global.

Li, G., Bian, Y., & Martinez-Hinestroza, J. (2018). "I don't have the resources to learn, or… the time to do that": Teacher educators' perspectives and practices of preparing pre-service teachers for English language learners. In A. E. Lopez & E. L. Olan (Eds.), *Transformative pedagogies for teacher education: Moving towards critical praxis in an era of change* (pp. 175–194). Greenwich, CT: Information Age Publishing.

Li, G., & Jee, Y. (2021). Pan-diversity integration as an equity trap: Lessons from pre-service teachers' experiences of preparation for teaching English language learners in the United States. *Teachers College Record, 123*(12), 125–54. https://doi.org/10.1177/01614681211070873

Li, G., & Sun, Z. (2023). "COVID has brought us closer": A proleptic approach to understanding ESL teachers' practices in supporting ELLs in and after the pandemic. *Language and Literacy, 25*(1), 32–56.

Li, G., Bian, Y., & Martinez, J. M. (2019). Learning to teach English language learners as "a side note": TESOL pre-service teachers' perspectives of their professional preparation. In S. Keengwe & G. Onchwari (Eds.), *Handbook of research on assessment practices and pedagogical models for immigrant students* (pp. 311–34). IGI Global.

Li, G., Dobrin-De, G. R., Sun, Z., Haslip, M., Burchell, D., Rivard Dexter, J., & Chen, X. (2021). Promoting second language learning during COVID-19 pandemic: Parents and teachers' coping strategies. *Royal Society of Canada COVID-19 Series*, Publication No. 72. https://rsc-src.ca/en/voices/promoting-second-language-learning-during-covid-19-pandemic-parents'-and-teachers'-coping

Lipika. (2016). *What is Web 2.0?* ZnetLive. https://www.znetlive.com/blog/web-2-0/

Lucas, T., & Villegas, A. M. (2013). Preparing linguistically responsive teachers: Laying the foundation in preservice teacher education. *Theory into Practice, 52*, 98–109. https://doi.org/10.1080/00405841.2013.770327

Mahnken, K. (2022). "Nation's report card": Two decades of growth wiped out by two years of pandemic. The 74. https://www.the74million.org/article/nations-report-card-two-decades-of-growth-wiped-out-by-two-years-of-pandemic/

Pawan, F., Paulus, T. M., Yalcin, S., & Chang, C. F. (2003). Online learning: Patterns of engagement and interaction among in-service teachers. *Language Learning and Technology, 7*(3), 119–40. https://doi.org/10125/25217

Philip, T. M., Souto-Manning, M., Anderson, L., Horn, I., Carter Andrews, D. J., Stillman, J., & Varghese, M. (2019). Making justice peripheral by constructing practice as "core": How the increasing prominence of core practices challenges teacher education. *Journal of Teacher Education, 70*(3), 251–64. https://doi.org/10.1177/0022487118798324

Rule, P. (2004). Dialogic Spaces: Adult education projects and social engagement. *International Journal of Lifelong Education, 23*(4), 319–34. https://doi.org/10.1080/026037042000233476

Stringer, E. (2014). *Action research in education* (2nd Ed). Pearson.

Appendix: Reading List of the TESOL Online Modules

Baecher, L., Artigliere, M., Patterson, D. K., & Spatzer, A. (2012). Differentiated instruction for English language learners as "variations on a theme" teachers can differentiate instruction to support English language learners. *Middle School Journal, 43*(3), 14–21. https://doi.org/10.1080/00940771.2012.11461807

Baecher, L. H. (2011). Differentiated instruction for English language learners: Strategies for the secondary English teacher. *The Wisconsin English Journal, 53*(2), 64–73.

Brown, C. L. (2007). Strategies for making social studies texts more comprehensible for English-language learners. *The Social Studies, 98*(5), 185–8. https://doi.org/10.3200/TSSS.98.5.185-188

Brown, K. (2014). The power of family engagement for English language learners. *Curriculum in Context, 40*(1), 5–6.

Buteau, G., & True, M. (2009). Differentiating instructional strategies to support English language learners. *New England Reading Association Journal, 44*(2), 23–5.

Carlo, M. S., August, D., McLaughlin, B., Snow, C. E., Dressler, C., Lippman, D. N., & White, C. E. (2004). Closing the gap: Addressing the vocabulary needs of English-language learners in bilingual and mainstream classrooms. *Reading Research Quarterly, 39*(2), 188–215. https://doi.org/10.1598/RRQ.39.2.3

Chambers, J. (2008). *ESL: Information gap*. YouTube. https://www.youtube.com/watch?v=KjyC-Q1kznQ

Colorín, C. (2012). *Parents as partners*. YouTube. https://www.youtube.com/watch?v=FOmDO3IjQ-Y&list=PLoU659hwTdDZ9CzQtrrDo01D3Fy1OeW67

Fry, R. (2008). *The role of schools in the English language learner achievement gap*. Pew Hispanic Center. https://files.eric.ed.gov/fulltext/ED502050.pdf

Gándara, P., & Orfield, G. (2012). Segregating arizona's English learners: A return to the "Mexican room"? *Teachers College Record, 114*(9), 1–27. https://doi.org/10.1177/016146811211400905

Gersten, R. (1999). Lost opportunities: Challenges confronting four teachers of English-language learners. *The Elementary School Journal, 100*(1), 37–56. https://doi.org/10.1086/461942

Haynes, J. (n.d.). *Challenges for ELLs in content area learning*. http://ftp.everythingesl.net/inservices/challenges_ells_content_area_1_65322.php

Haynes, J., & Zacarian, D. (2010). *Teaching English language learners across the content areas*. ASCD.

Hernández, A. (2003). Making content instruction accessible for English language learners. In G. G. Garcia (Ed.), *English learners: Reaching the highest level of English literacy*, (pp. 125–49). International Reading Association.

Keshav. (n.d.). *Teaching science to English learners*. Vimeo. https://vimeo.com/6256139

Lee, O., & Buxton, C. A. (2013). Integrating science and English proficiency for English language learners. *Theory into Practice, 52*(1), 36–42. https://doi.org/10.1080/07351690.2013.743772

Li, G. (2008). *Culturally contested literacies: America's "rainbow underclass" and urban schools.* Routledge. https://doi.org/10.4324/9780203935576

Mid-Atlantic Equity Consortium, Inc. (2016). *Engaging families of English learners.* https://maec.org/wp-content/uploads/2016/04/Engaging-Families-of-English-Learners.pdf

Moughamian, A. C., Rivera, M. O., & Francis, D. J. (2009). Instructional models and strategies for teaching English language learners. *Center on Instruction.* https://www.centeroninstruction.org/files/Instructional%20Models%20for%20ELLs1.pdf

Murrey, D. L. (2008). Differentiating instruction in mathematics for the English language learner. *Mathematics Teaching in the Middle School, 14*(3), 146–53. https://www.jstor.org/stable/i40053116

Pawan, F., & Craig, D. A. (2011). ESL and content area teacher responses to discussions on English language learner instruction. *TESOL Journal, 2*(3), 293–311. https://doi.org/10.5054/tj.2011.259956

Rogers, C., & Helman, L. (2009). One size does not fit all: How assessment guides instruction in word study with English learners. *New England Reading Association, 44*(2), 17–22.

SouthernEdDesk. (2012). *Teaching out of the box: Algebra for ESL students.* YouTube. https://www.youtube.com/watch?v=U2jrKRRAruc

Teaching Channel. (n.d.a). *Series internationals network deeper learning: Deeper learning for English language learners.* https://learn.teachingchannel.com/video/deeper-learning-for-ell-inps

Teaching Channel. (n.d.b). *Series ELA for ELL: Scaffolding understanding for complex text: Extending understanding: Vocabulary development.* https://learn.teachingchannel.com/video/middle-school-vocabulary-development

Thammineni, H. B. (2013). Teaching/learning English as a second language in mixed ability classrooms: A stimulating challenge. *International Journal of English: Literature, Language and Skills, 2*(3), 83–6.

8

Interrogating Raciolinguistic Ideologies through Role-Play: A Critical Dialogic Approach

Fares J. Karam, Amanda K. Kibler, and Patricia J. Arnold

Introduction

Completing this role-playing assignment was unlike any other graduate assignment I have had so far. It was an interesting experience to work with a partner to not only create a dialogue between two people but to also have to put yourself in the shoes of someone else and act it out. Reflecting on the assignment, having to use the readings and lecture notes to help formulate a conversation was surprisingly helpful. It was a unique way to better comprehend raciolinguistic ideologies. It made the assignment come alive and feel so much more realistic.

(Kora, reflection)

In the above excerpt, a graduate student reflects on a role-playing assignment as part of an asynchronous online TESOL course on language and the identities of multilingual learners. Students enrolled in this course included licensed teachers pursuing a TESOL endorsement or non-licensed graduate students pursuing a graduate degree in equity and diversity. The assignment presented students with two prompts describing real-life scenarios or events at the intersection of race, language, and identity (see Appendix: Assignment Description). For example, one of the scenarios described how a bilingual Latinx teacher candidate was asked by her mentor teacher in field placement training to "fix" her accent and speak "proper" English in order to be able to teach the children "correct" English. Working in small groups, students were asked to write a dialogue inspired by these scenarios in order to critically challenge and question raciolinguistic ideologies (Flores & Rosa, 2015), making connections to class readings about raciolinguistics (Alim, 2016) as appropriate. Students were also asked to enact their dialogues, videotape their interactions, and write a reflection on their experiences. Through analyzing students' understandings and enactments of raciolinguistic ideologies, the study aims to examine how intersections of race, identity, and language ideologies can be addressed through a critical and dialogic process.

One of the objectives of the assignment was to provide students with an opportunity to grapple with the complex processes of racialization through critical and dialogic pedagogical strategies such as role-play. Such a task can help deepen students' understanding of language/ideologies and prepare them to better serve language-minoritized students and families in K-12 classrooms. Such thinking is in line with what Kibler and her colleagues' (2021) call to re-envision curricula and teaching pedagogies for linguistically minoritized students through critical dialogic education (CDE) which promotes "equity-focused classroom pedagogies that are dialogic, critical, and inclusive" (p. 2). CDE emphasizes dialogic approaches to education and goes further to question inequities in language learning and bring social justice issues into the classroom (e.g., Karam, 2021). In a time when raciolingusitic ideologies continue to "produce racialized speaking subjects who are constructed as linguistically deviant even when engaging in linguistic practices positioned as normative or innovative when produced by privileged white subjects" (Flores & Rosa, 2015, p. 150), it becomes increasingly important to provide TESOL professionals with opportunities and tools to interrogate linguistic inequities in the classroom and beyond. We argue that adopting critical and dialogic approaches in creating and facilitating such spaces is of paramount importance, and we emphasize the potential of role-play as a strategy that can allow students to voice and perform their understandings of such complex issues at the intersection of language and race (Seltzer, 2019).

Framed within raciolingusitic ideologies and CDE, this study asks: How does a group of graduate students in an asynchronous TESOL course negotiate their understandings of raciolinguistic ideologies? How do they use critical and dialogic means to interrogate inequities at the intersection of race and language? In what follows, we first review the literature on Critical Dialogic Education and raciolinguistics, then discuss the specifics of the role-play assignment and the context of the study, and finally share our results, with a discussion of implications with respect to TESOL teacher education.

Raciolinguistic Ideologies from a Critical and Dialogic Perspective

In conceptualizing CDE, Kibler, Valdés, and Walqui (2021) placed issues of equity and social justice at the very center of dialogic and critical pedagogies. This is in line with raciolinguistics' focus on challenging dominant discourses that position racialized speakers as deficient (Flores & Rosa, 2015), and breaking the biased associations that are often formed between "correct" language use and the racial identities of students (Ricklefs, 2021a; Wortham & Reyes, 2011).

Dialogic and critical approaches such as CDE can be an effective tool in achieving those goals. Dialogic approaches, where knowledge is co-constructed (e.g., Haneda, 2017), can be particularly useful in challenging dominant narratives and ideologies. Indeed, multivocality (or the multiplicity of student voices and opinions in the classroom) is a central tenet of CDE. Kibler, Valdés, and Walqui (2021) argue that CDE invites multivocality "without seeking to unify or resolve it, which can be an ongoing tension in critical and dialogic environments" (p. 186). One of the aims of raciolinguistics is to challenge the dominant ideology of whiteness that marginalizes the literacy practices of racialized and multilingual students who are often deemed as deficient and ascribed labels such as English learners or long-term English learners in ways that can serve to limit their educational opportunities (Glick & Walqui, 2021; Kibler et al., 2018). The raciolinguistic assignment that this study analyzes was dialogic and multivocal in the sense that graduate students worked in pairs or small groups to interrogate the White gaze that Flores and Rosa (2015) described, experimenting with and negotiating the unpredictability of complex conversations about race and language, and exploring ways to resist ideologies of whiteness.

In addition, the scenarios described in the raciolinguistic assignment provide the graduate students with the opportunity to practice their agency in wrestling with critical interrogations of language ideologies that can challenge the superiority of the White gaze and its self-ascribed right to judge racialized speakers (Alim, 2016). In line with CDE's call to reimagine the role of teachers and students in creating dialogic and critical spaces, the assignment provides an opportunity for graduate students to not only make connections to important issues at the intersection of language and race, but also to draw upon their personal experiences and backgrounds. Such an approach aligns with raciolinguistics' calls to go beyond additive approaches in instructing multilingual learners and "placing the conflict that language-minoritized students experience in negotiating the many different linguistic communities that they must navigate at the center of instruction" (Flores & Rosa, 2015, p. 168). Research on teachers' language ideologies shows that although such ideologies are multiple, complex, and conflicting (Palmer, 2011; Ricklefs, 2021b), they can still be influenced through teacher education since universities often represent spaces where language ideologies are formed, negotiated, and transformed (Thoma, 2022; Woodward & Rao, 2020). In short, centering issues of equity, language ideologies, and race are all primary concerns to both raciolinguistics and CDE, which make both theoretical lenses a good fit for this study that aims at examining how graduate students negotiate and resist raciolinguistic ideologies involving fictional scenarios, co-constructing dialogues, and role-play.

Methods

Context and Participants

This qualitative case study (Merriam, 1998) examines an asynchronous online course for graduate students at a public university in the western United States. The course is part of a series of courses leading to a graduate certificate in TESOL and is also a required course for masters and doctoral students pursuing a degree in Equity, Diversity and Language Education. There were twenty-two students initially enrolled in this class (five males and seventeen females), but two of them later on withdrew from the course and did not complete the assignment on raciolinguistics. It is important to note that students were offered the opportunity (an alternative assignment) to write a mini literature review on raciolinguistic ideologies instead of completing the role-play assignment. Five students opted for that choice. Offering alternative modes and assignments was in line with first author's (the instructor's) aims of providing flexibility to graduate students who did not have the time or means to engage in collaborative tasks that required extensive planning and meetings. For example, some students were full-time professionals and found it difficult to schedule meetings with colleagues to coordinate work, especially since some of them were participating from different time zones across the United States.

Data Collection and Analysis

Data were collected after the course concluded in May of 2022 in order not to influence the instructor's evaluations of student work. IRB approval was sought to collect and analyze archival data from the course. Data included students' work on the assignment pertaining to raciolinguistics, including their written dialogues for the role-play, video recordings of their role-play, and reflections. As the focus of this chapter is on role-play, literature reviews (in the case of the five students who opted for the alternative assignment) were excluded from analysis. Participants were assigned pseudonyms and data were stored on a secure and password-protected server.

We adopted a hybrid inductive-deductive process to data analysis. Dialogues and reflections written by students were primary data sources while videos were a secondary data source used for triangulation. We simultaneously coded the data both at an inductive level via a process coding approach (Saldaña & Omasta, 2021) while also utilizing deductive codes derived from our theoretical frameworks. At an inductive level, we used our research questions as an anchor to guide our analysis, focusing on how students negotiated their understanding of raciolinguistics in critical and dialogic ways. Some of our emergent codes included drawing upon or ignoring class readings, reporting empathy or discomfort, self-reflecting as teachers, and making commitments or suggestions related to advocacy. At a deductive level, we adopted codes reflecting raciolinguistic ideologies (e.g., amplifying/marginalizing the voices of multilingual students; undermining/challenging monoglossic language ideologies) and CDE as well (e.g., engaging in multivocal dialogic discussions; eliciting connections to personal experiences and identities). In relation to our first research question pertaining to how a group of graduate students in an asynchronous TESOL course negotiated their understandings of raciolinguistic ideologies, we found that students either challenged or reified dominant language ideologies through drawing upon or ignoring class readings, and creating scenarios that amplified or marginalized the voices of multilingual individuals and advocates of multilingualism. As for our second research question related to how students used critical and dialogic means to interrogate inequities at the intersection of race and language, we found that students adopted such critical and dialogic means to discuss race and language through making connections to personal experiences and identities, engaging in multivocal dialogic discussions (grappling with tensions leading to both empathy and discomfort), self-reflecting as teachers, and making commitments or suggestions related to advocacy.

Positionality

All three co-authors are bi/multilingual, and we are committed to critical and dialogic approaches to teacher education, social justice, and equity. We believe in the importance of preparing critical and dialogic TESOL professionals who are well equipped to address complex issues relating to language ideologies both within and outside classroom contexts. Within the classroom, TESOL professionals are at the forefront of supporting and advocating for an increasingly diverse and multilingual student population (e.g., Duran, 2019; Karam, 2021). Outside the realm of the classroom, we also believe that language teachers should be able to challenge dominant language ideologies through conversations with relevant stakeholders (e.g., parents and families) and through home visits as well (e.g., Karam et al., 2021; Paulick et al., 2022).

Limitations

This study is limited by scope to the context of one asynchronous online TESOL course. Students enrolled in this course could have been more naturally inclined to be proponents of multilingualism and more invested in critical examinations of race and language. Another limitation is that readings related to CDE were not assigned to students in conjunction with readings on raciolinguistics. In the future, students can benefit from assigned readings on CDE to guide and complement their completion of this assignment.

Findings

Findings from this chapter revealed how students negotiated their understandings of raciolinguistic ideologies through either problematizing, or in some cases, reifying dominant language ideologies. Findings also showed how students grappled with difficult topics and opposing views related to language and race through dialogic and critical approaches.

Challenging and Reifying Dominant Language Ideologies

Students engaged creatively with the role-play assignment on raciolinguistics and with variable degrees of success—sometimes challenging, but at other times, reifying dominant monolingual ideologies.

In challenging such ideologies, students resorted to two key strategies: 1) creating scenarios that amplified the voices of multilingual individuals and advocates of multilingualism, and 2) drawing upon key constructs from raciolinguistics presented in class readings to construct dialogues and surface monoglossic language ideologies of dialoguers. More specifically, students created scenarios where multilingual individuals and proponents of multilingualism were empowered to challenge dehumanizing discourses that positioned speakers of languages other than English as inferior and deficient. Those characters used arguments drawn from class readings to undermine monoglossic language ideologies held by other characters.

To illustrate, we present a vignette from one of the scenarios written by two in-service teachers, Brenda and Sylvia (all names are pseudonyms). "A scenario that takes place in an elementary school felt the most authentic to us because [it] is the closest to what we may experience in reality," explained Brenda in her reflection. Characters in their scenario included a graduate from the same university where their TESOL course was offered, and an upset teacher who was frustrated with her students speaking Spanish in her class.

> **Upset Teacher**: Students are constantly talking in Spanish during class time. I keep telling them to practice their English, but I can't get them to stop. It's frustrating! Sometimes I speak Spanish with them when it's appropriate, but they keep choosing to speak in Spanish at inappropriate times.
>
> **Teacher/Graduate Student**: Which times do you think are appropriate and which times do you think are inappropriate?
>
> **Upset Teacher**: Well ... I'll try to ask them about their weekend in Spanish in the hallway on our way to lunch or during breaks. But they're having conversations in Spanish when they're supposed to be doing their work.
>
> **Teacher/Graduate Student**: It sounds like you value your students speaking Spanish since you're trying to speak Spanish with them. However, when you tell them to stop speaking Spanish during class time, you're signaling to them that you don't value their Spanish in an academic setting or that English is a language better used or more appropriate in an academic setting. Do you think that?
>
> **Upset Teacher**: Yes! They really need to be practicing standard English in the classroom so that they can work towards English proficiency. I'm just trying to make sure they're set up for success later in life.
>
> **Teacher/Graduate Student**: Have you ever thought about how we praise the skill set of English speakers with a second language, but we view speakers of other languages who also speak English as a deficit? In our society, which is dominated by white listeners, we overvalue proficiency in English and undervalue multilingualism when the first language is not English.

Upset Teacher: But isn't it my job to make sure they're learning English? They already know Spanish, and if we can get them to be proficient in English in school then they'll truly be bilingual which will help them get to college or get a good job, right?

Teacher/Graduate Student: I learned about something in my graduate class called monoglossic language ideologies. This means that people have ideas that languages bilinguals speak are used in isolation from one another, when really they're most often used interchangeably. So, some research suggests that instead of viewing language use this way, we should instead look at students' linguistic practices from a more multilingual perspective. I think it's our job to appreciate the multiple ways that students express their understanding of what they're learning.

In response to the Upset Teacher's frustration, the teacher/graduate student questions what contexts are deemed appropriate or inappropriate. It is worth noting that the response was professional in nature and not antagonistic. As Sylvia explains, they tried to frame their responses as they would "in real life." Responding through a question allows the Upset Teacher character to clarify her stance and presents an opportunity for the Teacher/Graduate Student to better understand her colleague's beliefs. The Upset Teacher explains that it is appropriate to use Spanish in hallways to discuss personal matters, but in the classroom, students should use English to complete their academic work. In their reflections, both Brenda and Sylvia explain that in creating this fictional context, they aimed at challenging the Upset Teacher's perceptions of appropriateness of language use, drawing upon Flores and Rosa (2015). Sylvia explains:

> We decided to have the Teacher/Graduate Student probe this teacher about which times are appropriate and inappropriate. This was a way to speak about Flores and Rosa's (2015) explanation of "appropriateness" and how even when we use additive approaches to language use in our classroom, it still regulates the use and deems non-English languages as inappropriate for academic settings.

Thus, the role of the Teacher/Graduate Student as revealed through Sylvia's reflection was to probe appropriateness in a professional manner. The conversation continues with the Teacher/Graduate Student acknowledging the Upset Teacher's valuing of her students' multilingual repertoire but further probing her on the appropriateness of using Spanish in academic contexts and how denying students the opportunity to do so may signal to them that Spanish is inferior to English. The Upset Teacher's response further cements her association of English with success, revealing another raciolinguistic ideology that equates success with standard English alone.

In her reflection, Brenda explains how her "thinking has shifted away from ideas of expecting students to model their linguistic practices after the white speaking subject" (Flores & Rosa, 2015). She counters such an ideology citing Alim (2005) who advocates that language-minoritized students use their diverse linguistic practices in the classroom. However, she further explains that Flores and Rosa (2015) call for an approach that places the focus on the listening subject and advocates for going beyond additive approaches in education that "fail to challenge appropriateness-based discourses and reify the racial status quo by perpetuating the presumption that individuals can control the ways their speech patterns are interpreted by their interlocutors" (Flores & Rosa, 2015, p. 155). Brenda reflects, "this is why we wanted to focus on critiquing the teacher's listening in our scenario, rather than encouraging the teacher to simply value their students' linguistic repertoires."

By taking this stance, both Brenda and Sylvia amplify the voices of proponents of multilingualism through applying "Flores and Rosa's (2015) framework of examining the 'mouth' and 'ears' of the white gaze, not just the 'eyes'" (Brenda's Reflection). In other words, the Upset Teacher's stance of classifying the use of Spanish as inappropriate reflects what Flores and Rosa (2015) describe as a situation where a white-speaking subject classifies and judges the practices of language-minoritized populations as "deviant based on their racial positioning in society as opposed to any objective characteristics of their language use" (p. 151). And it is exactly this raciolinguistic ideology that is called into question by the Teacher/Graduate Student.

The Upset Teacher moves on to emphasize her role in teaching the students English, since they already know Spanish. However, the Teacher/Graduate Student brings up the concept of monoglossic language ideologies that perceives bilingualism as separate languages that should be used separately. Furthermore, she highlights another important role of the teacher (in addition to teaching English), which is valuing the multiple and multilingual ways through which students express themselves and learn at the same time. In short, Brenda's and Sylvia's scenario represented a pattern of other scenarios where students successfully drew upon raciolinguistic concepts and arguments to challenge monoglossic language ideologies and empower proponents of multilingualism to present counter arguments that emphasized a multilingual perspective.

Nonetheless, other scenarios inadvertently reified some dominant language ideologies as we will see in the next scenario written by Rosario and Alina. The characters in their scenario included a Graduate Student and another character described as the Interviewer who starts the interview by asking how the

Graduate Student felt about people speaking a language other than English in informal settings such as the supermarket where Rosario and her mother were scolded for speaking Spanish. The Graduate Student replies that she is OK with this. "It is not anything formal like a business area, so I think that is ok, and I don't understand why people would be mad?" The Interviewer agrees with the Graduate Student, recounting how she speaks Spanish but in contexts as such medical appointments with her family so she can translate to her parents. The interview continues:

> **Graduate student**: My dad can speak Spanish. Just last week we went to a store and the people who saw us automatically started to speak Spanish to us. [...]
> **Interviewer**: I think that is something that I have done. I am guilty of charge because sometimes it is something that the person looks so Latina to me or looks Hispanic to me that I feel it is normal and natural for me to talk to them in Spanish.
> [...]
> **Graduate student**: I guess in that environment, the place I was in, [there were] many people who spoke Spanish. I don't want to sound like that. A lot of Mexicans go there, but it is kind of like a market. It is normal to them, so I can understand where she is coming from.
> **Interviewer**: That is an excellent example because I have done that before. [...] We discussed informal settings, but what about formal settings? Do you think in more formal settings could be considered rude to speak in a different language than the rest of the room?
> **Graduate student**: I think there is a time and a place when being bilingual is good for yourself. If one of my students is understanding what I am saying, and I have another student that can speak the same language being able to translate that, in a sense, I think that is OK. But if they are in separate groups going off talking about who knows what because I do not know another language. I feel they could be talking about other people in the group or me in a certain way. I don't think that would be an appropriate time to do so. If they do not understand what I am saying, I think it could be applicable to get better instructions.
> **Interviewer**: Right, I agree.

In the above excerpt, both characters role-played by Rosario and Alina agree that it is only appropriate to use languages other than English in informal settings. They role-play a scenario where the Graduate Student is assumed to be a Spanish speaker and the Graduate Student gets upset for being positioned as such just because she looks Latina. The Interviewer confesses that she has been guilty of making similar assumptions. While explicit references to raciolinguistics were not made by Rosario or Alina (who did not submit her reflection), it is clear that the scenario reflects raciolinguistic ideologies of assuming how people should sound based on their race. Perhaps inadvertently, the scenario reifies the raciolinguistic assumption that languages other than English are not appropriate in formal settings, and Rosario asserts in her reflection that both she and Alina

> conclude that [speaking Spanish in] informal settings should not be considered rude as they are private interactions between particular groups that share language, identity, and cultural values. However, we do consider formal settings to be conservative in using different languages that might create confusion or distorted communication.

Instead of *undoing* appropriateness, the scenario reifies appropriateness and Rosario emphasizes that "there is time and place for everything." It is worth noting that in her reflection, Rosario did not did not analyze the dialogue through a raciolinguistic lens.

Critical and Dialogic Tensions and Grappling with Race and Language

Through their responses to the assignment on raciolinguistics, students used various critical and dialogic means to interrogate inequities at the intersection of race and language. More specifically, they made connections to personal experiences and identities, engaged in multivocal dialogic discussions, self-reflected on their practice as teachers, and made thoughtful commitments or suggestions related to advocacy.

Most students reported enjoying working collaboratively with peers and described how the assignment allowed them to make connections to personal experiences related to race and language. For example, Adelina could personally relate to Rosita and her mother.

> I really enjoyed working on this week's assignment with my group. We worked with scenario one, where Rosita explains how people get angry when she speaks Spanish in public places. This scenario provides me with the opportunity to share my personal experiences in a similar scenario. As a Puerto Rican, I'm an American citizen but the truth is that those individuals shouting at us for speaking a different language don't only not know, but don't seem to care either. Families after generations of feeling shame, felt the urge of not teaching

their children their mother tongue as a way of preventing them from having to experience the constant harassment from many of their new country hosts. [...] For years immigrants have experienced being looked down, yelled at, marginalized and discriminated due to the way they look or the way they talk (i.e. accent, language fluidity).

Adelina makes a connection to her experiences as a Puerto Rican and draws upon the readings to show how raciolingusitic ideologies have debilitating effects on employment and professional opportunities afforded or denied. Similar stories were shared by other students in their reflections where they (or people they know) were the subject of discriminatory practices based on race, language, or both. Kim, a female teacher, described how some students at her school started crying because teachers did not allow them to speak Spanish based on the belief that the students were using Spanish to cheat on their work. Others recounted how they frequently hear, "You're in America, speak English!" yelled at immigrant families and students.

Such connections to personal experiences strengthened feelings of empathy. Through dialogic role-play, students were able to put themselves in other people's shoes, as reported by Kora at the beginning of this chapter. In addition, it was an opportunity to learn about the experiences of other colleagues in this class. For example, one student reflected that her work partner "has more personal experiences being a multilingual person living in the United States, so she added a different view to the whole scenario. Her unique perspective allowed me to see more of the emotional effects these attitudes [raciolinguistic ideologies] can have on a person."

On the other hand, engaging in multivocal dialogic discussion sometimes led to feelings of discomfort when students grappled with the complex topic of race and language. More specifically, role-playing characters who held raciolingusitic and monoglossic language ideologies was difficult for some students. As most students were pursuing degrees in language education or equity and diversity, they were self-professed allies of multilingual students and proponents of multilingual approaches to education, which made role-playing the opposite point of view difficult. In her reflection, Glenn explained

> this has been a challenge because it included the assimilationist perspective that would never be accepted by my side. I really had a lot of difficult time putting these unacceptable phrases into words. I realized that it was really challenging for my partner as well. To use a language that doesn't belong to you and even that you are totally against is not an easy task. The part of the scenario which

included "to fix" Maria's [character representing a bilingual teacher in the scenario] accent has been really difficult to put into words. I would never use such an expression to anyone, especially to a teacher candidate.

Thus, while some students found it helpful to be in someone else's shoes through role-play, others like Glenn found it tremendously difficult to use what she describes as "unacceptable phrases" to express discriminatory opinions or practices that can have dire consequences, especially if used by individuals in power such as a mentor who is trying to "fix" a bilingual in-service teacher's accent as Glenn's scenario describes.

However, such unresolved tensions where one's own beliefs are challenged can lead to critical and thoughtful reflections. For example, Miranda reported in her reflection on the assignment, "After reading Flores and Rosa (2015), I was really grappling with many of the concepts. I've taught first-year composition since 2015, and I've spent a lot of time contemplating how much time to spend teaching conventions." She goes on to explain how grading for correctness has consequences on "the assessment and placement practices that result in higher percentages of multilingual students enrolling in five-credit corequisite courses instead of the traditional three-credit first-year composition course." Although such a reflection was mainly driven by the readings and not the role-play, the readings were an essential part of the overall assignment.

Layla reflects on her own identity as a White, English-speaking teacher with more than ten years of experience who "can be confident that any critiques about my teaching will be focused on the actual teaching skills, not how I sound. Because it is outside of my personal experience, one of the most challenging parts of the assignment was putting ourselves in the shoes of someone who would actually suggest this!" Layla's partner reflected that

> When creating the scenario, I had mixed feelings. I was the mentor teacher who asked the bilingual teaching candidate to fix her Spanish accent. I felt disrespectful, inconsiderate, and uncomfortable with my character's ignorance. [...] While this was a re-enactment, I still felt that pit in my stomach that this happens today. It made me realize how close-minded people can be and how crucial it is for educators to continue educating themselves. Also, how the bilingual teacher candidate [character] stood her ground made me hope that we are teaching new teachers how to stand up for themselves.

It is this discomfort that led students to confront the fact that such scenarios still happen today. In fact, scenario 2 (see Appendix) was inspired by a real incident that one bilingual teaching candidate experienced during her field placement: designing the assignment on raciolinguistics through role-play was the one of the ways the instructor (as part of a wider group of faculty members) decided to respond by trying to better prepare teacher educators for such instances. Layla emphasized this point in her reflection explaining how the assignment reminded her "of how important it is to include these concepts [raciolinguistics] in teacher preparation programs. In our scenario, the bilingual teacher candidate was able to draw on what she had learned and read to support her claims." Layla goes on to argue that institutes of higher education mostly perpetuate White middle-class values and that is why "exposing teacher candidates to these readings and concepts early in their careers could help prevent such macro and microaggressions in the classroom." In short, despite the fact that the scenarios invoked discomfort, such conversations "could potentially be brought up by a coworker in my own practice as a teacher, so it was beneficial to practice how I might disprove those arguments when the situation arises," Lilly explains. Although there were no data to support such a hypothesis (e.g., student reflections), discomfort could have also arisen from the way the assignment pushed students to confront and self-interrogate their monoglossic ideologies/practices.

Similar calls for advocacy and suggestions for taking action were also voiced by students. For example, one scenario created by two students described a mother's recount of how her son was bullied at school because he was speaking Spanish and his classmates "told my son, Carlos, that he should speak English because he's in America and that's what you're 'supposed to speak.' They weren't even playing with the kids that were made fun of (Spanish speakers)." In that scenario played by the characters of Carlos's mother and a graduate student studying language and identity, the graduate student listens to the mother and explains that "even when language-minoritized individuals speak English, stigmatization is still incredibly prevalent," and that the white listener still looks for deviances or linguistic differences that still mark folks apart such as accents or dialects. The graduate student further adds:

> In terms of advocating for change at his school, I have some ideas. The first is to talk with his teacher about his experience and how he now feels unsafe and nervous.
>
> Continue to advocate for changes within the classroom and school overall to create a safe learning environment for Carlos and everyone else. For example, you can advocate for things such as a more inclusive and culturally responsive curriculum … more diverse books and materials … things that make students feel seen and represented.

Beyond listening and trying to use raciolinguistic references to explain to the mother the process of stigmatization, the graduate student also advises on how to advocate for Carlos and other linguistically minoritized students. Offering additional advice for the mother, the student shares, "To take your advocacy in the school even further, you can even request to administrators that teachers get proper and ongoing diversity, equity, and inclusion training so that they can change their practices to meet the needs of all students and families, especially multilingual families and families who do not speak English."

Discussion and Implications

Findings from this study revealed how a group of graduate students negotiated their understanding of raciolinguistics through writing and enacting fictional scenarios at the intersection of race and language. While some of them successfully challenged dominant language ideologies, others inadvertently reified such ideologies. The success of the first group was mainly attributed to creating scenarios that empowered multilingual individuals and their allies through drawing upon the arguments associated with the readings assigned as part of the course they were enrolled in. Less successful attempts of role-playing raciolinguistic ideologies did not draw upon the constructs and arguments from class readings on raciolinguistics. In any case, all students engaged and grappled with raciolinguistics through their fictional scenarios, presenting conflicting views regarding race and language and adopting critical and dialogic ways of doing so. In this section, we discuss theoretical and pedagogical implications of this study that can inform teacher educator efforts of preparing more critical TESOL educators that can support and advocate on behalf of multilingual learners in their future classrooms and other contexts as well.

On a theoretical level, we argue that CDE is a promising framework that can facilitate dialogic and critical conversations and reflections on such complex topics as raciolinguistics. More specifically, the assignment was critical by nature in the sense that it provided students with a frame to interrogate monoglossic language ideologies within the context of fictional scenarios that were inspired from reality. As students reported, the scenarios were similar to events that they have experienced or witnessed and as many shared, such critical examinations within the context of fiction were helpful in preparing them to face similar (but real) scenarios when they do take place.

The assignment was also dialogic by nature in the sense that students had to work collaboratively to represent multiple and often opposing points of view regarding language and race. This is in line with CDE's concept of multivocality that invites the incorporation of multiple points of view. The purpose is not to resolve such conflicting views, but more to engage with more than one perspective and critically explore more than one way of seeing the world. In doing so, students reported experiencing an array of feelings including discomfort and difficulty in putting oneself in another's shoes. One challenge for us as teacher educators to reflect on is how to address this "multivocality" that perpetuates and reinforces the deficit framing on non-dominant languages and speakers of those languages. One way to do this is to have students share their work and viewpoints in an open discussion forum facilitated by the instructors. Having such an opportunity for critical and dialogic discussions of their colleagues' work can deepen understanding of raciolingusitic ideologies and how they function to marginalize multilingual learners. Even without the open online discussions, the assignment still provided students with a chance to engage in deeper reflections on their identities, practices in the classroom, and language ideologies.

As such, on a pedagogical level, we argue that role-playing in particular accentuated such powerful engagement. Similar to Seltzer (2019), this study affirms the importance of role-play as an efficient pedagogical tool to facilitate students' negotiation of complex topics such as language ideologies through carefully designed dialogic engagement. Multivocality was facilitated by the writing of fictional scenarios where students did not have to disclose their own personal beliefs (although many of them did through their reflections). Thus, we believe that fictional scenarios provide an additional layer of safety for students to critically engage in complex topics. As teacher educators, it is sometimes easy to assume that students enrolled in a TESOL course on language and identity will probably have a multilingual perspective that informs their pedagogical beliefs on language education. However, findings from this study reveal how students are constantly grappling with their own beliefs that are by no means static or fixed. Consequently, it is important to provide classroom opportunities for students to be able to engage with and reflect on topics from multiple perspectives.

Providing such opportunities within the context of an asynchronous online course can be a challenge on its own. Many educators have expressed doubts about the limitations of online courses and videos to address such important issues as equity, social justice, and language ideologies (e.g., Karam et al., 2020). Nonetheless, online spaces offer an important opportunity to incorporate CDE approaches to address complex issues related to race, language, and identity. An asynchronous online platform can provide students with added time to reflect more deeply on their beliefs and language ideologies vis-à-vis arguments from core readings related to raciolinguistics. Findings from this study present one way of accomplishing this through adopting a critical and dialogic approach to curricular design and through the use of role-play and video. Despite the fact that there were no in-person discussions, students were still able to work collaboratively and role-play their scenarios.

Conclusion

In this work, analysis revealed how students grappled with race and language to challenge and sometimes inadvertently reify monoglossic language ideologies. Although difficult conversations on raciolinguistics led to feelings of discomfort for some students, engaging in such conversations through crafting fictional scenarios and enacting them led to deeper connections to students' own personal experiences with linguistic discrimination, thoughtful reflections on their own identities and language ideologies, and in some cases students reported being better prepared to support and advocate for multilingual learners. As Sylvia explains, "after creating this script with Brenda and enacting it, I now have ways that I could approach this situation if it happened at my school. There is value in sticking up for your students and advocating for them." It is our hope that TESOL teacher educators see CDE and role-play as promising theoretical and pedagogical tools to reimagine TESOL teacher education and help teachers like Sylvia to stick up for multilingual learners.

References

Alim, H. S. (2005). Critical language awareness in the United States: Revisiting issues and revising pedagogies in a resegregated society. *Educational Researcher, 34*(7), 24–31.

Alim, H. S. (2016). Introducing raciolinguistics: Racing language and languaging race in hyperracial times. In H. S. Alim, J. R. Rickford, & A. F. Ball (Eds.), *Raciolinguistics: How language shapes our ideas about race* (pp. 1–30). Oxford University Press.

Aneja, G. A. (2016). (Non)native speakered: Rethinking (non)nativeness and teacher identity in TESOL teacher education. *TESOL Quarterly, 50*(3), 572–96.

Duran, C. S. (2019). On issues of discrimination and xenophobia: What can TESOL practitioners do to support and advocate for refugee students? *TESOL Quarterly, 53*(3), 818–27.

Flores, N., & Rosa, J. (2015). Undoing appropriateness: Raciolinguistic ideologies and language diversity in education. *Harvard Educational Review, 85*(2), 149–71.

Glick, Y., & Walqui, A. (2021). Affordances in the development of student voice and agency: The case of bureaucratically labeled long-term English learners. In A. Kibler, G. Valdés, & A. Walqui (Eds.), *Reconceptualizing the role of critical dialogue in American classrooms: Promoting equity through dialogic education* (pp. 23–51). Routledge.

Haneda, M. (2017). Dialogic learning and teaching across diverse contexts: Promises and challenges. *Language and Education, 31*(1), 1–5.

Karam, F. J. (2021). Re-envisioning the ESOL classroom through a virtues-based curriculum: Contributions to critical dialogic education. *TESOL Journal, 12*(3), e582.

Karam, F. J., Warren, A. N., Kersten-Parrish, S., Lucas, J., & Talso, M. (2020). Practicums in online language teacher education: Instructors' perceptions of online teaching and using video as a key practice. In H.-S. Kang, D.-S. Shin, & T. Cimasko's (Eds.), *Online education for teachers of English as a global language* (pp. 39–59). Routledge.

Karam, F. J., Oikonomidoy, E., & Kibler, A. K. (2021). Artifactual literacies and TESOL: Narratives of a Syrian refugee-background family. *TESOL Quarterly, 55*(2), 510–35.

Kibler, A. K., Karam, F. J., Futch Ehrlich, V. A., Bergey, R., Wang, C., & Molloy Elreda, L. (2018). Who are "long-term English learners"? Using classroom interactions to deconstruct a manufactured learner label. *Applied Linguistics, 39*(5), 741–65.

Kibler, A. K., Valdés, G., & Walqui, A. (2021). Introduction: A vision for critical dialogic education. In A. Kibler, G. Valdés, & A. Walqui (Eds.), *Reconceptualizing the role of critical dialogue in American classrooms: Promoting equity through dialogic education* (pp. 1–22). Routledge.

Lu, M. Z. (1992). Conflict and struggle: The enemies or preconditions of basic writing? *College English, 54*(8), 887–913.

Merriam, S. B. (1998). *Qualitative research and case study applications in education.* Jossey-Bass.

Palmer, D. (2011). The discourse of transition: Teachers' language ideologies within transitional bilingual education programs. *International multilingual research journal, 5*(2), 103–22.

Paulick, J. H., Karam, F. J., & Kibler, A. K. (2022). Everyday objects and home visits: A window into the cultural models of families of culturally and linguistically marginalized students. *Language Arts, 99*(6), 390–401.

Ricklefs, M. A. (2021a). Functions of language use and raciolinguistic ideologies in students' interactions. *Bilingual Research Journal, 44*(1), 90–107.

Ricklefs, M. A. (2021b). Variables influencing ESL teacher candidates' language ideologies. *Language and Education.* Advance online publication.

Saldaña, J., & Omasta, M. (2016). *Qualitative research: Analyzing life*. Sage.
Saldaña, J., & Omasta, M. (2021). *Qualitative research: Analyzing life* (2nd ed.). Sage.
Seltzer, K. (2019). Performing ideologies: Fostering raciolinguistic literacies through role-play in a high school English classroom. *Journal of Adolescent & Adult Literacy*, 63(2), 147–55.
Thoma, N. (2022). Biographical perspectives on language ideologies in teacher education. *Language and Education*, 36(5), 419–36.
Woodard, R., & Rao, A. (2020). Tensions and possibilities in fostering critical language ideologies in elementary teacher education. *Studying Teacher Education*, 16(2), 183–203.
Wortham, S., & Reyes, A. (2011). Linguistic anthropology of education. In B. A. U. Levinson & M. Pollock (Eds.), *A companion to the anthropology of education* (pp. 137–53). Wiley-Blackwell.

Appendix: Assignment Description

Assignment Description

This assignment is to be completed in small groups of two to four people. The professor will facilitate a signing-up process or assign individuals to small groups.

Duration: Videos can be around 10–15 minutes. You do not have to meet in person to record the videos [Covid-19 mitigation efforts], and interactions/role-playing can take place over Zoom.

Groups may choose one of the two following scenarios, or please feel free to create your own similar scenarios.

Scenario 1

Please watch the following video: https://www.youtube.com/watch?v=YXmnUQrHE6s.

In the video, Rosita recounts how "People didn't like that we were speaking Spanish and they got mad at us," when she was playing *Veo, Veo* (I Spy) with her mother at the market. "They yelled at us that we should speak English and they looked so angry. I was so scared I hold my mommy's hand and she told me that we had to leave."

Nelson Flores tweeted about this:

https://twitter.com/nelsonlflores/status/1376886472951918592

Please respond to Flores's invitation by drafting a scenario and enacting it. More specifically, imagine Rosita's mother, or any other character(s) in a different setting asking a graduate student at our university why some people are OK with monolingual English-speaking individuals learning Spanish, but are not OK with adults speaking languages other than English in the workplace or in other public settings. In your conversations, explain why and allow an active exchange of thoughts and ideas. Videotape the interactions and submit both the written scenario and a link to the video. Remember to start your video by explaining the context, the characters involved in your sketch, and who will be playing which role. You can upload your video to the course's online platform and then share the link here. For each group member, also submit an individual reflection where you share your learning, thoughts, and experiences in creating this video, making connections to the readings as appropriate. Reflections can be between 400–700 words in length.

Scenario 2

As part of her field-placement experiences, a bilingual teacher candidate was asked by her mentor teacher to "fix" her accent and speak proper English in order to be able to teach the children appropriately. Seriously, this happened to one of the bilingual in-service teachers at our university! And unfortunately similar incidents are common both in school and out-of-school settings.

Draft a dialogue between the student and their mentor teacher. Use what we learned from the readings this semester to enable the teacher candidate to respond to the mentor teacher's request of fixing their accent. In addition, include some of the assimilationist and monolingual perspectives that are common in such scenarios. Enact the dialogue (you may want to have additional characters) and videotape the interactions. Remember to start your video by explaining the context, the characters involved in your sketch, and who will be playing which role. Submit both the written scenario/dialogue and a link to the video. You can upload your video to the course's online platform and then share the link here. For each group member, also submit an individual reflection where you share your learning, thoughts, and experiences in creating this video, making connections to the readings as appropriate. Reflections can be between 400–700 words in length.

Part Three

Commentary: Reimagining Online TESOL Teacher Education: Creating Dialogic and Critical Online Spaces

Yasemin Tezgiden-Cakcak

My Identity, Positionality, and Perceptions of Critical and Dialogic Education

Identifying myself as a middle-class, cisgender, able-bodied woman born and raised in a small conservative town in Western Turkey, I have both experienced the privileges of growing up in a middle-class educated household and suffered from the overwhelming pressures of leading life as a young girl under the dominant patriarchal, conservative, and religious norms of society. As a bilingual educator, I am privileged enough to enjoy the intellectually fulfilling exchange of ideas on a global realm, but I am also positioned as a "non-native" English-speaking educator both at home and abroad. As an academic, I benefit from the privilege of working at one of the prestigious public universities of Turkey, but I also feel marginalized at times as I am located far away from the Western academia. As a critical educator working in Turkey, I enjoy connecting with teacher-candidates but I also encounter the day-to-day challenges and risks of my critical endeavors under the authoritarian regime in the country (Babacan et al., 2021).

English is taught as a foreign language in Turkey for cross-cultural communication and/or for gaining access to "better" jobs. I work in a Foreign Language Education department and teach mostly undergraduate level English Language Teaching (ELT) courses. Because teacher candidates are not prepared for a specific target group of learners in Turkey, I try to help them (re)gain a critical lens for reading their students' worlds in relation to broader political-economic, socio-cultural, and educational issues. Depending on their institution type and the region they work, they may have students coming from privileged backgrounds as well as linguistically or culturally minoritized students, poor and hungry students, young girls who face the risk of forced marriages by their families, sexually abused students, LGBTQ students, neurodivergent students, disabled students, and/or victimized students due to the earthquake in February 2023 in Turkey and Syria.

Following Paulo Freire (2005), I believe in the unity of reflection and action (praxis) for critical transformation to occur. Therefore, I aim to educate teachers as transformative intellectuals, who exercise their agency to create change in and out of the classroom (Giroux, 1988). For me, critical pedagogy is the name of a political and educational movement focusing on democratic and emancipatory education practices for the well-being of all. Striving to question the reasons behind the systematic malfunctioning of mainstream education systems, critical pedagogy argues suppression, discrimination, exclusion, and silencing of an overwhelming majority of students are intrinsic to the maintenance of the neocolonial and neoliberal world order. For the ruling classes to continue exploiting the ruled, the capitalist system has to reproduce itself by educating submissive workers, citizens, and consumers, who would not question, recognize, or challenge the classist, racist, sexist, heteronormative, and ableist ideologies (Hooks, 2000). Critical pedagogy, however, aims to build a participatory dialogic space to deconstruct the traditional education system and to reconstruct an equitable and just education system for a truly democratic society (Kincheloe, 2008).

Drawing from critical pedagogy, I interpret critical language teacher education as a praxis-oriented approach to educating teachers as change agents. Adopting this approach does not mean that teacher candidates educated in this paradigm will necessarily embrace the role of a teacher as a transformative intellectual. Based on their identities, ideologies, positionality, and teaching contexts, they may choose to stay "neutral" and just teach the subject matter without envisioning a role for themselves to work for social justice. Even in that case, their experience in a critical language teacher education program/course might help them develop a new lens to have a three-dimensional understanding of students' life worlds, the structural inequities, and the challenges they face and may prevent them from harming students (un)intentionally. My first and foremost principle in teacher education has become "first do no harm" as in the Hippocratic oath. I raise critical consciousness for teacher candidates to realize and refrain from the normalized discriminatory acts, remarks, and ideas in the schooling system (Tezgiden-Cakcak, 2019). Even if they do not actively raise critical consciousness, their care and attention not to harm students and helping them develop their academic and linguistic skills would be an important step forward for the marginalized students. Although this might be regarded as minimizing expectations from critical language teacher education, it is in fact grounding our work on the solid basis of our sociohistorical, political-economic, and ideologic conditions (Shor, 2022).

Under repressive regimes, you might have to exercise critical action implicitly through your stance, your body language, your facial expression, your identity, or through the relationships you build with your students. We need to acknowledge that exercising critical pedagogy is risky and not everyone might be ready to face the consequences of such work, especially in an ideologically hostile space. If educators do not oppress, humiliate, or discriminate students, but help them develop their curiosity, creativity, and collaborative skills, provide them with a dialogic, participatory, and inclusive environment for finding and expressing their voice(s), then they might actually be fulfilling the bare minimum of becoming a critical dialogic educator.

For those who would like to take up a more explicit role as a transformative intellectual teacher, critical language teacher education has more to offer. Even though individual commitment, courage, and investment would be necessary to engage in struggle against power and injustice, critical education underscores the equal importance of working collectively for the common good instead of egoistic competition (Dewey, 1956). Therefore, critical teacher educators model relationship and community-building efforts for teacher candidates to imagine enacting such relationships of solidarity in their current and future practices. After encountering such egalitarian relationships and joining a professional community of critical educators, they may feel more competent and confident to raise critical consciousness, to exercise problem-posing liberatory pedagogy, and to work as critical allies with their students, families, and the school community for equitable democratic participation and voice.

Firmly believing in the vitality of dialogic relationship-building in critical language teacher education, I don't think I was able to achieve genuine relationships with my teacher candidates during the online teaching period during the pandemic, especially if I met the cohort for the first time on an online platform. Even though our online classes were synchronous, most of the students did not open their cameras and I did not have a chance to have eye contact with them. I did not find the occasion to chat with them during the breaks or after class, as I would in face-to-face teaching. Still, I continued to problematize educational, linguistic, and professional issues in my classes, strove to co-construct a dialogic, democratic, and inclusive space for the classroom community to express ideas and pose questions, and to talk with students on issues relevant to our lives. I asked them to reflect on critical pedagogy, how they would implement it in their real or imaginary teaching contexts, and to prepare critical lesson plans to raise consciousness in their students. Yet, I always felt one crucial dimension of my critical pedagogic work was missing during distance education. That is why I appreciate the efforts of fellow critical teacher educators in this section in creating dialogic spaces among teacher candidates on an online platform. If we have to reimagine TESOL teacher education in an online space because of the neoliberal/neoconservative push for distance education, we will have to find innovative ways to reconstruct our work without giving up on our struggles for face-to-face education. In this respect, the chapters in this section offer us critical ideas and practical tools to "reimagine" critical dialogic online TESOL teacher education.

Having introduced my identity, positionality, and my understanding of critical and dialogic language teacher education, I should now highlight the overlaps and divergences from the main premise of this book, CDE as conceptualized in Kibler et al. (2021). My view of critical and dialogic education is inclusive, respectful, and reciprocal similar to Kibler et al.'s vision of CDE. Like Kibler et al. (2021), I aim to challenge inequitable and discriminatory ideological and institutional policies and practices excluding minoritized students from equitable opportunities for learning, voice, and participation in and beyond the classroom. I highlight multiple ways of being and languaging in the school and society. As in their CDE framework, I problematize global and local issues and center my pedagogy and research on posing questions relevant to our lives. I also acknowledge the tensions arising from the unpredictable, dynamic, and multivocal nature of critical dialogue in exploring complex topics, as Kibler et al. (2021) suggest. When it comes to building relationships among the classroom community, I agree with Kibler et al.'s (2021) idea that "classroom dialogue is built upon personal relationships" (p. 187). However, in my view, teacher-student relationships should also be given equal importance to disrupt the traditional power relations. For me, critical teacher education should model equitable relationships for teacher candidates to build similar relations with their own learners. While I acknowledge Kibler et al.'s (2021) focus on creating "equitable and inclusive *learning spaces* for linguistically minoritized students inside and outside the classroom" (p. 192, italics mine), I believe we should also foreground helping and joining minoritized language learners in their individual and collective struggles against the hegemonic policies, discourses, and practices in and outside the school setting to build inclusive and democratic schools and societies. My commentary as to the chapters in this section will therefore be informed both by the CDE approach conceptualized by Kibler et al. (2021) and by my own understanding of CDE.

Creating Critical Dialogic Online Spaces

Even though distance education was predominantly characterized by individualized learning and atomization of students, teachers, and school communities especially during the Covid-19 pandemic (Miller & Liu, 2021; Sayılan & Alica, 2022), chapters in this section indicate it might in fact be possible to create *dialogic* online spaces for critical TESOL teacher education as long as students have access to digital technologies. There is no doubt learners, teacher candidates, and teacher educators benefit from in-person interactions during class discussions. However, we need to realize they learn as much, if not more, outside the classroom from their dialogic interactions with their peers and the school community. Therefore, both chapters imply CDE cannot be reduced to real-time, face-to-face interactions within the classroom setting and showcase how CDE can actually take place on an online platform asynchronously.

Without ignoring the constraints of distance education, Li and Bian (this volume) highlighted the affordances that advanced digital technologies could bring for sharing, communicating, working together, and co-constructing knowledge. Li and Bian (this volume) maintained that preparing teacher candidates to address the unique needs of culturally and linguistically minorized students in teacher education programs is a must in our increasingly multilingual and multicultural world in line with the main purposes of CDE. They thought preparing teacher candidates in teaching multilingual learners requires special and careful planning involving critical dialogic reflections as well as hands-on, field-based learning. Their online teacher education module was based on co-constructed dialogic, multivocal interactions among teacher candidates and the school community, as suggested by Kibler et al. (2021). In addition to gaining a critical understanding of structural inequities and raciolinguistic ideologies multilingual learners face, they believed it is important for teacher candidates to hear the perspectives of all stakeholders. They incorporated field experience into their six-module training program, with the help of which teacher candidates found a chance to connect with linguistically and culturally minorized students, their families, and teachers. This experience was invaluable for them to understand the life worlds of immigrant students, which showcases the need for critical personal encounters with minoritized communities in CDE. On the other hand, the authors thought asynchronous mode of interaction enabled teacher candidates to interact with each other on their own times taking low risks. Therefore, they asked teacher candidates to write critical reflections on an online forum responding to one another's posts dialogically and to form critical friendships to support one another. This chapter shows it is possible for classroom community to interact with each other through carefully planned dialogic tasks online.

Karam, Kibler, and Arnold (this volume) benefitted from role-play as an innovative pedagogic tool for critical and dialogic online TESOL teacher education. Graduate students enrolled in the course worked in groups to think over the fictional case scenarios drawn from real-life experiences. With the help of advanced interactive technologies, they could meet online to write and enact role-plays for their chosen scenarios. This role-play task aimed to provide teacher candidates with a chance to critically reflect on the given situation and to think of ways to disrupt the dominant discourses. For carrying out the task, teacher candidates needed to work in close interaction and to exchange ideas, experiences and insights. Collaboratively, they identified the white gaze inherent in racialized discourses. This was an innovative task synthesizing multiple tenets of CDE conceptualized by Kibler et al. (2021): problematizing dominant discourses and standardized curricula, benefiting from multivocal, multilingual, and multimodal resources, working dialogically to support one another's learning, and developing agency to challenge deficit views of minoritized students. While some groups challenged the deficit perspective in the given scenarios through their dialogue, others could not refrain from reproducing the dominant discourses in their role-plays. The fact that some groups could not challenge the deficit perspective might mean two things: a) They might not have engaged with course content sufficiently, or b) they might still be processing the critical content they were exposed to, not yet feeling ready to oppose the dominant narratives (Gonsalves, 2008). These findings support critical teacher educators' calls for not restricting critical teacher education to particular courses but implementing it program wide (Li & Bian, this volume; Potts et al., 2008). Only through constant encounters with critical content can we support teacher candidates in their struggles for unlearning some of the taken for granted notions in their minds, which must be emphasized in CDE.

Contributions to Critical Dialogic TESOL Teacher Education

Addressing the need to prepare teacher candidates for educating linguistically and culturally marginalized students, both chapters in this section contribute to critical and dialogic TESOL teacher education with innovative pedagogic tools. Li and Bian (this volume) developed and piloted online training modules with notes for instructors while Karam, Kibler, & Arnold (this volume) benefitted from role-plays for deeper dialogic engagement with the course content. Their innovative pedagogic experiments provide US-based critical and dialogic teacher educators with practical teaching tools and inspire colleagues working in other settings to develop similar tools for and in their local contexts.

The strength of Li and Bian's contribution (this volume) comes from their collaborative action-research to create change in their teacher education context. The authors first looked thoroughly into their own experience and the feedback they received from their students. Teacher candidates expressed they did not feel prepared to teach multilingual learners. Most teacher candidates participating in the study had grown up in linguistically homogeneous communities and needed to connect with the immigrant students. They also asked for practical strategies, resources, and coaching to teach this particular group of students. To meet teacher candidates' needs, the authors designed a specialized teacher training program synthesizing critical reflection, dialogic interaction, and fieldwork experience. Most strikingly, they used their recorded interviews with immigrant families as course materials, which enabled teacher candidates to hear the experiences of multilingual learners from firsthand. The field experiences of teacher candidates showed them the complexity of teaching multilingual students from different angles. For teacher candidates to envision acting differently, they wrote reflection papers about their future actions. I believe collaborative action research Li and Bian (this volume) used is a fruitful instrument for professional development and enacting locally grounded change. Still, to problematize power relations in the educational and research context further and to enable all stakeholders take part in research studies as equal contributors and problem posers/solvers (Brydon-Miller et al., 2011), researchers could consider engaging in participatory action research (PAR) projects in future studies, as recommended by Kibler et al. (2021), as well.

For graduate TESOL students to develop understanding of intersectionality of race, language ideologies, and identity, Karam, Kibler, and Arnold (this volume) used role-play as a creative and collaborative pedagogic tool. Fictional scenarios were used to give students the room for imagining what they would do when they encountered dominant language ideologies in their personal and professional lives. Students wrote dialogues, enacted, and videotaped them. As Kibler et al. (2021) highlighted, learners and teachers need to learn how to navigate tension in critical dialogic interactions around controversial issues and this task provided students with a non-threatening environment to experiment with a difficult topic. It enabled teacher candidates to express their controversial or conflicting ideas without revealing their personal beliefs. Findings of the study showed students felt empathy and discomfort writing and enacting their multivocal role-plays. Some of them also expressed commitment for advocacy. I believe this role-playing experience is priceless considering many of us are caught unprepared for racio-linguicist discourses and practices and we do not usually know how to challenge them in daily conversations. As Kubota (2023) noted, it is quite crucial for us critical educators to learn how to challenge dominant ideas among non-academic audiences. In this sense, I find Karam, Kibler, and Arnold's (this volume) contribution unique and exemplary because they not only provide an empowering instrument for teacher candidates to raise their voices against injustice, but they also give teacher educators a new learning activity for problematizing a marginalized issue.

Contributions to Critical Dialogic Education

Chapters in this section embody characteristics of CDE in preparing TESOL teacher candidates to cater for the specific academic and linguistic needs of multilingual learners. Showing teacher candidates the structural inequities and the raciolinguistic discourses multilingual learners have to confront, authors in both chapters provide a chance for teacher candidates to empathize with their learners and to see them as strengths. Li and Bian (this volume) give them practical teaching strategies as well as experiential knowledge to connect with multilingual communities to learn from and with them. On the other hand, Karam, Kibler, and Arnold (this volume) strive to equip language teachers with the practical experience to negotiate and resist dominant racio-linguistic perspectives to advocate on behalf of multilingual learners. By raising authentic and relevant questions in their role-plays, language teachers encounter and question multiple voices and perspectives. In this way, they learn how to negotiate power dynamics beyond their classroom communities to disrupt and transform dominant discourses for more democratic participation.

While I appreciate the dedication of authors in this section to prepare teacher candidates to support multilingual language learners to develop their full potential and to become legitimate contributors of the class community, I also think that we should give equal importance to helping multilingual learners become change agents, who can use their agency to liberate themselves and their communities from the oppression they face. Therefore, we should not limit our CDE efforts solely to supporting marginalized students learn and/or use English language effectively. Rather, we should take the next step to help multilingual learners read the world from a critical perspective, just as we do with teacher candidates, so that minorized students can also better understand the structural reasons behind their oppression. They should be able to grasp the political behind their personal issues, so that they can liberate themselves and take action for transforming the oppressive conditions individually and collectively.

In their emancipation process, we should become their allies and accompany them in this painstaking journey for individual and social change. Following Freire (2005), I don't think we should work *for* them but work *with* them in their struggles. Rather than speaking *for* them, we should help them find their voices and speak up for themselves disrupting the culture of silence. Although this might sound too ambitious, we should not stop believing in the *possibility* we could create for change through critical and dialogic (teacher) education. Without imagining such a possibility, our vision will not challenge the deficit perspective of minoritized learners, rather, it will reproduce the dominant perspective that "multilingual learners can also learn." Rather than seeing them "as objects to be saved" (Freire, 2005, p. 65), we should regard multilingual learners as agents who can actively take part in civic, democratic engagement, as highlighted in CDE. Although Kibler et al. (2021) are right in believing that following CDE does not necessarily lead to empowerment or transformation in all marginalized learners, I still have a firm belief in the agentive potential of marginalized learners to enact change. As Freire argued, "who are better prepared than the oppressed to understand the terrible significance of an oppressive society?" (Freire, 2005, p. 45).

For helping multilingual learners to realize the inequitable structural conditions they are exposed to and to foster their reflection and action to challenge them, I believe we could add another component into Li and Bian's (this volume) teacher education program, where teacher candidates engage in critical consciousness-raising activities among multilingual learners for personal and social transformation. The opportunity Karam, Kibler, and Arnold (this volume) gave teacher candidates to learn to speak on behalf of marginalized learners was excellent. But we could also give that role-playing task to multilingual learners for them to learn how to negotiate power hierarchies as a way of talking back at the dominant powers in future studies. Hence, I suggest critical and dialogic teacher education should foreground fostering the agentive potential of minoritized language learners for transformative action along with teacher candidates.

Implications for Teacher Educators and TESOL Professionals

Dedicated to CDE, authors contributing to this section use praxis in their pedagogic and scholarly endeavors. They problematize inequity and injustice in their class readings/discussions, create dialogic safe spaces for all teacher candidates to participate as legitimate contributors, and take pedagogic action to enable teacher candidates to experiment with their new insights in dialogue with teacher educators, their peers, and the school community in line with the tenets of CDE. The findings of the studies reported in both chapters indicate teacher candidates have increasing awareness of complex structural issues of inequity and injustice multilingual learners face and express commitment for advocacy.

Even though dialogue among teacher candidates and the school community is essential for critical dialogic language teacher education, I still think we should not disregard the importance of the relationship built between teacher educators and teacher candidates, either. The relationship we build with teacher candidates sets an example for them for the relationships they will build with their students. As Freire (2005) argued, an indispensable element of critical education is overcoming the teacher-student contradiction in which teachers become students and students become teachers. Teachers and learners should learn and grow together in this new egalitarian relationship without ignoring the power dynamics. For such a relationship to be built, Freire (2005) asserted, educators need to have humility, respect, and love for the students, trust in their reasoning power, impatience to realize their dreams, and patience to devote necessary time and energy for those dreams to come true. Embodying these values in our teacher educator persona as much as possible, we should model how becoming a critical educator informs one's presence in the world from body language to overall stance toward life. The value and respect we give to our own teacher candidates, or lack thereof, will tell them more than our lectures will convey. In other words, we should not overlook the potential of the bonds we make with teacher candidates for their future teacher personas and/or for our collective well-being. We should perhaps think more thoroughly about how to reconstruct such relationships during online teacher education. In a parallel vein, the way we include our teacher candidates/students or not in designing and reshaping our classes and/or our research studies will make an impact on their future actions as educators/researchers and expand our view of teacher education/research, as maintained by Kibler et al. (2021).

Concluding Remarks

My interpretations of the work of authors writing in this section were naturally informed by my positionality and my own understanding of critical and dialogic language teacher education. However, writing this commentary on their work helped me reconsider my own approach from a new perspective. Transformative actions of teacher educators in online spaces enlarged my perspective of the possibilities of distance education for CDE. I learnt that critical dialogic encounters do not necessarily occur only in real time, in person and synchronously, but they could be fostered with critical pedagogic tools beyond the classroom, which enable teacher candidates to reconsider their beliefs, ideas, and perceptions in close interaction with their peers and the school community. I also saw how the critical class readings and discussions came alive in dialogic co-constructions of teacher candidates and how reflection turned into (possible) action in both chapters. The chapters also helped me think of innovative pedagogic tools that could be adapted in Turkey. Interviews with school communities and role-plays to challenge racio-linguistic bias were truly inspiring. They could be used to disrupt the dominant neoconservative ideologies in Turkey.

Both chapters in this section embodied characteristics of CDE (Kibler et al., 2021) in their pedagogy and research with their focus on preparing teacher candidates for teaching multilingual learners, problematizing structural inequities and dominant ideologies, incorporating multiple voices and perspectives of different stakeholders, and implementing problem-posing pedagogy. Still, I argue critical and dialogic teacher education should not disregard a) relationship-building between teacher educators and teacher candidates, b) helping not only teacher candidates but also multilingual language learners develop their agency to take transformative action individually and collectively to create a democratic and equitable school and society, and c) working with, not for, the minoritized language learners and teacher candidates in their struggles as allies. I suggest research in critical and dialogic education could use PAR research for future studies to disrupt power inequalities in research studies as in Park et al. (2021).

In this commentary, I shared my interpretations of the common threads of the contributions in this section in relation to CDE (Kibler et al., 2021) and I added my own response. Seeing the engagement of teacher candidates in critical praxis as well as their growing understanding of the complexity of teaching multilingual learners refreshed my hopes for the possibility of change both in the school and the society at large. Reflecting on the works of fellow teacher educators along with mine allowed me to see how we all strive to open counter-hegemonic spaces within the restricting institutional spaces in our worlds apart. Our critical dialogic encounters in meaningful projects like this volume are valuable for they give us motivation, inspiration, and strength to expand our efforts individually and collectively. As a final word, I would like to thank the editors for inviting me to contribute to this volume because the very act of writing this commentary helped me reconnect with my international peers and overcome some of my feelings of marginalization and isolation as a critical teacher educator situated in Turkey.

References

Babacan, E., Kutun, M., Pinar, E., & Yilmaz, Z. (Eds.). (2021). *Regime change in Turkey: Neoliberal authoritarianism, Islamism and hegemony.* Routledge.

Brydon-Miller, M., Kral, M., Maguire, P., Noffke, S., & Sabhlok, A. (2011). Jazz and the banyan tree: Roots and riffs on participatory action research. In Y. S. Lincoln & N. K. Denzin (Eds.), *The Sage handbook of qualitative research* (4th Ed., pp. 387–400). Sage.

Dewey, J. (1956). *The child and the curriculum the school and the society.* Chicago University Press.

Freire, P. (2005). *Pedagogy of the oppressed 30th anniversary edition.* Continuum.

Giroux, H. (1988). *Teachers as intellectuals. Toward a critical pedagogy of learning.* Bergin & Garvey.

Gonsalves, R. (2008). Hysterical blindness and the ideology of denial: Preservice teachers' resistance to multicultural education. In I. Bartolomé (Ed.) *Ideologies in education: Unmasking the trap of teacher neutrality* (pp. 3–27). Peter Lang AG.

Hooks, B. (2000). *Where we stand: Class matters.* Routledge.

Kibler, A., Valdés, G., & Walqui, A. (2021). Introduction: A vision for critical dialogic education. In A. Kibler, G. Valdés, & A. Walqui (Eds.), *Reconceptualizing the role of critical dialogue in American classrooms: Promoting equity through dialogic education* (pp. 1–22). Routledge.

Kincheloe, J. (2008). *Critical pedagogy* (2nd Ed.). Peter Lang Publishing.

Kubota, R. (2023). Linking research to transforming the real world: Critical language studies for the next 20 years. *Critical Inquiry in Language Studies, 20*(1), 1–16. https://doi.org/10.1080/15427587.2022.2159826

Miller, R., & Liu, K. (2021). After the virus: Disaster capitalism, digital inequity, and transformative education for the future of schooling. *Education and Urban Society, 55*(5), 1–22. https://doi.org/10.1177/00131245211065419

Park, J., Simpson, L., Hernandez, C., Hernandez, S., Isom, O., Nguyen, T., Michaels, S., & O'Connor, C. (2021). Translating words and worlds in poetry inside out: Intergenerational research with multilingual youth on productive group talk. In *Reconceptualizing the role of critical dialogue in American classrooms* (pp. 105–31). Routledge.

Potts, A., Foster-Triplett, C., & Rose, D. (2008). An infused approach to multicultural education in a pre-service teacher program: Perspectives of teacher educators. *International Journal of Multicultural Education, 10*(1), 1–15.

Sayılan, F., & Alica, Z. (2022). The agenda of critical pedagogy during the Covid-19 pandemic in Turkey. In F. Mızıkacı & E. Ata (Eds.), *Critical pedagogy and the Covid-19 pandemic* (pp. 187–94). Bloomsbury.

Shor, I. (2022). Paulo Freire at 100, still inspiring: An interview with Ira Shor. In F. Mızıkacı & E. Ata (Eds.), *Critical pedagogy and the Covid-19 pandemic* (pp. 111–23). Bloomsbury.

Tezgiden-Cakcak, Y. (2019). *Moving beyond technicism in English language teacher education*. Lexington Press.

Conclusion: Toward a Future CDE Research Agenda

Fares J. Karam and Amanda K. Kibler

The chapters in this volume drew upon critical dialogic education (CDE) (Kibler et al., 2021) as a framework for preparing TESOL teachers in diverse contexts such as the United States, Macau, Türkiye, and New Zealand. Authors engaged with different aspects of CDE with the common goal of helping prepare future educators and advocates of multilingual students who are ready to "aggressively challenge the implicit and explicit ways that schools fit minoritized students into singular or monolithic forms of behavior, thinking, and […] discourse" (p. 1). Each in their own way, the contributing chapters presented their visions for reimagining curricula, pedagogies, online spaces, and the roles of students, teachers, and teacher educators—through the lens of CDE. In an effort to capture the richness of these contributions, we attempt to align these reimaginings to the critical dialogic transformations we discussed in the volume's introduction before we present our vision for a future CDE research agenda.

Critical Dialogic Transformations in TESOL Teacher Education

In the introduction, we discussed six common dialogic talk features (as being co-constructed, intellectually purposeful, respectful, adaptive, contextually responsive, and learnable), in addition to each feature's corresponding critical dialogic transformation that can put dialogic classrooms on a path to becoming critical *and* dialogic (see Table I.1, p. 10). In this section, we draw upon examples form chapters in this volume to highlight some of these transformations. We acknowledge that transforming classrooms and teacher education is an ongoing effort, but it is our hope that these transformative examples can inspire similar efforts in other settings where teacher educators are engaged in reimagining how to prepare TESOL professionals.

First, an important dialogic talk feature is how knowledge is co-constructed. In CDE classrooms, knowledge is not only co-constructed, but students are also positioned as agentive co-engineers and co-constructors of this knowledge in that they have a say in identifying authentic and relevant questions and issues essential to their learning and intellectual and professional development. In translating this into TESOL teacher education contexts, pre-service or in-service teachers become agentive co-constructors of their knowledge and training, in collaboration with teacher educators. This is evident in several chapters in this volume, especially in the chapter by Meston and Galloway (this volume) who work collaboratively with four in-service teachers as part of a Critical Friends Group (CFG). The CFG is part of a professional development effort where participants share their problems of practice and discuss solutions to those problems in a dialogic and critical manner. More specifically, the in-service teachers discuss the challenges of implementing CDE in their respective classrooms. Notable in the CFG meetings is how the discussions are centered around the in-service teachers' visions of critical and dialogic classrooms, positioning them as agentive sources of knowledge. In a way, the curriculum underlying these CFG discussions is determined by the in-service teachers' problems of practice, and they enact dialogic and critical discussion to learn from and encourage each other, centering issues of equity and social justice to better address the needs of their students. Meston and Galloway, as teacher educators, play a role that facilitated the in-service teachers' efforts of realizing their visions of critical and dialogic classrooms. They do not provide the in-service teachers with solutions to their problems or with the "right" answers to their questions. Through collaborative participation in the CFG, both the researchers and the in-service teachers engage in dialogic and critical teaching and learning that they can potentially carry into their classrooms in both school and teacher education settings.

A second feature of dialogic talk is that it is intellectually purposeful. From a CDE perspective, this purposeful feature is enriched through multivocality. Through the elicitation of multiple voices and perspectives that are traditionally silenced, teacher educators can foster a critical stance among TESOL professionals through dialogic interactions. We observe this taking place in the chapter by Yuan et al. (this volume), where the authors facilitate critical and dialogic learning activities that assist their pre-service teachers in developing their critical multilingual language awareness. One of the main implications of that chapter is how curricular design needs to be purposeful to provide pre-service teachers with the opportunities needed to address critical issues related to English language education (e.g., the role of colonialism in shaping language ideologies), in which multiple minoritized views are explored and thoughtfully considered. Helping TESOL professionals engage in such discussions that directly address biases, discriminatory practices, and power structures may involve difficult conversations. In Karam et al. (this volume), we observe how graduate students reported some of that discomfort when they explore both assimilationist and pluralist perspectives of multilingualism. Through role-play, they are able to explore the positioning and perspectives of linguistically minoritized individuals as they grapple with how to challenge raciolinguistic ideologies that position multilingual learners of English from racialized backgrounds as deficient.

Two additional features of dialogic talk include the prominence of respectful and adaptive interactions. A CDE transformation in classrooms and teacher education contexts means that every participant in dialogic and critical interactions is positioned as a "talk-worthy partner" (Alvarez et al., 2021, p. 89) through reciprocal norms, and that discussions are adapted—both a priori through intentional design of classroom talk and, in the moment, toward creating an equitable environment where all voices are heard. In the chapter by Kızıldağ and Kaçar (this volume), the authors not only have respectful interactions with their pre-service teachers within a field placement context: they integrate reciprocity by allowing their students to reimagine the role of both teacher educators and mentor teachers through adopting a Notice-Problematize-Implement (NPI) cycle. In short, the pre-service teachers are encouraged to put on a critical lens to identify inequities in their field placements through noticing and problematizing non-inclusive practices. Then they are invited to implement solutions to these problematic practices based on dialogic and critical conversations with their teacher educators. Instead of a top-down approach that is common within the Turkish context, where teacher educators are perceived as the source of knowledge, the authors provide their pre-service teachers with the chance to reimagine themselves as worthy sources of knowledge through collaborative learning and dialogic and critical discussions via the NPI model.

Dialogic talk is also contextually responsive—the next feature of CDE. From a CDE perspective, emphasis in contextual responsiveness is placed on power structures within these contexts that are never neutral. Special attention is given to how multilingual learners can potentially be disadvantaged in a surface level approach of seeing talk as responsive to context without addressing inequalities and practices that privilege some students at the expense of others. For example, Mohamed et al. (this volume) decentered such practices as starting the class with personal statements or anecdotes to honor the feelings of some students who preferred to get to know personal information about their classmates in contexts and ways beyond the traditional self-introductions that are used as common icebreakers to kick-start classes. Another example of being contextually responsive from a CDE perspective comes from Turner and Fránquiz (this volume), whose findings emphasize the importance of context in whether pre-service teachers are able to sustain their beliefs in an inclusive stance on language ideologies. Their chapter calls for us to broaden our thinking of "context" to include not only teacher education courses prior to course completion, but also field placements, professional development, and work settings where different stakeholders and power dynamics can play an important role in how pre-service teachers (transitioning into in-service teachers) can sustain their beliefs in dialogic, critical, and inclusive approaches to teaching and learning.

A final feature of dialogic talk is how it is learnable, with the CDE caveat that engagement in dialogic talk is not a direct path to empowerment. Such an acknowledgment is evident in Walqui's chapter (this volume) where the author documents teachers' hesitancy to shift away from prescriptive curricula and practices into more creative and dialogic ways of teaching multilingual students. Despite the careful professional development and scaffolding provided to both teachers and their students, teachers still needed time and additional experiences to develop their understanding of CDE and learn how they can incorporate CDE tenets to address the needs of multilingual students. Walqui's chapter underscores the importance of dialogic professional development and collaborative work with teachers on helping them envision and use supportive materials and curricula. For those reasons, Walqui reports ongoing work on reimaging the curriculum with their teacher collaborators, including the incorporation of videos, streamlining activities, and strengthening conceptual connections across the curriculum in order to better support teachers. Similarly, one important implication from the chapter by Li and Bian is that it is not enough to create online spaces for dialogic discussions without helping teachers look, think, and act differently. To help accomplish this goal, they propose engagement "in locally-grounded, collaborative, problem-solving inquiries" (p. 200) such as action research conducted by TESOL practitioners and teacher educators (modeled through the authors' chapter) to critically examine their own educational settings and enact changes that will help prepare critical reflective teachers for multilingual learners.

What we learn from all these chapters is that creating critical and dialogic spaces both within P-12 and teacher education contexts requires drawing upon an array of CDE tools and transformative actions, including reimaging curricula, language pedagogies, online spaces, and the roles of students, teachers, and teacher educators. All of these are areas that the three commentaries included in this volume discuss at length, highlighting how the chapters draw upon and extend CDE in each of these areas. The commentaries also address Kibler et al.'s (2021) invitation to "explore, question, refine, reframe, and even replace" (p. 192) CDE tenets in efforts to create dialogic and critical classrooms.

The commentary by Ungco and Varghese adds to CDE by highlighting the importance of accounting for identities, lived experiences, and contexts. By extending the original conceptualization of CDE to further emphasize the concept of identity, Ungco and Varghese (this volume) draw our attention to the fact that subsumed under CDE's call to reimagine the roles of teachers and students is a call to reimagine their identities. The chapter by Mohamed et al. in particular is an example of how the authors' identities have shaped their practice as teacher educators and their implementation of CDE. Ungco and Varghese elaborate that reimagining the roles of students, pre- and in-service teachers, and teacher educators involves decentering authority and re-envisioning classroom talk, particularly in teacher education contexts. They identify specific multivocal pedagogies (found in the chapters they reviewed) that are used toward those objectives: Duoethnography with teacher educators (Mohamed et al., this volume), a Notice-Problematize-Implement (NPI) approach with teacher candidates (Kızıldağ & Kaçar, this volume), and Critical Friends Group (CFG) with current teachers (Meston & Philips Galloway, this volume).

Madigan Peercy's commentary (this volume) also adds to CDE through a specific focus on the power of CDE—especially when combined with or examined alongside other critical lenses. Madigan Peercy discusses such powerful intersections of CDE with translanguaging (e.g., Turner & Fránquiz, this volume) and critical multilingual language awareness (Yuan et al., this volume), arguing for the need to "explore how CDE—and the ways in which it can be applied to both the creation and analysis of curricula and pedagogies—intersects with, complements, and diverges from other critical and dialogic approaches to education" (p. 97). In a way, Madigan Peercy's call is an example of CDE's concept of multivocality, applied at a theoretical level. In this case, other theories can dialogically speak to CDE and be operationalized to further leverage the CDE framework to prepare critical and dialogic teachers. In line with this concept of multivocality, Madigan Peercy underscores Walqui's (this volume) effort of collaborating with teachers and drawing upon their perspectives to reimage curricula and pedagogies.

Transitioning from curricula to learning contexts, the commentary by Tezgiden-Cakcak (this volume) shifts our attention to online spaces. She explains how the chapters she reviewed (Guofang & Bian, this volume; Karam et al., this volume) demonstrate that "CDE cannot be reduced to real time, face to face interactions within the classroom setting and showcase how CDE can actually take place on an online platform asynchronously" (p. 229). Noteworthy in this commentary is how Tezgiden-Cakcak critically reflects upon her own beliefs and perceptions of online learning, sharing how critical and dialogic conversations can be facilitated via online contexts and starting to imagine how such applications "could be used to disrupt the dominant neoconservative ideologies in Turkey" (p. 235) where she is engaged in the education of language teachers.

While the chapters (and commentaries) included in this volume reveal innovative and original ways through which CDE can contribute to powerful transformations in TESOL teacher education, they also show how there is no one recipe for preparing critical and dialogic TESOL professionals. However, it is our hope that these chapters highlight some of the ways that this important goal can be accomplished.

Suggestions for Future CDE Research

Where should educators and scholars go from here, as they explore the potential of CDE in TESOL teacher education? In this section, we highlight different pathways for future research with CDE on theoretical, methodological, and contextual levels.

On a theoretical level, we echo Madigan Peercy's call to further examine how CDE resonates with, complements, or diverges from other critical and/or dialogic lenses. For example, chapters in this volume utilized CDE in tandem with raciolinguistics (Karam et al.), translanguaging (Turner & Fránquiz), critical multilingual language awareness (Yuan et al.), and visioning (Meston & Phillips Galloway). Other intersections may include investment (Darvin & Norton, 2015), language teacher agency and positioning (e.g., Kayi-Aydar, 2015), and language teachers' identities (e.g., Varghese et al., 2005), among others. CDE can perhaps be both a macro-level concept under which critical and dialogic work can take place, as well as a micro-level theoretical lens on classroom discourse that can be combined with other theoretical perspectives to examine critical and dialogic work and settings.

Methodologically, CDE has been utilized with various qualitative designs in this volume such as case study (Karam et al.; Turner & Fránquiz), duoethnography (Mohamed et al.), and self-study (Li & Bian). Other studies drawing upon CDE beyond this volume also adopted case study design (Karam, 2021; Kleyn & López, 2021), discourse analysis (Alvarez et al., 2021; Lee et al., 2021), youth participatory action research (Lee et al., 2021; Park et al., 2021), and interviews alongside self-study (Charity Hudley et al., 2021). Within a TESOL teacher education context, we believe there is huge potential in longitudinal studies that track individual or cohorts of pre- or in-service teachers as they pursue their TESOL teacher education degrees or endorsements, throughout their field placements, and eventually to professional work settings. This longitudinal design can allow researchers to see how CDE tenets are sustained or not, and how CDE is carried into the classroom and implemented with multilingual learners of English. Although not longitudinal in design, the chapter by Turner and Fránquiz in this volume provides valuable insights for such future studies.

Other methodological innovations with CDE can include adopting an ecological view toward CDE (e.g., Kibler, 2023) in order to better understand CDE across macro, meso, micro settings in both TESOL teacher education and P-12 classroom settings. At a micro level, discourse analysis can be particularly helpful to showcase how multivocality is enacted, and how classroom talk is negotiated and adapted in critical and dialogic ways. We also agree with Tezgiden-Cakcak's recommendation of adopting participatory action research (PAR) projects in future studies in order to include the perspectives of different stakeholders in reimagining TESOL teacher education. In line with CDE's tenet of multivocality, we strongly believe that future studies that address multiple global contexts will represent valuable contributions to how we understand and implement CDE. Studies in this volume include such settings as Macau, New Zealand, the United States, and Türkiye; however, more is needed—especially from multilingual countries with complex colonial histories and different language policies and ideologies. We are also curious about international students pursuing undergraduate or graduate degrees in TESOL or Applied Linguistics—how do they grapple with, interpret, and implement CDE in their various roles as students, graduate teacher assistants, and eventually perhaps teacher educators?

To conclude, we echo Kibler et al.'s (2021) invitation to continue to explore, question, refine, reframe, and examine inequities through the lens of CDE in order to prepare critical, dialogic, and inclusive teachers who are ready to support and advocate on behalf of multilingual learners of English and see them as worthy partners in the ongoing quest to challenge and dismantle the inequities that abound in TESOL as a field.

References

Alvarez, L., Capitelli, S., De Loney, M., & Valdés, G. (2021). English learners as agents: Collaborative sense-making in an NGSS-aligned science classroom. In A. Kibler, G. Valdés, & A. Walqui (Eds.), *Reconceptualizing the role of critical dialogue in American classrooms: Promoting equity through dialogic education* (pp. 78–104). Routledge.

Charity Hudley, A. H., Mallison, C., Berry-McCrea, E. L., & Muwwakkil, J. (2021). Empowering African-American students voices in college. In A. Kibler, G. Valdés, & A. Walqui (Eds.), *Reconceptualizing the role of critical dialogue in American classrooms: Promoting equity through dialogic education* (pp. 157–84). Routledge.

Darvin, R., & Norton, B. (2015). Identity and a model of investment in applied linguistics. *Annual review of applied linguistics, 35*, 36–56.

Karam, F. J. (2021). Re-envisioning the ESOL classroom through a virtues-based curriculum: Contributions to critical dialogic education. *TESOL Journal, 12*(3), e582.

Kayi-Aydar, H. (2015). Teacher agency, positioning, and English language learners: Voices of pre-service classroom teachers. *Teaching and teacher education, 45*, 94–103.

Kibler, A. K. (2023). Critical and dialogic perspectives on why ecologies matter: Commentary on "Mid-adolescents' language learning at school: Towards more just and scientifically rigorous practices in research and education." *Language Learning, 73*S2, 225–9. https://doi.org/10.1111/lang.12562

Kibler, A. K., Valdés, G., & Walqui, A. (Eds.). (2021). *Reconceptualizing the role of critical dialogue in American classrooms: Promoting equity through dialogic education.* Routledge.

Kleyn, T., & López, D. (2021). Teaching current immigration issues to secondary immigrant and U.S.-born students: Interdisciplinary dialogic learning for critical understandings. In A. Kibler, G. Valdés, & A. Walqui (Eds.), *Reconceptualizing the role of critical dialogue in American classrooms: Promoting equity through dialogic education* (pp. 132–56). Routledge.

Lee, J. S., Meier, V., Harris, S., Bucholtz, M., & Casillas, D. I. (2021). School kids investigating language in life and society: Growing pains in creating equitable and dialogic learning environments. In A. Kibler, G. Valdés, & A. Walqui (Eds.), *Reconceptualizing the role of critical dialogue in American classrooms: Promoting equity through dialogic education* (pp. 52–77). Routledge.

Park, J., Simpson, L., Hernandez, C., Hernandez, S., Isom, O., Nguyen, T., Micaels, S., & O'Connor, C. (2021). Translating words and worlds in poetry inside out: Intergenerational research with multilingual youth on productive group talk. In A. Kibler, G. Valdés, & A. Walqui (Eds.), *Reconceptualizing the role of critical dialogue in American classrooms: Promoting equity through dialogic education* (pp. 105–31). Routledge.

Varghese, M., Morgan, B., Johnston, B., & Johnson, K. A. (2005). Theorizing language teacher identity: Three perspectives and beyond. *Journal of language, Identity, and Education*, 4(1), 21–44.

List of Contributors

Yue Bian is Assistant Professor and the ESOL Program Coordinator at the University of Washington Bothell in the School of Educational Studies. Her research interests revolve around teacher education, with a specific focus on linguistically and culturally sustaining and thriving pedagogy for multilingual learners in general education and English language development classrooms. As a transnational and bilingual scholar, she also dedicates her attention to issues of diversifying the teacher workforce and supporting first-generation immigrant educators. She has published in the *Journal of Literacy Research, Linguistics and Education, International Journal of TESOL Studies*, and *Beijing International Review of Education*, among others.

Christine Biebricher is Senior Lecturer in the Faculty of Education and Social Work at the University of Auckland. She leads the Bachelor of Education in TESOL. Christine is a trained teacher, who has worked in pre- and in-service language teacher education in several countries. Her research interests focus on teacher education and teacher professional development in languages and literacies. Her latest, co-authored book is *Journeys Towards Intercultural Capability in Language Classrooms: Voices from Students, Teachers and Researchers* (2022).

Rosemary Erlam is Associate Professor in the School of Curriculum and Pedagogy at the Faculty of Education, the University of Auckland. She leads the Postgraduate Certificate/Diploma in Teaching Linguistically Diverse Learners. Her research interests include a focus on language assessment, form-focused instruction, and language teacher education. Her latest, co-authored book is *Pedagogical Realities of Implementing Task-Based Language Teaching* (2022).

María E. Fránquiz is Professor of Curriculum and Instruction at the University of Texas, Austin. She is former Dean of the College of Education at the University of Utah and President of the National Council of Teachers of English. She is long-time editor of the *Bilingual Research Journal*. Her research focuses on language and literacy practices in bi/multilingual educational settings. She is published in top literacy journals and co-authored the books, *Inside the Latin@ Experience: A Latin@ Reader* and *Scholars in the Field: The*

Challenges of Migrant Education. Her most recent co-authored book is *Cultivating Young Multilingual Writers: Nurturing Voices and Stories in and Beyond the Classroom Walls* (2023).

Emily Phillips Galloway is Assistant Professor in the Department of Teaching and Learning at Vanderbilt University's Peabody College. Her quantitative and qualitative research explores the relationships between school-relevant language development and language expression and comprehension during middle childhood, focusing on linguistically and culturally minoritized learners. With the goal of advancing anti-racist pedagogy, Emily's work positions school-relevant language as a semiotic resource for critically examining inequality, envisioning change, fostering learner agency, and nurturing minoritized learners' socioemotional, professional, and political aspirations. Her scholarship appears in multiple journals, including *Reading Research Quarterly*, *Journal of Literacy Research*, *TESOL Quarterly*, and *Linguistics and Education*.

Işıl Günseli Kaçar is a lecturer (Ph.D), researcher, and teacher educator at the Department of Foreign Language Education at Middle East Technical University (METU). Her research interests include ELT methodology, academic writing, technology enhanced language learning, flipped learning, intercultural communication, virtual exchange/telecollaboration, pre-service teacher education, mentoring, e-mentoring, ELF-aware teacher education, and Global Englishes. She has published on pre-service teacher education and technology-enhanced language learning. Her most recent publications are as follows: *Designing a Complementary E-mentoring Program for Pre-service ELT Teachers: Online Co-mentoring Project* (2023), *Online Flipped Tasks and Universal Design for Learning: A Means to an Inclusive and Motivating EFL Environment* (2023).

Fares J. Karam is Associate Professor of TESOL at the University of Nevada, Reno. His scholarship focuses on the language and literacy development of multilingual learners from immigrant and refugee backgrounds. His research has appeared in such journals as *TESOL Quarterly*, *International Journal of Multilingualism*, *Applied Linguistics*, and *Research in the Teaching of English*, among others. He is currently working with Dr. Amanda K. Kibler on a co-edited volume titled *Innovative Qualitative Methodologies in Multilingual Literacy Development Research: Amplifying Voices from Immigrant, Transnational, and Refugee Communities*.

Amanda K. Kibler is Professor in the College of Education at Oregon State University. Her research focuses on the interactional and ecological contexts through which multilingual children and adolescents develop language and literacy expertise, and on using these insights to support pedagogical change. This work has been funded by the Spencer Foundation, William T. Grant Foundation, and Institute of Education Sciences. Selected recent publications can be found in *Language Learning*, *International Journal of Bilingual Education and Bilingualism*, and *TESOL Quarterly*, and her co-edited volume, *Reconceptualizing the Role of Critical Dialogue in American Classrooms: Promoting Equity through Dialogic Education* (2021).

Ayşe Kızıldağ is Associate Professor at Aksaray University in the Department of English Language Teaching. Her research interest basically focuses on foreign language teacher learning, that is, teacher cognition, professional identity, and mentoring. She has extensively published in EFL pre-service teacher learning and teacher education. Her most recent publication is *Mentoring for Professional Identity Construction in EFL Pre-Service Teacher Education: A Case Study from Turkey* (2023).

Guofang Li is Professor and Tier 1 Canada Research Chair in Transnational/Global Perspectives of Language and Literacy Education of Children and Youth in the Department of Language and Literacy Education, University of British Columbia, Canada. Her program of research focuses on bilingualism and biliteracy development, pre- and in-service teacher education, and current language and educational policy and practice in globalized contexts. Her recent books include *Handbook on Promoting Equity in Education for Inclusive Systems and Societies* (forthcoming), *Superdiversity and Teacher Education* (2021), *Languages, Identities, Power and Cross-Cultural Pedagogies in Transnational Literacy Education* (2019), and *Educating Chinese-heritage Students in the Global-Local Nexus: Identities, Challenges, and Opportunities* (2017).

Jiahui Li is currently an MA student at the Faculty of Education, University of Macau. Her research is about language teacher education, particularly regarding teacher beliefs and motivation.

Heather M. Meston, Ph.D., is Senior Humanities Content Creator at Khan Academy. Shaped by her experiences as a middle grades literacy educator, she uses her research to examine links between classroom discussion, agency, and teacher practice in classrooms serving minoritized youth, with the goal of identifying practices that foster equitable classroom discourse communities. Recent co-authored publications include "'They're the ones who hold the answers': Exploring educators' and students' conceptions of academic conversation" (2021), "Pedagogy of possibility: Proleptic teaching and language learning" (2022), and "Co-constructing agency: Weaving academic discussion" (2022).

Naashia Mohamed is Senior Lecturer of TESOL at the University of Auckland, New Zealand. Her teaching and research contribute to understanding how school and society can empower racially and linguistically marginalized children, youth, and families to achieve greater social equity. Through her scholarship, Naashia illustrates how home languages serve as powerful resources for students, helping them not only to attain academic success, but also to promote second language and literacy development. Her publications critically analyze educational policies and practices in the Maldives and New Zealand contexts to promote those that validate multilingual learners' assets while building on their ethnolinguistic identities.

Megan Madigan Peercy is Professor and Special Assistant to the Provost at the University of Maryland. Her research examines pedagogies of teacher education and the preparation and development of teachers throughout their careers, as they work with linguistically and culturally diverse learners. She is deeply invested in understanding the ways in which practice and theory can be in dialogue. Her research has been funded by the Spencer Foundation, the Institute of Education Sciences, and the Maryland State Department of Education. Examples of her recent work appear in *Teaching and Teacher Education, TESOL Quarterly,* and *TESOL Journal.*

Yasemin Tezgiden-Cakcak is Lecturer (Ph.D.) at Middle East Technical University in Ankara, Turkey, in the Department of Foreign Language Education. Her research interests focus on critical pedagogy, L2 teacher education, and critical applied linguistics. She has published on teacher agency, transformative educational action, and native-speakerism. She problematized technicist language teacher education in Turkey and theorized her own critical teacher education practices in her book titled *Moving Beyond Technicism in English Language Teacher Education* (2019). She is one of the associate editors of the book called *A Language of Freedom and Teacher's Authority Case Comparisons from Turkey and the United States* (2017).

Laura D. Turner is Co-Director of the international project, Refuteach: Lingüística Aplicada para la inclusion de personas refugiadas. She also serves as Applied Linguistics Coordinator with Madrid for Refugees. Her research interests focus on preservice teachers' positionings toward language and multilingualism, the disproportionate representation of multilingual children in special education programs, and in supporting future educators to develop holistic portraits of multilingual children. Laura serves on the editorial board of the Texas Education Review. She is published in the *Handbook of Latinos and Education: Theory, Research and Practice* and the *Bilingual Research Journal*.

Camille Ungco is a doctoral candidate at the University of Washington, College of Education in Language, Literacy, and Culture. Her research and teaching interests focus on Asian Critical Race Theory and anti-colonial pedagogies in teacher education. She has recently published in *Journal for Southeast Asian American Education and Advancement, Northwest Journal of Teacher Education,* and *Asian American Policy Review*.

Manka Varghese is Professor at the University of Washington, College of Education in Language, Literacy, and Culture. Her research and teaching interests focus on anti-oppressive identities and pedagogies for multilingual students and their teachers. She has published in numerous journals such as *TESOL Quarterly* and *Journal of Language, Identity, and Education, Teachers College Record,* and *Educational Researcher* as well as being an editor for special issues and monographs.

Aída Walqui directs the National Research and Development Center for Improving Education for English Learners in Secondary Schools and the Quality Teaching for English Learners Initiative at WestEd, both efforts focused on improving teacher and educational leadership ability to deepen and accelerate the linguistic and academic disciplinary achievement of English learners. A native Peruvian, Walqui holds a Ph.D. in Education from Stanford and a Masters in Sociolinguistics from Georgetown University. During her extensive career, she has taught at all levels and at universities in Perú, Mexico, the UK, and the United States, and published thirteen books and multiple articles.

Kailun Wang is a Ph.D. student at the Faculty of Education, University of Macau. His research interests include language teacher education, English medium instruction (EMI), and English for specific purposes (ESP) in higher education.

Rui Eric Yuan is Associate Professor at the Faculty of Education of the University of Macau. His research focuses on language teacher education, critical thinking, and English-medium instruction (EMI) in higher education. He has published extensively on these research topics in different international journals such as *TESOL Quarterly*, *Language Teaching*, and *Teaching and Teacher Education*.

Index

Act Cycle 186, 200
adolescent English Learners 24
affordances 31, 33–4, 90, 95, 98, 108, 111, 113, 116, 147, 184, 229
Alim, H. S. 213
Allwright, D. 28–9
American Dream 40
Andrei, E. 7
Aneja, G. 7
applied linguistics xi, 6, 13, 67, 245
Arias, M. B. 196
Arnold, P. J. 15, 230–3
Asian immigration 132
Athanases, S. Z. 82
Atwood, M., "Bread" 26, 28

Bakhtin, M.
    dialogism 3
    multivoicedness 9
banking pedagogies 109
Barros-del Rio, M. A. 4–5
Benade, L. 184
Bian, Y. 15, 186, 229, 231–3, 242
Biebricher, C. 14, 130, 135–7, 139, 168–9, 171, 174–5, 176
bi/multilingual (bi/multilingualism) children 49–52, 54–7, 60, 67, 77–8, 81–2, 89–99, 107, 133, 168, 183–8, 192, 194–5, 198–200, 207, 209–11, 213, 217, 219–21, 229, 231–6, 241, 245
Bloom's Revised Taxonomy (BRT) 152–3, 158
Brookfield, S. D. 184, 192, 198

classroom talk 3–4, 9, 69, 127, 175–7, 241, 245
    good 35, 93
    re-envisioning 15, 171–4, 178, 243
Cochran-Smith, M. 98
collaboration 30, 69, 83, 90, 149, 195, 240
    and decentering authority 174–5

    and dialogue in planning and teaching 136–9
    learning 72, 84, 241, 244
collaborative analysis (problems of practice) 14, 95, 108–9, 122–3, 176
    CDE 109–10
    changes 119–22
    context, participants and 114
    data collection and analysis 114–16
    participants' visions changed 116–19
    positionality 116
    professional learning experience, design 112–13
    visioning 110–11, 113, 118, 123–4
Collaborative Dialog Writing 38–9
colleague-to-colleague learning 174, 177
Coombe, C. 2
course with CDE 71–5
    data collection and analysis 74–5
    forum tasks 72
    "Introduction to Applied English Studies" 71, 91
    participants 73–4
    researcher positionality 75
    topics 71
Covid-19 pandemic 38, 50, 52, 183, 229
critical and dialogic approaches 1, 13, 46–8, 50, 97, 128, 148, 165, 206, 209, 221, 243
critical dialogic education (CDE) xiv, 1, 8, 24, 30, 47, 66, 91, 107, 129, 134, 137, 147, 164, 167–8, 176–7, 206, 239, 242
    centers 127
    CMLA with 69–71
    contributions to 232–4
    in course structure and assessment 139–41
    course with (*see* course with CDE)
    expanding work on 95–8
    features gravitating 25–9

fostering through NPI 156–8
framework for preparing language
    teachers 8–13
identity, positionality, and perceptions
    225–9
multivocality 83
in peer communication 162
principles 89, 94, 97
research, future 244–6
studies 94–5
TESOL teacher education,
    contributions to 91–4
transformations 10–12, 15
and translanguaging stance 48, 52–3,
    58, 91–2, 94, 243
visions of 108, 113, 124, 228, 239
Critical Educational Curriculum 41
critical friends 193, 230
Critical Friends Group (CFG) 109, 118,
    121, 172, 175–7, 240, 243
criticality xi–xiv, 128
critical language teacher education xiv, 3,
    6–8, 226–7, 235
critical multilingual language awareness
    (CMLA) 3, 6, 13, 65, 91, 99 n.3,
    240–241, 243–4
  with CDE 69–71
  critical view, English and use with 79–81
  English as subject 75–7
  implications 81–4
  language teachers 65–6, 68–9
  limitations 84
  multilingualism and plurilingualism
    77–9
  pre-service language teacher education
    66, 84, 91
  understanding 67–9
critical pedagogies 68, 84, 128–9, 207,
    226–8, 235
critical reflection, teachers' 7, 14, 82,
    183–4, 230, 242
  advancement of educational
    technologies 184–5
  and dialogic learning in modules 188–94
  methods 185–6
  modules and learning outcomes 194–8
  remote learning 184–5
  teacher educators/candidates,
    perspectives of 186–8
Cui, R. 4

culturally and linguistically diverse 131,
    142
curriculum 11–12, 23–4, 37, 90, 97,
    129, 132–3, 135, 149, 152–4,
    157, 187, 240, 242. See also
    innovation/innovative
    curriculum
  educative notes 40
  and language pedagogies (see language
    and language pedagogies)
  lessons and across units 40
  streamline activities 39–40
  virtue-based 69

Darling-Hammond, L. 111
decolonial pedagogy 2
Deroo, M. R. 7, 68, 82
Dhivehi language 129
dialogic gatherings (DGs) 4
dialogic language teacher education 3–6,
    228, 234–5
  advocacy work 5
  communities 5
  components 4
  interactions, educators and teachers
    4
  models 4
  online discussion prompts 5
dialogic learning 109, 184, 195, 199, 240
  critically reflective and 188, 192–4
  in virtual spaces 193, 198
dialogic talk 9, 11, 239–42
dialogic teaching 2–4, 9–11, 69, 124, 169,
    171–2, 194
dialogue 40, 66, 136–9, 141, 159, 184–5,
    196, 209
Dubiner, D. 68
Duffy, G. G. 108
duoethnography 14, 128–9, 141, 169–70,
    172, 174–5, 177, 243, 245
  dialogic practices and critical
    pedagogy 128–9
  differences 134
  methodology 133–41
  and self study 245
  sharedness and differences 170

educational settings 69, 107, 110, 147, 185,
    242
ELT Journal 73

engineered texts 33
English-as-a-foreign-language (EFL) 4, 66, 148
English as a lingua franca (ELF) 71
English as the medium of instruction (EMI) 81
English for Speakers of Other Languages (ESOL) teacher education 5, 69, 137, 195
English language arts (ELA) teachers 91, 93
English language learners (ELLs) 137–8, 140, 196. *See also* English Learners (ELs); Multilingual Learners (MLs)
English Language Teaching (ELT) 148, 225
English Learners (ELs) 5, 24, 27–8, 37, 41 n.3, 93, 110, 133. *See also* English Language Learners (ELLs); Multilingual Learners (MLs)
　adolescent 24
　long-term 13, 24–5, 29–30, 33, 35, 40, 93, 207
　with opportunities 27
equity 3, 8–9, 47, 53, 109, 117, 123, 142, 167
　centering bilingualism 54–6
　inclusion and 69, 148, 154
　and justice 90, 172, 175–7, 192, 240
　-oriented pedagogy 1, 11, 14, 69, 89–91, 94–5, 120, 206
　problem 98
Erlam, R. 14, 130–1, 135, 137, 168–9, 171, 174–5, 176
exploratory talk 193

face-to-face education 199, 227–9, 244
fallacies, language teachers xii
family engagement 195–6, 198
Farooq, S. 184
Farrell, T. S. C. 4, 7
Feldman, S. 30
Flores, N. 7, 207, 212–13, 217, 223–4
Fránquiz, M. E. 13, 89–92, 94, 96–7, 242, 245
Freire, P. 127, 142, 148, 184, 192, 226, 233–4
　problem-posing pedagogies 9, 127, 142, 192, 200

funds of knowledge 32, 108–10, 115, 117, 119, 133, 136
　student agency and 121–2

Galloway, E. P. 14, 168, 170–1, 174–7, 240
García, O. 46, 65, 67–8, 77, 81. *See also* critical multilingual language awareness (CMLA)
Glick, Y. 30
Godley, A. J. 67, 69, 83
Google Jamboard 112
Gorski, P. 142
Graduate Diploma (GradDip) TESSOL 130, 133
Günseli Kaçar, I. 168, 170–1, 173–6, 241

Hartman, L. 30
Hawkins, M. 6
holistic languaging pedagogies 13, 45, 49, 52, 54–5, 58, 60, 92, 98–9

ideologies (LTE) xii–xiii
inclusion 148, 153, 155, 158, 172
　vs. exclusion 151–2, 156–7
　inclusive pedagogy 66, 156–8, 162
innovation/innovative curriculum xi, 35, 68, 91, 94, 245
　changes to 39–40
　design 13
　instructional materials 23, 25–9
　replacement educative materials 29–30
instructional materials 23, 25–9, 148
　coverage 26
　focus on language 28
　high intellectual challenge, absence 27
　lack of academic rigor 26
　linear progressions 26
　monolingual and essentialized student audience 25–6
　transmission-oriented approaches 26–7
instructor overt facilitation 193
intentional curricular design 14

Johnson, K. E., dialogic interactions 4

Karam, F. J. xiv, 15, 69, 162, 230–3, 241
Kettle, M. 170
Kibler, A. K. xiv, 1, 3, 8–9, 15, 30–1, 69, 96, 129, 167, 171, 184, 194, 206–7, 228–33, 235, 243, 245

Kızıldağ, A. 168, 170–1, 174–6, 241
Kleyn, T. 46
Kubota, R. 232
Kumaravadivelu, B. 163

language and language pedagogies xii, 12–13, 28, 67, 92, 98, 129, 243
  and bilingualism/multilingualism 50, 60
  identity and power 68, 80, 218, 220
  and ideological issues 80
  learning xii, 65, 69–70, 80, 82–3, 206
  methods
    contexts 49–50
    data collection and procedures 50–2
    democratic vision 58–9
    equity 54–8
    findings 53–4
    participants 50–1, 53
  monolingual approaches 45, 59, 66, 68
  and power relations 98
  society and power 67
  teaching xii, 12, 65, 74, 79, 82, 130, 177
language learning histories (LLHs) 51
language-minoritized students 45, 47, 206–8, 213, 218
language teacher education (LTE) xi–xii, 68, 91, 134
  critical (*see* critical language teacher education)
  dialogic (*see* dialogic language teacher education)
  ideologies in xii–xiii
  mission of xiii
lesson architecture 32–3
Li, G. 15, 186
Li, J. 13, 91, 229, 231–3, 242
linguistic diversity 5, 66, 68, 82, 183
look cycle 185, 198–9
Los Angeles Unified School District (LAUSD) ELA teachers 30, 34, 40
Lourenço, M. 68
Luke, A. 170

Macau perspective, CMLA 91
Māori language Act of 1987 131
Mattie's vision 117–21
McClure, G. 5

Menken, K. 46
Merriam, S. B. 153
Meston, H. M. 14, 168, 170–1, 174–7, 240
methodology, duoethnography
  CDE embodies teaching 136–41
  lived experiences shaping practice 135–6
Michener, C. J. 5, 82
migration 131, 183
misguided system 127
modules 188–94
  critically reflective and dialogic learning 188–94
  and learning outcomes 194–8
  online 15, 186, 231
Mohamed, N. 14, 129, 136–8, 168–71, 174–5, 176, 242–3
monoglossic ideologies 7, 68, 211, 213, 216, 219, 221
multilingual language awareness 6–7, 13, 241, 243–4
multilingual learners (MLs) 1–2, 4, 8, 10–11, 13, 15, 23, 183, 185, 187, 195, 198–200, 211, 213, 229, 231–3, 241–2, 245–6. *See also* English Language Learners (ELLs); English Learners (ELs)
  practical pedagogical knowledge 192
  structural challenges 192
multilingual students/multilingualism 45–6, 51–2, 55, 77, 81–2, 89–91, 93, 95, 97–9, 107, 168, 209–10, 217, 241
  curriculum 97
  language and 50, 60
  P-12 90
  and plurilingualism 77–9
  SIFE 107, 171
multivocality 55, 83, 147, 149, 152, 154, 162, 172–3, 176, 207, 220, 240, 243, 245

native-speakerism xii, 45, 71, 80, 82
New Zealand 14, 127, 131–2, 142
  Auckland, population breakdown of 131–2
  educational context 132–3
  Māori 131–2, 135, 171
  Ministry of Education (MOE) 132
  minoritized students in 170

population 132
TESOL teacher education programs 128
Norton, B. 6
Notice-Problematize-Implement (NPI) approach 14, 148, 154, 162, 164, 172–3, 175, 177, 241, 243
  implementation 153
  noticing 151–2
  problematizing and modifying 152–3

Oedipus myth 36
online spaces 6, 15, 185, 220–1, 235
  creating critical dialogic 229–30
  online learning 185, 193, 199, 244
oracy, simultaneous development of 33
Otheguy, R. 46

pan-diversity approach 187
Park, J. 236
participatory action research (PAR) projects 231, 245
paternalistic leadership model 163–4
pedagogy-oriented research xi
Peercy, M. 14, 243–4
peer-to-peer learning 153, 173–4, 176
Phaeton myth 34
Phillipson, R. xii
plurilingualism 67, 77, 81
Poe, E. A., Masque of the Red Death 38
political and ideological clarity xiv
Ponzio, C. M. 7, 68, 82
power relations xiii–xiv, 6, 81, 84, 163, 228, 231
pre-/in-service teachers 7, 10–13, 15, 46–8, 50, 60–1, 90–2, 96–7, 123, 148–9, 152, 155–6, 159, 161, 164, 240–3, 245
  critical multilingual language awareness 13, 66, 84
  participants 51
  problems of practice 240
  self-reports 96
  of SIFE 108
  in SLTE programs 82
  sociopolitical consciousness 163
problem-posing education 9, 127, 142, 192, 200, 227, 235

professional learning 15, 35, 37, 41 n.4, 66, 83, 108–10, 141, 159, 183, 188
  and development 163
  experience, design 112–13
  experience, pedagogically enriching 160
  teacher visioning 110–11
Prospero, P. 38

race and language 15, 48, 206–7, 209–10, 215–19, 220–1
raciolinguistics/raciolinguistic ideologies 15, 68, 220, 241, 244
  assignment description on 223–4
  and CDE 206, 208
  critical and dialogic perspective 207–8
  dominant language, challenging/reifying 210–15
  implications 219–21
  methods
    context and participants 208
    data collection and analysis 208–9
    limitations 210
    positionality 209–10
  race and language 215–19, 221
  role-play 15, 205–6, 208–10, 214, 216–21, 230–2, 234–5, 241
Reid, W. 46
RELC Journal 73
remote learning 184–5
replacement educative curriculum 29–30
  assumptions and components 30–4
  for eighth grade English Language Arts 41 n.1
  lessons learned 34–9
    old habits die hard 37
    rich, demanding, and longer texts 38
    sustained, critical student talk 35–6
    task structure to foment 36
    teachers need support to grow 37
    teachers' vision of students 35
role-play 15, 205–6, 208, 210, 214, 216–21, 230–2, 234–5, 241
Rosa, J. 207, 212–13, 217

Sánchez, M. T. 46
Schmida, M. 30
school 11, 30, 112, 121, 128, 184, 198, 239
second-language acquisition (SLA) 60, 131, 135

second language teacher education (SLTE) 65, 68–70, 84, 163, 184
self-reflection and self-reflexivity 11–12, 83, 95, 99 n.4, 215
Seltzer, K. 220
Sharkey, J. 99 n.4
Spanish language practice 55, 59
spiraling organization 32
Stringer, E. 185
students 49–50, 93, 112, 205, 210, 243
    academic, discipline-specific practices 31
    as agentive learners and collaborators 116
    interthink 31
    juntos 58–9
    as knowers and researchers 148
    linguistically minoritized 1, 3, 45, 107, 206, 219, 228–9, 241
    linguistic repertoires 213
    power of talk 31
    undergraduate/graduate 49–50, 206–9, 218–19, 230, 241
students with interrupted formal education (SIFE) 14, 107–8, 110, 112, 114, 116, 121–3, 170–1, 176–7
Suh, S. 5, 82

teacher education xii, 1, 4, 11, 46, 60, 84, 89, 92, 95–6, 98, 128, 134, 141–2, 162, 167–8, 172–3, 177, 208, 235. *See also* language teacher education (LTE)
    equity problem 98
    K-12 and 98
    TESOL (*see* Teaching English to Speakers of Other Languages (TESOL) teacher education)
teacher educators/candidates xii, xiv, 1, 4, 6, 8, 10, 12, 47, 61, 99, 108, 134, 167, 174, 234, 241
    action research 200
    as facilitators and supporters 14
    identities, lived experiences, and contexts 172
    implications for 234–5
    "look/see" differently 198–9
    perspectives of 186–8
    and students *juntos* 58–9
    "think/act" differently 199–200
teacher expertise, development 13, 23–5, 29–30
teacher language awareness (TLA) 67
Teaching English as a Foreign Language (TEFL) 4, 14, 149
Teaching English to Speakers of Other Languages (TESOL) teacher education xi, xiv, 1–2, 60, 91, 128, 177–8, 183, 228
    CDE to make contributions 91–4
    contributions to critical dialogic 231–2
    critical awareness 6
    critical dialogic transformations in 239–44
    dialogic and critical approaches 3, 46–8
    identity-oriented approach 7
    modules 188–94
    P-12 classroom settings 245
    professionals, implications for 234–5
    qualities 2
    in Spain 4
    teachers 7
    transformations 244
    translanguaging stance and 46–8
Teo, P. 3–4
Te Tiriti o Waitangi (Treaty of Waitangi) 131
Tezgiden-Cakcak, Y. 15, 244–5
thematically organized learning tools 32
think cycle 185–6, 199–200
transformative intellectual teacher 227
translanguaging theory/stance 7, 13, 45–8, 50, 52–3, 60, 68, 78–9, 82, 91–2, 94, 96–7, 141, 243–4
    democratic vision 58–9
    dual correspondence theory 46
    equity 54–6
    implications 60–1
    pedagogies 98–9
    power dynamics 56–8
Tuning Protocol 113
Turkish ELT 148, 236
    compulsory school system 150, 164
    English 225
    field placement 149, 159–65

findings 155–62
methodology 153–5
NPI model (*see* Notice-Problematize-Implement (NPI) approach)
study 149–50
theoretical framework 148–9
transmission model of learning 170, 173
Turner, L. D. 13, 89–92, 94, 96–7, 242, 245

undergraduate students 49–50
Ungco, C. 15, 168, 243
Universal Design for Learning (UDL) 152–3, 158

Valdés, G. 1, 30–1, 129, 167, 207
van Lier, L. 31
Varghese, M. 15, 168, 243

Vasconcelos, E. F. D. S. 5
Veo, Veo (I Spy) 223
virtue-based curriculum 69
visioning 14, 110–11, 113, 123–4, 244
Vygotsky, L., sociocultural theory of learning 3

Walqui, A. 1, 13, 89, 91, 93–4, 97, 129, 167, 207, 242–3
Wang, K. 13, 91
white English 80–1
Wiley, T. G. 196

Yazan, B., critical autoethnographic narrative (CAN) 7–8
Yuan, E. R. 13, 89, 91–2, 94–7, 240

Zeichner, K. 96

www.ingramcontent.com/pod-product-compliance
Lightning Source LLC
Chambersburg PA
CBHW071813300426
44116CB00009B/1302